The Mechanic and the Luddite

The Mechanic and the Luddite

A RUTHLESS CRITICISM OF TECHNOLOGY AND CAPITALISM

Jathan Sadowski

UNIVERSITY OF CALIFORNIA PRESS

University of California Press

Oakland, California

© 2025 by Jathan Sadowski

Library of Congress Cataloging-in-Publication Data

Names: Sadowski, Jathan, author.
Title: The mechanic and the Luddite : a ruthless criticism of technology
and capitalism / Jathan Sadowski.
Description: Oakland, California : University of California Press, [2025] |
Includes bibliographical references and index.
Identifiers: LCCN 2024021717 (print) | LCCN 2024021718 (ebook) |
ISBN 9780520398061 (hardback) | ISBN 9780520398078 (paperback) |
ISBN 9780520398085 (ebook)
Subjects: LCSH: Technology—Economic aspects. | Technology—
Political aspects. | Capitalism—Political aspects.
Classification: LCC HC79.T4 S43 2025 (print) | LCC HC79.T4 (ebook) |
DDC 338/.064—dc23/eng/20240816
LC record available at https://lccn.loc.gov/2024021717
LC ebook record available at https://lccn.loc.gov/2024021718

Manufactured in the United States of America

33 32 31 30 29 28 27 26 25 24
10 9 8 7 6 5 4 3 2 1

Contents

Acknowledgments

This book would not exist in anything like the form it does now—in fact, it might have never been written at all—without my editor at UC Press, Michelle Lipinski, who first emailed me out of the blue all the way back in June 2021 after seeing a tweet of mine musing about writing a second book. Michelle made contact to ask if I wanted to chat about my ideas and see if UC Press might be a good home for them. We vibed instantly, the rapport was immediate, and working with Michelle felt natural. I knew she was the exact fit for whatever it was I wanted to do, which at that point was still nebulous. Soon after our initial meeting, Michelle went on maternity leave and I got busy starting a fellowship I had just been awarded, so the book went on the back burner.

Then twelve months later, Michelle emailed me again to say she was back and still keen to work with me. I like to say that I waited for Michelle to come back before actually starting to work on the book because I didn't want to write it with anybody else. The first part might be a nice way to say I just got really busy with other stuff, but the second part is true. By late 2022, we had together turned my loose idea for just repackaging some previous work into a killer proposal for an original piece of synthetic analysis that pushed my work to a new level. From the moment of first contact, and throughout every phase and process after, Michelle has been the biggest champion and advocate for this book. I feel lucky and grateful for her support.

This book is also the product of so many other people who work at UC Press, or were contracted through the publisher, and devoted their time, energy, and expertise to supporting and improving this book. It was a joy to work with them. The least I can do is acknowledge their crucial work: Artemis Brod (copy editor), Jyoti Arvey (editorial assistant), Teresa Iafolla (marketing communication manager), Katryce Lassle (senior publicist), Julie Van Pelt (senior production editor), Amber DeDerick (independent indexer).

I didn't really talk much about this book while I was writing it. A lot of people had no idea I was even writing a book until it was either almost done or totally finished. I try not to take credit for work I'm doing before it's done. That way I don't trick myself into feeling all the satisfaction from a job well done before the job is actually done (and hopefully done well). But Emma was the one person whom I spoke regularly with about the project and who shared the process with me and who celebrated little wins like finishing a chapter or commiserated with me about setbacks like falling behind. When I started the book we were dating, by the time it was published we were married. And I'm happy to now return all the love and support Emma gave me while she finishes her own book!

There are many others who deserve to be recognized for all the support they provided—social, intellectual, professional—both directly and indirectly, whether they know it or not. So much of my analysis has been sharpened through the weekly discussions about the political economy of technology I have with Edward Ongweso

Jr. and Jereme Brown during the podcast we produce together, *This Machine Kills*. Not to mention the roster of brilliant guests, many of whom are world leading experts in their fields, who take time to come on TMK and talk about their work with us. I also have to give a big shout out to my core crew in Melbourne who are easily among the smartest and cleverest people I have ever known, and who I feel very lucky to be such close friends with: Thao Phan, Chris O'Neill, Jake Goldenfein, Lauren Kelly.

Last but certainly not least, the Emerging Technologies Research Lab at Monash University has provided such an amazing environment to work in. I am deeply appreciative of Yolande Strengers and Sarah Pink for bringing me into the lab, making space for me, and then giving me lots of space to do my work. With their invaluable support, I successfully received a DECRA Fellowship from the Australian Research Council (DE220100417), which allowed me to really focus on writing this book.

I'm very lucky to have so much support, in so many different ways. This book is a product of that luck.

1 *Two Systems*

Miasma

We are constantly being made to serve the needs of two systems: technology and capitalism. Their purposes and goals are almost always prioritized above all others. Their imperatives and logics very often have more influence than any others. These systems could also be called structures. They are structures in the sense that they force social life into specific forms. But also in the sense that we live inside—we are completely entombed by—these social constructs.

Neither exists outside humans, but both are treated as beyond humans. They are products of human values, choices, and actions, but they are also larger-than-life institutions that even the most powerful people claim to have no control over. At the same time, they deny anybody else the agency to exert control over them. In this way, technology and capitalism are more like religions and states. In a relatively short amount of time, just a few hundred years really, these modern systems have altered human society and the natural world at every scale. They are not totalizing in the way that destiny is inescapable or that god is omniscient. Rather, they are totalizing in a way that is more like a toxic miasma, an oppressive cloud, emanating from everywhere, choking and trapping anything caught in its atmospheric existence—which is now essentially everything. Technology and capitalism work in tandem to create mutually reinforcing systems, which we must then work for, within, and against. We cannot understand one without seeing how it is connected to the other. They have fused together into a dual system: technological capitalism.

It is a tricky business trying to define either of these two things. They are so familiar that we all already have everyday definitions of them—even if they are as simple as "technology is about using tools" and "capitalism is about making money." Yet they are so multifaceted that no dictionary entry could do them justice. They are so central to life that we engage with both constantly, and yet they are so contentious that any normal person likely has internally contradictory feelings about them, not to mention disagreements with other people's perceptions. I'm not interested in trying to advance the most superior, holistic, bullet-proof definitions of technology and capitalism. That is a fool's errand for many reasons, not least of which is that, as I argue, the real complexity of these systems—and our complex understanding of them as ideological and material forces—is only truly revealed by seeing their parts in action and in dynamic relation with each other. This book shows that action, studies that relation, and demystifies these systems.

For the sake of establishing shared ground to build on, however, basic working descriptions of technology and capitalism will be useful. My aim here is not to be encyclopedic. There is a reason why Karl Marx alone wrote millions of words analyzing capitalism or why there are multiple interdisciplinary academic fields dedicated to studying technology from various angles. There will always be quibbles with any framing of these two things. But thankfully we don't need to comprehend the entirety of complex systems to see their patterns and discern their trajectories. The specific features, details, and examples that each chapter will dig into provide ways of understanding the larger structural foundations and operations of technological capitalism. What we need, as a starting point, is just a quick orientation for how to think about technology and capitalism.

I don't assume you have expertise; nor do I write as if you were born yesterday. This book is not the first time you have encountered technology or capitalism. In fact, your engagement with them is far more pervasive and invasive than you probably realize. Yes, it is the computer you use and the job you work, but it is so much more. You don't need to be a professional deep thinker to recognize your own experiences of living in a specific type of society. Common aphorisms like "cash is king" and "privacy is dead" already reveal something about the role of profit and data in our society. Over the course of this book, readers who are familiar with theories about technology and capitalism will be offered ways of rethinking what they know. Readers who are newcomers to the subject will be offered ways of understanding what they need to know.

Technology Is Power

As a social scientist, I'm often asked how I got into studying technology. Did I turn a hobby as a geek into a profession as a nerd? Not quite (but also not wrong). I always answer truthfully: technology is not actually what I study. I'm far more interested in the material operations of power and the forms it takes in society. Technology—the things, the industry, the system—is one of the most important vectors of power today. This is not a new development in society, but it is one that continues to grow in familiar and strange ways. It is also a feature that many people, including those who study and make technology, are only starting to recognize and confront. Being fascinated by technology for its own sake is perfectly fine. There's nothing wrong with liking gadgets. I have my own share of devices I really quite enjoy and care too much about. The problem comes when we fetishize technology by only seeing the object in front of us without considering any of the broader networks of social, political, and economic relationships that the object is embedded within. In other words, all the things that are behind what technology gets made, why it's made, how it's made, where it's made, who it's made for, and all the consequences that follow from its being made.

All technologies—even the most seemingly advanced, autonomous artificial intelligence systems—are ultimately products of people. They give concrete form to human values and material structure to social relations. However, except for an elite minority who have the power and resources to make decisions about investment, purpose, and design, technology is something that happens to us. Not by us, or with us, or even for us. We largely have to live with the major choices made by a few. We might benefit from some things that happen to us, while being harmed by other things. We aren't really given a choice in those tradeoffs. We have to figure out how to navigate the world they build—and the ones they want to build. A few people get to exercise their influence and realize their visions; the rest of us don't have that ability or opportunity. Not because this is the only way things could possibly be. Not because nobody else could make those choices for lack of knowledge, imagination, or aspiration. Not because anybody else would just mess things up. But because this is how the technological system is currently organized and perpetuated.

"For most consumers—who learn about new technologies only when they brighten the windows of an Apple store or after they've already gone viral—it's easy to imagine that technological progress is dictated by a kind of divine logic; that machines are dropped into our lives on their own accord, like strange gifts from the gods," writes Meghan O'Gieblyn.[1] Technological fetishism means more than treating these machines as objects of desire for consumerist urges. More critically, it also makes us passive users of machines that seem to come from nowhere. All we can do is pray that the gifts are beneficial and the gods are benevolent. Prayers that have been going unanswered more and more regularly.

Importantly, when I talk about technology as a system I do not mean to erase the multiplicities—to equate all technologies and unify them into one totalized thing like a divine force with its own essence and endpoint.[2] This is an approach taken by many who are treated as thought leaders and trend whispers for the future of technology.[3] It is based in deterministic thinking that blends various (and contradictory) beliefs about technology as a singularly progressive force that develops in a predictable and linear fashion while also being out of our control, like a primal force of nature.[4] For them, the main purpose of analyzing its trajectory is to better anticipate and adapt to its changes, harness its evolution for a competitive edge in the market, and perhaps convince others to accept its effects. Exercising agency over how it develops—or, heaven forbid, stopping its development—is not an option.

Just as importantly, I want to avoid treating technology as a loose, assorted collection of the latest devices and emerging innovations that appear on the market. Far too much of the time spent talking about technology—by both advocates and critics, enthusiasts and pessimists—is taken up by an approach that treats gadget reviews as the model for how to engage critically with technology. No doubt we need clear reporting on the specs and uses of devices, but that has to be the starting point for our analysis. If we study each new technology in isolation, then we will never see the more important (and more interesting) connections that create a system. This is a classic case of missing the forest by counting the number of leaves on each tree. As we will see, the development of technology tends to follow patterns—patterns that have been closely enmeshed with the dynamics and dictates of capitalism for hundreds of years. Capital controls the resources needed to innovate, produce, and take advantage of technology at a large scale.

Technologies articulate broader dynamics—political, economic, social, cultural, moral—and give them material form in the world. They come from certain decisions, objectives, desires, and goals being prioritized over other alternatives. They are a deck that has been stacked in ways obvious and unnoticed, intended and accidental. They are embedded with values and intentions. They are encoded with logics and imperatives. They are entangled with infrastructures and institutions. They expand human agency, making it concrete and durable, across time and space. The issues of whose interests are included in technological choices, which imperatives drive the movement of this power system, and what impacts result from its production and operation are matters of critical concern.[5]

Legal systems are sets of rules for what is (not) allowed, frameworks for what rights people (don't) have, and plans for what kind of society we will (not) live in. Technical systems do all the same things in different ways and often to far greater degrees than many laws. Technologies are like legislation: there are a lot of them, they don't all do the same thing, and some are more significant; but together as a system they form the foundation of society.[6] Just as with law, technologies are also created and harnessed by the class with the political influence and economic resources to advance their own positions in the world. Unlike the law, technology as a system of power tends to operate outside the close scrutiny that comes with statecraft while it also structures our lives in ways that are more intimate than any government service.[7] Technology escapes even the bare minimum of public accountability, let alone public control, that we demand from other forms of power that "shape the basic pattern and content of human activity" to a much lesser extent than technology does.[8]

Not long ago, this critical understanding of technology would have been quite radical outside of specialized areas of academic research. Now, however, it is impossible to keep up with news of the latest algorithm that denied people housing or the latest digital platform that used sensitive mental health data to target consumers or the latest tech company that received multibillion-dollar contracts with military and intelligence agencies or the latest innovation bubble that caused users to lose all their money while already rich boosters got even richer or the latest [fill in the blank with the most recent ethically egregious and socially toxic tech-sector activity]. This now also means it has become impossible—for all except the most zealous believers and cynical investors—to deny the political nature and social impacts of technology. I want to push our analysis beyond blame and outrage over single cases of bad technologies or bad billionaires. Undoubtedly some apples are more rotten than others, and they should be among the first to be disposed of. Yet they are symptoms of a problem. Agents of rot that spread it further. In reality, the whole damn apple orchard is rotten to its roots. The rot of capitalism.

Value in Motion

If I say technology, you should think of *power*. If I say capitalism, you might think of *profit*. This is not wrong. The drive to capture as much profit as possible by any means available is a core feature of the capitalist system. This one human desire elevated to inhuman—and inhumane—levels has left a deep scar on all of society and the planet. The search for profit, in all its forms and sources, has given us the world as it exists today. Making profit, in the simple sense of pocketing more than you invest, had been a human desire for many millennia before the system of capitalism. People have always wanted to produce more value from their time and energy. What capitalism successfully did was turn that desire into an infernal engine sitting at the center of society, pushing and pulling everything else according to its logics.

Over time, the financial interest in profit transformed into the social imperative of profit-making. Milton Friedman, Nobel Prize-winning economist, champion of the free market, and granddaddy of neoliberalism explicitly advocated for this transformation. He did not originate this argument, but he crystallized it and slapped his name on it in a 1970 essay for the *New York Times* titled "A Friedman Doctrine—The Social Responsibility of Business Is to Increase Its Profits."[9] The article itself is a convoluted argument about how, actually, the singular pursuit of profit in a system of free enterprise is the most efficient and most ethical way to organize society. At this time, people still mostly thought of finance as only one part of society and believed that corporations had social obligations beyond profit. Today, Friedman's doctrine is simply treated as common sense. No longer does capitalism need to justify its existence or offer defensive cases for profit-making. The system is now focused on advancing offensive tactics for profit-taking and bulldozing any barriers to its endless expansion.

This is a good starting point for thinking critically about capitalism, but capitalism is driven by much more than cultural attitudes that prioritize profit and lionize entrepreneurs. Things start getting a bit more heady when we move from defining capitalism in basic terms of profit-making to studying its dynamics as a complex socio-technical system in which a small class of capital owners extract and control the surplus-value created by a large class of wage-laborers. In this way, we can also further analyze the profit motive as the basic impetus of capitalism by redescribing it in terms of a more extensive *imperative of capital accumulation*. So just what is *capital* and this process of accumulation that gives the system its name? To answer that question, we need to take a quick journey into the foundational analysis that remains as relevant and revelatory now as it was nearly two hundred years ago.

In *Capital, Volume 1*, Marx describes capital as a relationship between money (M) and commodities (C); specifically, the ways they circulate and transform, which he simplifies into two general formulas.[10] The first formula represents consumption, C-M-C: a commodity is sold for money which is then used to buy another commodity. Therefore, C-M-C is the cycle of using money to turn one commodity (e.g., labor) into another different commodity (e.g., coffee). The cycle of consumption is motivated by the use-value of a commodity—the value you get by using the thing in your life—and it is completed when money is turned into a commodity. Most people's lives revolve around completing this cycle by using their paycheck—money for labor—to then buy food, housing, video games, and so on.

The second formula represents capital, M-C-M': money is used to buy a commodity, which is then sold for more money. The cycle of capital is motivated by exchange value—the value received by exchanging a thing in the market—and the cycle does not ever complete, because capital requires continuous circulation. When money is turned into a commodity for consumption rather than invested to make profit, it ceases to be capital. "The circulation of money as capital is an end in itself, for the valorization of value takes place only within this constantly renewed movement," Marx writes. "The movement of capital is therefore limitless."[11] The process of accumulation is unending. The formula does not stop at M-C-M'; it continues onward forever as money is turned into more money which is turned into even more money through the endless exchange, extraction, and exploitation of commodities. If that cycle is interrupted in some way, then capitalism is thrown into crisis.

In short, capital is value in motion, with money often standing in for value (but not always, as we will see in the chapter on data). There are many different types of capital, which correspond to the different ways value moves and different things it does in the process of producing and capturing profit. For example, constant capital is the means of producing commodities; variable capital is the cost of hiring workers; and financial capital is money invested in profit-seeking activities. Capital is not the *content* of wealth—like machinery or stocks—capital is the *forms* that value takes as it circulates, accumulates, and transforms in this system. Capital can "only be grasped as a movement, and not as a static thing," writes

Marx.[12] This need for capital to be always moving and growing is what makes capitalism so dynamic but also so voracious and rapacious. Capitalism is also built on the alchemy of abstraction. By this I mean it is a system that excels at taking a concrete, specific thing like the house you live in and turning it into an abstract, universal category called an *asset*. Or, taking a collection of similar but different things like varieties of apples grown in different places and turning them into a singular, standardized category called a *commodity*. Even the most basic features of capitalism, concepts like *property* and *wages*, which don't seem strange at all because they feel like they have always been part of society, are ultimately ways capitalism has abstracted how we relate to ourselves, other people, objects, labor, and value. As philosopher Søren Mau explains in *Mute Compulsion*:

> What distinguishes capitalism from pre-capitalist systems is not the mere existence of capital, but rather its social function. In pre-capitalist societies, the processes governed by the logic of capital were always marginal to social reproduction. From the sixteenth century onwards, however, a fundamental transformation took place: the logic of capital began to weave itself into the very fabric of social life, eventually reaching the point where people had become dependent upon it for their survival. Capital became "the all-dominating economic power," or, put differently: society became capitalist.[13]

I'm not taking us on a detour into the deeper waters of political economy just for the fun of it. These features of capital—motion, valuation, abstraction, accumulation—are essential to this book's analysis of technological capitalism. Major transformations in capitalism have been based on the creation of new technologies that increase and expand capital's powers of motion, valuation, abstraction, and accumulation. Doing capitalism harder, better, faster, stronger. Whether with innovations like steam trains and grain elevators or computer networks and data warehouses,[14] whether the historic era is called industrial, financial, or digital, we are talking about different guises for the same underlying features of capitalism. Ultimately these are all revolutions that advance the powers and processes of capital to another level. In large part, the task of analyzing these systems is figuring out how capitalism is both extremely dynamic in its means and remarkably consistent in its motivations.

As capitalism develops—and the easy, cheap ways of extracting value get more scarce—the methods of accumulating capital and capturing profit have grown more complex and abstract. The relation is not always a direct connection between consumers, workers, bosses, and landlords who are making, buying, selling, and renting commodities in the great big Mall of Capitalism. Some of the biggest engines of capital to ever exist are based on financial instruments and digital platforms that pull profit out of pure speculation. These engines are collectively called "fictitious capital" because they are seemingly removed from the real economy of material things and physical processes. It is not always easy to discern how profit is made, who it is made for, and on what time horizons. We will get more into these dynamics and their consequences for technological capitalism in the chapter on innovation.

As a core imperative, the accumulation of capital is a higher order process than the profit motive. Its driving logic is the perpetual acquisition, control, and mutation of anything needed to make and take profit. This includes money, machinery, and raw materials but also human labor power. A major argument in this book is that the imperative of capital accumulation is the dominant force that conditions society, generally, and that drives the design, creation, and use of technology, specifically. This does not mean capital accumulation is the only social force at play. There are, of course, other logics, structures, and imperatives that coexist and intersect in these complex systems. They include familiar demons like racism, sexism, ableism, homophobia, transphobia, among others. However, these are not different heads of a hydra acting independently from each other and only occasionally working together to cause havoc. They are coordinated parts of a collective whole. Capitalism needs to construct hierarchies of power based on social differences and to further inflame existing forms of control and inequality. It creates ways of dividing people and devaluing human life, making people easier to exploit, oppress, and discard like used up resources.

To be clear: capitalism is not deterministic in the sense that it is the only option possible and that there are no alternatives. Many non-capitalist ways of living do exist right now, simultaneously with capitalism, in complicated ways. For example, our home lives exist, to various degrees, as non-capitalist enclaves within a capitalist society. If capitalist imperatives like the profit motive start dictating how we treat friends and families, then we see that as perverting the social relations we care about. However, capitalism is *overdetermined*. This does not mean that society cannot develop in any other way but that many powerful forces are pushing society in a single direction toward more capitalism.

By understanding how capitalism is driven by this core imperative, we can track the various ways this system manifests that imperative. It is hard to underestimate the extent to which the entire structure of society, the resources of our planet, the vast productive forces of humanity, and the global networks of innovations and infrastructures have all been organized to meet the demands of capital accumulation for the very few via the exploitation of the many. In the never-ending battle to accumulate capital, all social relations are conditioned by constant competition and conflict. "It would be possible," Marx famously quipped, "to write a whole history of the inventions made since 1830 for the sole purpose of providing capital with weapons against working-class revolt."[15] Marx wrote that line in the 1860s. I think we could now say "a whole library of histories" could be written to cover the subsequent 160 years of inventions, bringing us to the present day in technological capitalism.

The class divide between workers and owners is not merely a by-product of the imperative for capital accumulation but essential to its functioning. We often talk about class in terms of cultural signifiers—Do you like wrestling or opera? Burgers or oysters?—but class in capitalism is much more specific. Class is not even strictly about your income, though that certainly matters for your place within the many hierarchies of capitalist society. Fundamentally, class is a relation to the means of production—or, the land, tools, infrastructure, factories, resources, and so on used to produce goods and capture value. Do you earn a wage for a living? Or do you own assets for a living? That is the real class divide of capitalism.

There is also much more to capitalism than just class. We should be wary of any reductive or obsessive focus on one aspect rather than an analysis of the whole system and its power dynamics. People's position relative to capital—and the domination of capital as a social logic—is also determined by many other historical and social forms of intersecting oppression, exploitation, and inequality that are endemic to capitalism and based on characteristics like race, gender, sexuality, ability, and geography. Capitalism is unbelievably good at creating, stoking, and taking advantage of differences between people—pitting groups against each other while capital profits off the fights staged in the arena it owns. You are likely well aware that the wealth divide keeps growing wider, though you may not realize just how yawning it is. According to the 2022 World Inequality Report, the richest 10 percent of the world own 76 percent of all the wealth—and the top 0.01 percent alone own 11 percent of global wealth. The bottom 50 percent possess a meager 2 percent.[16] The pandemic accelerated the concentration of wealth. This wealth chasm is not the result of major leaps in production or the economic pie growing bigger or a rising tide lifting all boats—as if some people just happened to leap a little further, eat a bit more, and rise a tad higher than everyone else who also did quite well. No, this dynamic must be seen as a direct transfer of wealth from the vast majority to the very top. From labor to capital. From people who work for a living to people who own stuff for a living.

The transfer is not unprecedented; it has been happening continuously and consistently. The only thing that changes is the speed at which this transfer happens, or as it is also called, the rate of exploitation. The direction of that transfer never changes, at least not without some kind of major force exerted on capitalism to reverse its momentum. Even when we talk about policies for redistributing wealth, in reality, these often involve redistributing income between different segments of the working class. It is like shuffling chairs between tables on the deck of the *Titanic*, while the top 1 percent have climbed into the lifeboats and the top .01 percent have escaped in helicopters with all the caviar and champagne.

Importantly, for our purposes of analyzing technological capitalism, those who control the means of production have the ability to dictate what, how, why, where, when, and by whom things are produced and used. It is their orders, their interests, their goals that guide the process of technological investment, innovation, and implementation. They are, in turn, driven by the imperatives and logics outlined above. The hunger for profit and the will to power. The development of technology is never inevitable, but under capitalism it is overdetermined in specific ways by certain groups for particular purposes. "Capital and labour, through a struggle over the design and manipulation of technology that one owns and the other sets in motion, contribute to forming each other in their class characters," explains Cynthia Cockburn, a feminist technology scholar.[17] We need to have a clear view of these overarching dynamics of technological capitalism so that we can then analyze the system in action: to see it happen, know why it happens, and understand the effects of it happening.

As systems, technology and capitalism are transformative in every sense. They change shape to suit their environments while also reshaping their environments to meet their needs. This is what theorists call "subsumption": the various ways in which already existing social practices—such as methods of organizing labor or producing goods—are plugged into a capitalist system and redirected to serve capitalist interests like exploiting surplus value. If subsumption continues, then these practices are totally remade and reorganized according to the imperatives of capital such that they become inherently capitalist in nature. We can see this shift historically when early capitalists initially captured profit from forms of artisan labor that existed before capitalism by enforcing new property regimes on their work—for example, by making artisans rent the tools needed to craft goods. Then with the rise of industrial capitalism, these forms of labor were fully transformed by the factory system; they were absorbed into capitalism, becoming appendages of capital. Subsumption has now come for everything. As political theorist Jodi Dean writes, "The world in the twenty-first century is entirely subsumed by capitalism. The capitalist system is global. Competition, crises, and precarity condition the lives of and futures of everyone on earth."[18]

Similar processes of subsumption are also enacted by technological systems. First the application of, for example, some new smart device is used to augment an already existing process. Before long, the process itself is being changed to feed the needs of smart tech: data is collected constantly about every aspect of its use and its functions are controlled automatically. So when a coffee maker is made smarter it gets some new features that usually add a bit of convenience and connectivity. Oh look, I can turn on the coffee maker using an app or I can get real-time updates on my bean levels. Kind of weird, but also maybe cool and useful. But then, very quickly, the coffee maker gets an update and now it's sharing all the data it collects about when, how, and what kind of coffee you drink—plus maybe other stranger data like pictures of your kitchen—with third parties who then use it for their own (unknown) reasons. And the coffee maker keeps sending notifications with sponsored advertisements for coffee beans and insisting that I set up an account to automatically order beans when it senses my supply is low. Also the coffee maker won't work unless it is always connected to the internet so it can stay in constant contact with the manufacturer's servers in another country.

This is the logic of solutionism taken to its natural endpoint.[19] However, no longer is it enough to create (nonexistent) social problems that justify the application of technological solutions. Now the focus is on re-creating our world to justify the supremacy of technological systems being built to govern it. In my previous book, I called this transformative subsumption a way of "terraforming society," or "creating conditions for a specific model of human life that is engineered according to the imperatives of digital capitalism."[20] The example of a coffee maker could stand in for a vast range of things, from vacuums and televisions to long-haul trucking and global shipping—and the process of subsumption by smart tech can be observed in all of them.

In a 2021 interview, science fiction author Ted Chiang, with his hallmark clarity, nailed the thesis of this book: "Most of our fears or anxieties about technology are best understood as fears or anxiety about how capitalism will use technology against us. And technology and capitalism have been so closely intertwined that it's hard to distinguish the two."[21] The relationship between these two systems, and their various uses and effects, takes many different forms, as we will see in the following chapters.

There is obviously much more to say about this fusion of technological capitalism than what's contained in this capsule primer. We are, after all, talking about a globally hegemonic, sociotechnical, political-economic system that has developed over long periods of time while interlocked with nation-states. That's a recipe for profound complexity. However, as I've said, attempting to comprehend the complexity in its entirety is unnecessary; trying to do so would actually impede our understanding. Try swallowing everything at once and you just end up choking. To mix metaphors: like any story, the characteristics we meet in the first scenes will get fleshed out as the plot moves along, and we will meet others as they become relevant to our adventure into technological capitalism.

Focus on IT

If it is not already apparent, my primary focus in this book is on (digital) information technology—its creation, application, integration, and implications across various sectors in society—rather than other types of technology and technoscience. There is a good chance you already assumed that to be the case. In our everyday ways of talking and thinking, people tend to equate technology with computers and the internet. However, it is good to be clear and explain why I'm focusing on this specific type of technology.

The digital information industry and its technologies are defined by their immense concentrations of power, wealth, influence, and impacts. And these concentrations continue to increase at an extreme rate. Consider that the elite club of companies valued at over $1 trillion is, at time of writing, dominated by the tech giants Apple, Alphabet, Amazon, Microsoft, and Nvidia. While Saudi Aramco, the country's national oil and gas company, is the only non-tech holdout in the $1 trillion club, Saudi Arabia's sovereign wealth fund has also famously injected billions of dollars into tech start-ups through its investments in massive venture capital funds like Softbank's $100 billion Vision Fund. With all that money sloshing around, big tech giants have also built powerful political machines for lobbying policymakers in places like the US, UK, and EU, thus securing their positions and protecting their interests in these markets.[22] As one headline in the *Guardian* put it, "Forget Wall Street—Silicon Valley is the new political power in Washington."[23]

As I explained earlier, I study technology as a way to study the power and values that technology materializes. So when I first started working on the social science of technology, I spent a lot of time trying to understand the culture, politics, and ideology of Silicon Valley. It is the mecca of innovation, the maker of progress, the model of growth. It is a place where significant futures and fortunes have been made in such a way, to such a degree, over such a short time, and by such a small number of people that I don't think we have yet fully reckoned with their consequences for how we live and our world. Over time, I have narrowed my attention on specific cases where the technologies and ideologies of Silicon Valley began intersecting in major ways with other key industries. These include my early research on smart cities and urban governance[24] and then subsequent projects on finance technology (fintech) and insurance technology (insurtech).[25] Analyzing how these emerging markets for digital technology augmented other sectors of society that were already major centers of power in their own right offered a way to better understand the nitty-gritty workings of technology and capitalism.

What's more, digital information technology is often deeply integrated into other areas of technoscientific research and development (R&D). Computers are more than just useful tools that enable us to send emails or run spreadsheets; they are the infrastructure for doing everything else. It's why big organizations have separate IT departments even if they have nothing to do with the tech sector. Advances in software and hardware have direct impacts on the practices of every other industry and institution, whether biochemical engineering or bureaucratic administration.

It is now cliche that when digital technology enters into a sector it does so not only by upgrading their capabilities and selling them products but also by trying to transform, disrupt, colonize, and monetize that sector. For example, cars are now described as complex computers on wheels that produce enormous data about their operations (and drivers). This is why the recent microchip shortage was, for many people, felt most strongly in the car market. Cars now run on microchips, and there just weren't enough to go around, which caused scarcity and rising prices. Back in 2018, the CEO of Ford declared that the future of automotive manufacturers is in being data miners. "[Ford] could make a fortune monetizing data. They won't need engineers, factories or dealers to do it. It's almost pure profit," explained automotive industry journalist John McElroy.[26] Meanwhile, artificial intelligence researchers have been claiming for over a decade that they will one day replace doctors and nurses—or at least drastically augment the practice of medicine—with superior machine learning trained on data from millions of patients.[27] Or consider that in the energy sector companies and regulators have suggested that digital platforms like Uber should be models for how to manage the energy markets that determine the flow and price of electricity.[28]

While my focus is on information technology, the relevance of my analysis extends beyond the digital. Ultimately, I am interested in fleshing out fundamental dynamics that drive technological capitalism. Throughout this book I'm drawing lessons from foundational studies and historical confrontations with technological capitalism that predate our digital age yet still hold crucial lessons for then, today, and tomorrow because of their ability to reveal patterns and processes that have persisted over time. It is not as if Silicon Valley is the one bastion of capitalist technoscience in the world. Other industries like mining, manufacturing, petrochemicals, pharmaceuticals, and agriculture would like a word with anybody trying to make that claim. And there are extremely good critical studies of those industries—by people who know far more than me about them—that show why they are also crucial case studies of technology and capitalism.[29] I do think, however, that the contemporary information technology sector and its intersections with other industries tend to heighten many of these dynamics and features to almost absurd degrees, making them more obviously apparent for critical analysis of the underlying systems.

Beyond Conclusions

There is a growing cottage industry of work that casts a skeptical eye on Silicon Valley. Thanks to recent shifts in public opinion—spurred by events like the "techlash" that kicked off in 2018 with worker protests at Google over the company's military contracts to build AI for weapons—it is now fairly common to no longer just assume the tech sector is a socially benevolent engine of progress. However, this mystifying fog has not been completely burned away. There are still many tech companies, along with the Great Men who lead them, that enjoy reputations as innovators, visionaries, and vanguards of the future. They are granted the benefit of the doubt. Their trespasses and failures are forgiven. Their legions of loyal followers run interference, perform apologia, and attack detractors. But there is at least some recognition by normal people that the whole spectacle is strange and maybe not the best way to "do innovation." We can now raise the question, in polite company, of whether Silicon Valley is building technology and thrusting it upon the public in ways that are ethical, safe, and socially beneficial—or not.

As historian Leo Marx has shown, the idea that "improved technology means progress" is an old one that traces a long way back to the Enlightenment project of using scientific knowledge and technological power to dominate nature and accumulate wealth.[30] This ideology evolved to prioritize technocratic progress on the assumption that other forms of progress (e.g., social, economic, political, moral) and other values (e.g., freedom, justice, autonomy, equity) will follow as long as the technocratic machine continues to advance. (Now, however, our expectations of how technology can improve our lives have been lowered to the degree that "innovation" doesn't even need to be "improved" in any meaningful sense to be lauded as progress. I'll expand on that point in a later chapter.) The belief in technocratic progress has since become "the fulcrum of the dominant American worldview," writes Leo Marx.[31] It is deeply embedded in stories we tell about how value is produced, what kind of work is valuable, and who is valued above others in the hierarchy of society. For that reason, I can't blame people for being reluctant to give up their faith in a deus ex machina—salvation by innovation or grace by genius— especially in the face of escalating social regression and climatic catastrophe.

The recent mainstreaming of tech skepticism has gone a long way toward dislodging some of these deeply entrenched beliefs. Most of the critical work in this area—which fueled that shift in public opinion and keeps pushing it forward—focuses on giving people a set of neatly packaged conclusions. They provide a list of problems (e.g., exclusion) and harms (e.g., bias), alongside some causes (e.g., racism, sexism) and broad solutions (e.g., algorithmic audits). There also tends to be a narrow focus on case studies of certain companies using specific technologies, such as Amazon's application of surveillance to enforce draconian rules and squeeze more profit from workers. Generally, this line of critical analysis is important and its conclusions are correct. It has put us on the right track and gotten us far. But now to get further we need to push even harder. Our ways of analyzing these systems must become more fundamental and more forceful.

Crucial to that work, I argue, is connecting these specific problems and discrete case studies to technological capitalism in a serious way. Too much of the tech criticism that exists today is happy to ignore, if not remain ignorant of, the links between technology and capitalism. We can see this anodyne style in the sudden burst of work on "AI ethics," which is content with offering superficial tweaks to, say, the training data for an algorithm without ever challenging how that algorithm will be used or why it should exist at all.[32] Setting aside the cynical capture of ethics by corporations and consultants who make a point of distracting us from these questions, even some of the best work on the social impacts of technology hasn't made the leap to confronting the role of capital in what they rightfully critique. These two systems don't just happen to coexist in parallel; they are mutually reinforcing, load-bearing structures of our society.

Conclusions are never enough if our aim is to truly stay on top of their consequences, let alone actually stop their causes. We need to understand more than just what is happening because of these systems; we need to understand how and why these dynamic systems operate in the way they do. We need an approach to studying them that goes beyond observing and chasing their effects—like an ambulance always arriving after a crash has occurred. With such an understanding we would be better able to anticipate new developments in technology and capitalism while also better identifying the vital points where we can apply pressure.

This book has a strong point of view and takes normative positions. Yet my goal is not just to tell you *what* to think but to show you the value of an approach for *how* to engage with technological capitalism. Indeed, this move from *what* to *how* also marks a transition between my first book, *Too Smart,* and this book. Previously I spent a lot of time explaining what smart technology and digital capitalism was doing in our cities, homes, and lives. But now I want to get deeper into the core dynamics of how technology and capitalism are operating, how they manifest in a variety of ways, and how we must dismantle them to create something much better.

Next Up

The next chapters focus on key features of technological capitalism. Each one offers provocative ways of understanding the operations, logics, and impacts of this dual system that orders our society. The subject is massive, sprawling, and dynamic. No single book could be a definitive account. This one equips readers with tools to take the analysis further and in different directions.

While I hope the book will be read as a holistic collection, I have also written the chapters as stand-alone essays that are thematically linked. Starting from the beginning and working to the conclusion is not necessary for understanding the arguments. Readers should feel free to jump around according to their own needs and wishes.

Chapter 2 outlines the difference between idealist and materialist approaches to analysis and then describes two role models—the mechanic and the Luddite—whom we should embody in our ruthless criticism of technological capitalism.

Chapter 3 takes a deeper look at the concept of innovation in our culture, the emergence of venture capital as the dominant financial model for planning technology, and the role of fictitious capital in how innovations are valued.

Chapter 4 examines the imperatives of data as a form of capital, the processes of abstraction that turn us all into objects for machines, the arms race driving the development of artificial intelligence, and the capture of cheap data that is essential for technological capitalism.

Chapter 5 uncovers the dynamics of labor in artificial intelligence, the Potemkin illusion of using hidden people to fake automation, and the capitalist dream of creating a perpetual value machine that will finally abolish the problem of human labor.

Chapter 6 focuses on the central position of landlords in technological capitalism, the powers of rent extraction and remote control at the heart of software business models, the vast enclosure of everything through smart systems, and the convergence between digital platforms and real estate.

Chapter 7 dissects the vital role of risk in modern forms of governance over society, the integration of financial logics and technological systems, the use of risk scores in operations of power and value, the hyper-personalization of actuarial practices, and the moral economy of making risk into a commodity.

Chapter 8 concludes with the business of producing futures, the role of (real) utopias in both the maintenance and dissolution of technological capitalism, and the need to combat the futurists of capital with the materialist alternatives of the mechanic and the Luddite: the former knows the future is always built on the past, and the latter knows the future doesn't just happen to us, but that it must be made—actively and constantly.

We have now named our objects of focus and outlined our plan of attack. From here each chapter digs deeper into core features of how these systems work, who they work for, and what work they do to both construct and constrain society in specific ways, for specific purposes. Let's start by getting better acquainted with the fundamentals of ruthless criticism and our avatars for materialist analysis.

2 *Two Models*

Beer's Maxim

Stafford Beer knew a thing or two about analyzing complex systems. Beer was a pioneer of management cybernetics, a field of theory and practice based on creating mechanisms of information control, communication, and computation to govern the operations of large organizations, both private (e.g., United Steel) and public (e.g., Chile's economy). While Beer's career was fascinating, and far too eclectic (and weird) to do justice here, I invoke him because later in his professional life Beer put forth a maxim that I think should be an essential rule of thumb for analyzing technology: "The purpose of a system is what it does. There is after all, no point in claiming that the purpose of a system is to do what it constantly fails to do."[1]

It seems that many people involved in the tech sector today missed this memo. From the most anonymous copywriter to the most famous executives, the public discourse about technology is absolutely dominated by people claiming systems have purposes—and capabilities—that they not only regularly fail to fulfill but that they seemingly never will.

More often, these claims just propel cycles of wild hype where a stupendous amount of money and noise results, at best, in products with dubious value. Here I'm thinking of the blinding flash of Web3, NFTs, crypto, and so on.[2] Many investors and consumers lose their shirts, a few make out like bandits, and some from both sides go do the same exact thing with another venture in the next hype cycle while calling themselves serial entrepreneurs who know the value of failing fast.

More rarely, these claims can really blow up in spectacular ways. Here I'm thinking of the infamous case study of Theranos: the start-up that raised over $700 million dollars based on claims it had created a high-tech blood diagnostics machine. In reality Theranos was selling snake oil.[3] This was a rare case where being guilty of constant failure turned into a conviction for criminal fraud. Theranos was held up as a symbol of the absurd excess of Silicon Valley. Or even worse, Theranos's founder, Elizabeth Holmes, was depicted as a con artist who took advantage of starry-eyed investors who truly wanted to make the world a better place.

In her defense while on trial, attorneys for Holmes made the case that "exaggeration is part of Silicon Valley's startup culture"[4] and that investors should have known better and done their due diligence. (What made this failure into a criminal case was that Theranos not only bilked its rich investors, it then rolled out its fake tech to patients, which was a step too far.) I'm the last person to say that Theranos and Holmes were unfairly made into scapegoats for cultural evils—if anything their fate should be a far more common one in Silicon Valley—but she has a point! Writing about allegations of fraud against the electric truck company Nikola, the financial columnist Matt Levine deftly explains how this culture of hand waving works in technological capitalism:

Startup investors understand that this is the game they are playing; they want to be sold an enthusiastic vision of the future by someone who believes it so purely and tangibly that he thinks it has already happened. Sometimes it works out great, the founder achieves his vision, the future is as predicted and the investors get rich. Other times—most times—it doesn't work out, the vision fails, the future is different and the investors lose their money. It's fine. That is the game they are in, betting on wild visions of the future sold to them by wild visionaries; only some of them have to come true for the investors to get rich.[5]

We will get much deeper into the speculative games played by those who largely control decisions about innovation in society in the next chapter. For now, looping back to Beer's maxim, we can see how it effectively draws a line between approaches to analyzing technology and society that are based on idealism and those that are based on materialism.

Mind Palace

Idealism describes kinds of claims made about a system that are based on what we intend for it to do, what we hope it will achieve, and what we fear it will cause—and on all the many other beliefs that might surround a technology. It is a headspace where many promoters and propagandists for technological systems spend most of their time. Idealism is not the same as being *idealistic* in the sense of being optimistic or utopian about technology, though they often come as a pair. Rather, in our context, it is an approach that prioritizes ideas, desires, visions, and vibes as the true engine of society. This ethereal engine is set apart from the practices of physical bodies and the conditions of social relations. "Mainstream theories of power rely on a social ontology in which the wills, wishes, thoughts, and intentions of individual human beings constitute the ultimate foundation of any social phenomenon," writes philosopher Søren Mau. "Most of these theories commit the idealist mistake of assuming that the subject's active, transformative relation to its environment—its 'agency'—resides in or springs from its intellectual capacities."[6] Ideas are abstracted away from—not dependent upon or even dominant over—the corporeal and social contexts they are embedded within. In short, mental capacities are privileged over material conditions.

Idealism is not totally disconnected from the material world, as if the idealists only exist within their own mind palaces. The more apt comparison comes from the best-selling self-help book *The Secret*: if the reality you want does not manifest, then it is because you did not envision it hard enough, your consciousness was not raised high enough. Contrary to the slogan from *Field of Dreams*— "If you build it, they will come"—a slogan for idealism could be: If you believe it, the world will change. It is an attractive theory of change for both the powerful—who have utmost faith in their ability to shape the world through sheer willpower alone—and the powerless who must rely on the audacity of hoping for something better.

Idealism can be found in the pitches for disruption by start-ups, in the predictions about technologies that are just around the corner, in the hype generated by venture capitalists and entrepreneurs, in the visions put forward by futurists and consultants, and in a shocking amount of media coverage about technology. If you have paid even slight attention to the digital tech sector over the last fifty years, you'll have noticed the relentless cacophony of idealist claims about how technologies like the internet, block-chain, and artificial intelligence—or whatever trend is the latest rage—will empower communities, redistribute wealth, secure investments, manage risk, improve fairness, and much more. The degree to which these technologies achieve these goals is doubtful at best. It seems that their real purposes, in terms of what they chiefly succeed at doing, are nowhere to be found in this long list of assertions and aspirations.

Idealism is not just the refuge of cynical boosters and true believers. Many critics and skeptics also engage in idealist analysis. That is, they base their critical analysis on claims about the purposes and implications of systems—often using the assertions made by those marketing the technologies—rather than on their actual capabilities and consequences. The historian Lee Vinsel has identified a popular strain of skeptical idealism that he calls "criti-hype." Vinsel writes, "The kinds of critics that I am talking about invert boosters' messages—they retain the picture of extraordinary change but focus instead on negative problems and risks. It's as if they take press releases from startups and cover them with hell-scapes."[7] At its most severe, criti-hype can amount to just repeating verbatim the ad copy from press releases and company websites but doing so with sarcasm in your voice or a flashlight under your chin.

The ultimate result of criti-hype, Vinsel argues, is that the critics ironically give further credence to the very things they are criticizing by conflating idealist claims with material reality. For example, Cory Doctorow argues that the blockbuster book *Surveillance Capitalism* by Shoshana Zuboff has constructed an elaborate analysis of big tech firms like Google and Facebook that all but assumes they are "able to perform sorcerous acts of mind control" over users.[8] These companies would love for everybody to believe they have such lucrative powers! Imagine how much more you could charge advertisers and political parties if you could convince them that you had the ability to do mass mind control over consumers. All the better if you don't have to make those false claims explicitly and can let your biggest critics do the talking for you. The dangers of idealism cut both ways, whether wielded by the boosters or the skeptics of technological capitalism.

This leads us to the other side of the dividing line drawn by Beer's maxim, which I'll repeat here: "The purpose of a system is what it does. There is after all, no point in claiming that the purpose of a system is to do what it constantly fails to do."[9] Materialism sets about shining the interrogative light on a system and demanding answers to the questions: What do you do? How do you work? Who do you work for? As simple as these questions are, their answers can be hidden under layers of obfuscation:[10] The technical obfuscation of black boxes and esoteric expertise. The legal obfuscation of trade secrets and nondisclosure contracts. The mystical obfuscation of technics as magic and progress as inevitable. Piercing that obfuscation is a tough but necessary task.

The emphasis for materialist analysis is on closely studying the world as a place constituted by a vast, integrated web of physical objects, social relations, economic interests, and power dynamics—all linked together in continuous processes of motion and change. I argue that a materialist method is the best way for uncovering the truth of how these systems actually operate and their real outcomes—and for informing our reactions to that knowledge. It all sounds very complicated in the abstract. But the goal of this book is to show you this theory in action.

The rest of this chapter will illustrate this approach to the critical study of technological capitalism through two metaphorical role models for how to do materialist analysis: the mechanic and the Luddite. The mechanic knows how a machine is put together, how its parts function, and what work it does. The Luddite knows why the machine was built, whose purposes it serves, and when it should be seized—in both senses of stopped or taken, destroyed or expropriated. We should always strive to embody both of these models. Neither is sufficient on its own. The materialist analysis of the mechanic provides the basis for the material action of the Luddite.

The Mechanic

I was born on the Gulf Coast of Mississippi, but I went to high school in the plains state of South Dakota between the Black Hills Forest and the Badlands canyons. This is the kind of place where my science teacher was also a cattle rancher. Where I grew up, most people didn't go to big universities. They learned a trade—a skilled job acquired through some combination of technical school, community college, and apprenticeship—as has been the norm for a very long time in most places. And I was exposed to many different trades.

My dad was an electrician at a shipyard all his life, crawling around and pulling wires through the guts of half-built ships. He apprenticed at eighteen years old and stayed until he retired forty-five years later. My grandfather was a supervisor at the same shipyard, and my grandmother worked the switch boards at AT&T in her younger years, then later opened a home bakery that specialized in wedding cakes. My mom is skilled in the lost art of domestic crafts: a seamstress with the sewing machine; a chef in the kitchen; and expert at knowing exactly what chemicals and tools are needed to clean, maintain, and repair anything in the home that needed cleaning, maintaining, or repairing. My stepdad entered the Air Force at a young age and trained as a carpenter and mason before retraining in pest control. Our garage was filled with woodworking tools and traps for bugs and animals of all kinds. My older brother spent over a decade assembling, repairing, and delivering medical equipment like wheelchairs, nebulizers, and hospital beds to patients' homes—and retrieving that equipment when it was no longer needed. My younger brother is now an HVAC—heating, ventilation, and air conditioning—technician who works both on construction sites and in building management.

As a kid, I loved machines. I had all the standard interests of an amateur tinkerer. I took apart small appliances found at thrift stores. I set up Linux on my first laptop so I could have more control over it. One of my favorite shows was *Junkyard Wars*, where teams of engineers would have to construct machines like a trebuchet or jet car using what they salvaged from the scrap heap. It was likely this show—though the exact reason is now lost to my memory— that sparked my desire to learn how to weld. Knowing my science teacher (the cattle rancher) also did metal working, I asked him to show me how to weld. After a bit of convincing, he agreed. During lunch period, we would go to the school district's machine shop, where he showed me the ropes of MIG and TIG welding. I only learned the basics, but I loved knowing how things were put together. I started noticing the welds on metal joints and silently judging their finish. I even considered going to the local automotive trade school so I could learn how to work on high-performance vehicles.

But I decided that I would go to a university and follow a different interest, in chemistry, with a focus on polymers (synthetic materials like rubbers and plastics). This was catalyzed by another of my high school science teachers who let me propose and conduct experiments in class as long as I could explain what was happening in the reaction. My interest in the material world extended to their physical properties and chemical makeup. Eventually that interest grew to incorporate social relations and political dynamics. I switched majors to do what I'm doing now: treating science, technology, and engineering as subjects of critical study. I like to say that I entered college as a materials scientist and left a dialectical materialist.

In a literal sense, being a mechanic means having a trade, a profession, a certification, a degree, a set of skills. But in the analytical sense I'm using here, being a mechanic is as simple as pursuing a curiosity about how the world really works and what you can do in it. Like many kids, I was already acting like a mechanic. And I was lucky enough to be surrounded by others who supported that tendency and showed me different ways it could be manifest. It is only after we are alienated from our own material conditions—constantly told that only those with special access and rarefied expertise can uncover their properties or that we don't have the right abilities and tools to turn the scrap into something different—that we then believe material power and knowledge are out of our reach.

I want us all to be mechanics because none of us should be shut out from the workings of technology and capital; instead we should all be empowered to get under the hood and tinker with the machines, as well as take apart and (re)build the machines for our own purposes.

Our stereotypical idea of mechanics as low-status, low-skilled grease monkeys is a relatively recent social invention. The shift happened around the 1930s at the same time that the term *technol-*

ogy gained its now popular usage describing all manner of tools and machines.[11] As these tools and machines became more complex and as both industrialists and intellectuals started granting technology the power to drive and determine the shape of modern society, the mechanic was supplanted by the engineer. While the engineer became the master of technology, the engineer was meant to serve another master: the imperatives of capital. The origins of engineering as a profession can be found in the need for capital to turn its abstract logics of accumulation, control, and efficiency into concrete processes.[12] In practice this looks like deploying the full force of technology and science for the purpose of rationalizing every step of production—mining resources, manufacturing commodities, managing workers, and much more.

As a lieutenant for capital, the engineer became a prestigious profession that stripped others of their knowledge and autonomy over the technical systems that came to dominate work and life, while also expanding the power and purview of those systems.[13] At the same time, the mechanic and other trades became downgraded as the kind of thing you did if you lacked the class position and education to do something more valuable in society (i.e., something that generates more value for capital). Some people are given the opportunity and guidance to be engineers, and others find their way to training in skilled trades; but the majority of people are steered in other directions and away from obtaining mechanical knowledge. Thus, they live in a world where they are largely dispossessed of the ability to decipher, let alone modify or program, as they see fit. The historian Leo Marx traced this divide between the mechanic and the engineer in an essay investigating the emergence of technology as a "hazardous concept" in contemporary times. It is worth quoting from him at length:

Whereas the term *mechanic* (or *industrial*, or *practical*) *arts* calls to mind men with soiled hands tinkering at workbenches, *technology* conjures clean, well-educated, white male technicians in control booths watching dials, instrument panels, or computer monitors. Whereas the *mechanic arts* belong to the mundane world of work, physicality, and practicality—of humdrum handicrafts and artisanal skills—*technology* belongs on the higher social and intellectual plane of book learning, scientific research, and the university. This dispassionate word, with its synthetic patina, its lack of a physical or sensory referent, its aura of sanitized, bloodless—indeed, disembodied—cerebration and precision, has eased the induction of what had been the *mechanic arts*—now practiced by engineers—into the precincts of the finer arts and higher learning.[14]

This quote also highlights another crucial feature of these figures: we can only recuperate the mechanic as a model for engaging in materialist analysis by firmly rejecting all masculine tropes and any other forms of exclusion and stratification that seek to limit who has access to technical know-how.[15] Only then can the model live up to its critical purpose and radical potential.

The class hierarchy outlined above is also sharply divided by gender and race.[16] Skilled crafts and trades have been cleaved away from the domain of technology and industry. Crafts like sewing are often treated as mere hobbies done during free time, and trades like carpentry are viewed as ways to merely make a paycheck. They are set apart from vocations or professions in which people are seen as devoting their life to a higher purpose, like priests and engineers. However, these boundaries shift: as soon as work once classified as menial, mundane, and mindless becomes especially valuable for capitalist exploitation, then suddenly it gets redefined as a high-status, high-skill, high-tech profession. The social category shifts from feminine to masculine, from racialized to white, from poor to prestigious. There is an extensive body of research tracing these divides and their consequences for how, why, and by whom technical knowledge and material power are deployed in society.[17]

A striking example is the fact that the first "computers" were women who did long-hand calculations and the first coders were women who programmed early analog and digital computers.[18] Once these skills and machines started becoming essential to industry and government, they were reclassified as jobs for male experts.[19] Women were then deskilled and downgraded, emerging "as the *operators* of machinery, [who] do not have, nor are expected to have, knowledge of the inner workings of those machines."[20] Thanks to successful campaigns of historical revision and cultural division, the belief that technical knowledge is an inherent trait reserved for a certain class of white men is now treated as a social fact.

The mechanic, in the model for materialist analysis I have sketched here, offers a way to repudiate the gatekeeping over who operates the machines and who oversees the machines. Beyond making all the stuff in this world more accessible to everybody and supporting people's abilities to tinker with that stuff, the mechanic should also set us on the pathway to a more subversive techno-politics. It is not enough to simply "fix" the systems that already exist—in the sense of restoring and maintaining the machinery of capital—we must also scrap and salvage, take apart and build anew.

The Luddite

I'm a Luddite. This is not a hesitant confession but a proud proclamation. For me, Luddism is not a naive belief but a considered position. It does not come from being ignorant of technology but from being informed of its functions. Once you know what Luddism actually stands for, I bet you will begin identifying as a Luddite too—or at least be more sympathetic to the position than you might have thought.

Luddism is now mostly lobbed as an insult. Examples are abundant and casual. Typically, being a Luddite is seen as synonymous with being primitive: backwards in your outlook, ignorant of innovation's wonders, and fearful of modern society. But the term's usage can be slippery, reduced to a vague negative label for any position that does not enthusiastically embrace technology. For instance, take this recent report by Accenture, a global consulting firm and trend forecaster, that argues the health care sector must adopt artificial intelligence: "Excessive caution can be detrimental, creating a *luddite* culture of following the herd instead of forging forward."[21] You don't even have to reject technology to be a Luddite. According to this warning, anybody who is not an early adopter of unproven innovations also risks the follies of Luddism.

This all-or-nothing approach to debates about technology and society is based on severe misconceptions of the real history and politics of the original Luddites. As historian E. P. Thompson observes, "Luddism lingers in the popular mind as an uncouth, spontaneous affair of illiterate handworkers, blindly resisting machinery."[22] However, our circumstances today are much more similar to theirs than it might seem.[23] Our lives and labor are dominated by the same structural imperatives of capitalist exploitation. New technologies are used now, as they were then, to transform our social and working conditions. And if we knew more about Luddism, we might see that their actions were more than a sudden burst of rage against the machine, and we might even learn a few lessons from them.

The Luddites were skilled craftworkers who, under the cover of night, smashed weaving machines in the textile factories of England in the early 1800s. This was a time of turmoil, with people's ways of life (and livelihoods) being radically disrupted on multiple fronts. Modern capitalism was taking hold, giving rise to markets and profits as the dominant logics for society. The industrial revolution was in full swing, giving rise to new methods for accelerating production and controlling labor. The factory system was being created at this time, giving rise to the brutal exploitation of what poet William Blake called the "dark satanic mills."[24] There were foreign wars with France and the United States, giving rise to economic hardship as the state demanded more taxes, supplies, and soldiers from the public. And there was a newly urban working class as droves of people moved to cities to find jobs in factories, giving rise to crowded slums, inhumane conditions, and social unrest.[25]

It was this context that birthed the Luddites, who took their name from the apocryphal tale of Ned Ludd, a weaver's apprentice who supposedly smashed two knitting machines in a fit of rage. The contemporary usage of Luddite has the part about smashing machines correct—but that's about all it gets right. The Luddites were not a small club of unruly grunts. They were a secret society with hundreds of members spread across England; they had the vocal support of celebrities like Lord Byron and were organized with military precision, since many of its leaders were veterans of the war against Napoleon. The Luddites were folk heroes of their day, heroes who took a stand against the capitalists who sought to bleed people for all they could produce, against the machinery used to rob artisans of their expertise and freedom, and against the factories that broke the bodies of children who were beaten by overseers and fed into their gears.[26]

Let me explain why I've chosen the Luddite as a role model for materialist action against technological capitalism by clearing up three myths and misconceptions about Luddism as a movement and philosophy.

First, the Luddites were *not indiscriminate* in the machines they broke; it is not as if they just picked up the nearest hammer and started swinging at any metal and wood in sight. They were intentional and purposeful about which machines they smashed. They targeted those owned by manufacturers who were known to pay low wages, disregard workers' safety, or speed up the pace of work. Even within a single factory—which might contain machines owned by different capitalists—some machines were destroyed and others passed over depending on the business practices of their owners. Thus, the machines were not their real targets; their targets were the owners of those machines and the type of society they were bringing into being. The Luddites were striking blows against capitalism as a social system of exploitation by smashing the material manifestations of capital. "The wealthy and powerful understood machines as a method to accumulate power, and so too did the toiling classes over whom they wished to exert it," writes Gavin Mueller in his book, *Breaking Things at Work*, which examines Luddism as a labor struggle that has persisted, in various ways, over the last two hundred years.[27]

Second, The Luddites were *not ignorant*; they were not scared or mystified by the alien machines that appeared one day in their workplaces. It is important to remember that the Luddites were also mechanics—sometimes in the literal sense and often in the figurative sense I use above—who pushed their knowledge into action. They were not mindless workers or moronic peasants; they were skilled artisans who knew better than most about how the technologies and factories were operated and how labor and capital was organized. Luddism was a working-class movement opposed to the political economic consequences of industrial capitalism. Far from being a kneejerk reaction to new technology, smashing machines was a tactical response by workers based on their understanding of how owners were using those machines and what purposes they were serving. The Luddites wanted technology to be deployed in ways that made work more humane and gave workers more autonomy. The bosses, on the other hand, wanted to drive down costs and increase productivity. As historian David Noble puts it, "the Luddites were perhaps the last people in the West to perceive technology in the present tense and to act upon that perception."[28]

Third, the Luddites were *not against innovation*. In fact, many of the machines they destroyed weren't even new inventions. One machine they targeted, the gig mill, had been used for more than a century in textile manufacturing. Similarly, wide stocking frames and power looms had been used for decades.[29] If it was fear of new things that drove the Luddites, then they would not have waited so long to act. If it was hatred of new innovation, then they would not have used the machines for so long before destroying them. "Protest stemmed not from the invention but from the application of these new technologies," writes historian Adrian Randall.[30] The Luddites were provoked to action when capitalists began using these machines to displace and disempower workers, make labor conditions more miserable, reduce the quality of outputs, and increase their own profits.

Spoiler alert: the factory owners won in the end. The capitalists convinced the government to deploy its military to crush the worker uprising, infiltrate the Luddite movement with spies, hunt down its members, and make machine breaking a treasonous crime punishable by hanging. This was an early, important case of the state using its full might to enforce the demands of industrial capital and to protect its machines and markets from workers who fought back against the colonization of their lives.

Randall has argued that we still use the term *Luddite* today—a rare case of remembering the villains of technological progress rather than the heroes of history—because Luddism has been twisted into a "cautionary moral tale."[31] The Luddites are now examples of what happens to people who stand in the way of progress (as defined by capital), who advocate for their own autonomy and communities, and who attempt to assert social control over the machinery of production. They will be hung as traitors to the future and vilified as relics of the past. Well, the good name of Ludd has been dragged through the mud for far too long. It is time we reclaim the mantle and all that it stood for. Being a Luddite is not a scarlet letter we wear with shame. It is a badge we should display with pride.

Being a Luddite today does not necessarily (or only) require swinging hammers against the smart fridge in your home or the data servers that power digital technologies. As was the case with the original Luddites, destroying a machine is not the first action to be taken but rather a conclusion based on a critical analysis of the roles, purposes, and impacts of technology in society; it comes after other alternatives for democratic governance have been foreclosed by those with power and wealth. The first step to being a Luddite is simply opening yourself to the radical possibility of evaluating the technologies that fill our lives and determining whose goals they primarily advance. Not all innovations deserve to exist, and many should never have been created in the first place. Yet we assume their legitimacy and acquiesce to their existence merely because they have already been made. Silicon Valley demands we accept their products like a cargo cult receiving gifts from the gods. Instead we need an approach modeled more closely after Marie Kondo. For every technology, we should hold it up and ask—not, Does this thing spark joy?—but, Does this thing contribute to human well-being or social welfare? If not, toss it away! Any technology should have to pass that very simple criterion. Once you start applying that criterion, though, you might be surprised at how many technologies fail the test.

Contrary to being an extremist position against technology, Luddism is founded on a radical politics of refusal—which in reality just means having the right and ability to say no to things that directly impact your life. This should not be a radical stance; and yet in our dominant approaches and discourses about technology, the right to refusal is radical. With growing concern about issues related to areas like AI ethics, tech corporations have quickly mobilized to co-opt the conversation, write their own ethical principles, and promise to create (and self-regulate) policies for responsible innovation.[32] In practice, this means the ethical problems raised, and the solutions adopted, rarely go beyond technical reforms like decreasing bias and improving accuracy. They don't get close to posing fundamental challenges that might hinder the ability of corporations to do what they are already doing—all in the name of progress (and profits).

Rather than a politics of refusal, we are given an ethics of acceptance. The driving concern is: How do you get people to trust a technology, integrate it into their lives, or just look the other way and not raise a fuss? Ethics is put in service of technology: What must we do to make you trust us and accept this thing? When tech workers at places like Google do actually pose serious ethical challenges about the technologies being created and decisions being made and do so in ways that might really threaten corporate interests, then they are quickly demoted or fired. There is a "near total absence of the word 'no' in discussions of data ethics," notes Anna Lauren Hoffmann. "It neutralizes critical calls to not collect certain kinds of data or build and deploy certain technologies by reframing the issue as exclusively one of iteration, improvement, and doing things more inclusively."[33] If saying no is not a real option on the table, then you don't actually have a choice. We should not just be content with clicking "disagree" on yet another terms of service agreement.

Luddism is about asserting the ability to make meaningful decisions about the directions and applications of technologies that structure our lives. Technology is far too important to be thought of as just a grab bag of neat gadgets. And it's far too powerful to be left in the hands of billionaire executives and venture capitalists. I want technology—I want the future—to work for the many, not against us. We deserve a say in who creates it and how it's controlled. Two centuries ago, Luddism was a rallying call used by the working class to build solidarity in the battle for their livelihoods and autonomy. Despite all the changes in technology and capitalism that have occurred, the purpose and philosophy of Luddism remains as vital as ever.

Ruthless Criticism

The mechanic knows how a machine operates, how it is put together, and how it can be repaired or reengineered. The Luddite knows why the machine was built, whose purposes it serves, and when it should be disassembled or destroyed. By becoming mechanics and Luddites, we get to the heart of how these systems work, who they work for, and what we can do to change them. Together these models provide us with the tools necessary for rejecting the systems thrust on us by others and, in their place, making our own future.

Ultimately, as a philosophy of analysis and a source for action, materialism is rooted in "*the ruthless criticism of the existing order*," as Karl Marx wrote, "ruthless in that it will shrink neither from its own discoveries, nor from conflict with the powers that be."[34] To be ruthless, we must also be dogged in our pursuit of truth about the concrete operations of abstract systems. Whether it is artificial intelligence or financial instruments, the inner workings of these things that have outsized power in society are shielded by layers of opacity. Sure, these abstract systems are complex, but they are mystified by design. We are told that only an elite few know how they are created, and even fewer know how they actually work. The result is that the vast majority of people are prevented from acquiring the threatening position of knowing how things work, saying no to the way they work now, and then demanding that they work differently. With our two models in mind, we can set about engaging in the ruthless criticism that technological capitalism deserves.

Before we continue onwards, a note on style: I avoid a contrived application of these two models in the chapters that follow. I wrestled with the idea of having the mechanic and the Luddite be recurring characters that are constantly popping up to frame specific points and drive the analysis forward, thus keeping the whole book anchored to them. However, I decided it would be clunky, stylistically and analytically, to try making continuous references to them.

Imagine if I were regularly saying things like, "If we think about this as a mechanic . . . " or, "As a Luddite would say . . . " In addition to avoiding a choice that would quickly become tiresome for me and you, it is also just unnecessary for this book's purposes. I want every chapter to stand alone as a complete essay like an anthology series where each episode is a wholly contained piece of work. But taken together they are clearly hitting on bigger themes and building a deeper argument. So I've tried to minimize features that might confuse readers who are only engaging with certain chapters. The mechanic and the Luddite have done their jobs by helping set up the series, illustrating the materialist approach and critical attitude that motivates this book and persists through every chapter. They are the title characters of our story—their presence is felt in every scene; I wrote the coming chapters with them always on my mind—but they do not appear on-screen again until the finale.

3   *Innovation*

Silent Modifier

Innovation is worshiped in our culture. It is the one true source of human progress and a mercurial force that cannot be controlled. We can only hope to create the right conditions, make the right offerings, and perform the right rituals such that innovations bless us with sacred revelations and actionable insights. Those entrepreneurs and engineers who are seen as conduits for innovation are held in high esteem and granted access to power, wealth, and status. States, cities, companies, universities, nonprofits, and every other organization spend money, enact policies, hire consultants, and build cultures for the single purpose of driving, attracting, and harnessing innovation. There are countless departments, agencies, schools, and other giant institutions and initiatives with the word "innovation" in their title. All evidence for our universal pursuit of innovation.

We could define innovation as what is new, novel, and original. Perhaps it is a significant advancement on what already exists, taking things to the next level. Or it might be a significant disruption that upends the status quo, pushing humanity in new directions.

While these definitions of innovation are not wrong, they also do not get at the qualities of innovation that really matter in terms of the effect that it has on people. Innovation is much more than just an empty buzzword on a mission statement. It does real work in the world. It is a value people prioritize over most others. It is a goal people strive to achieve. It is an end that justifies almost any means necessary. It is a pillar of technological capitalism.

Innovation is a fetish: an object of obsession. Innovation is a feeling: a sense of the sublime. Divorced from the conditions and systems that produce it, innovation is treated as a transcendent force purified of any external influences—one that stands outside of society, while acting directly upon it. It emerges in ways that are unable to be fully comprehended, let alone directed. Innovation springs forth from the minds of the brilliant and the chosen; the sudden moment of eureka combined with the long hours of meritocratic hustle. When boiled down in this way, the rhetoric of innovation sounds absolutely absurd. And yet, once you become attuned to this way of thinking and talking about innovation, its existence and influence in every part of society is inescapable.

I'm reminded of the way people in a previous era of technological development wrote in splendid terms about the raw power of industrial machinery and infrastructure projects. Take this passage from a magazine essay in the 1830s about the railroads cutting across the American West: "Objects of exalted power and grandeur elevate the mind that seriously dwells on them, and impart to it greater compass and strength. . . . Its vastness and magnificence will prove communicable, and add to the standard of the intellect of our country."[1] Filter the baroque language through the style of a start-up's pitch deck or McKinsey trend report and it might as well be about the latest innovation in chatbots.

This persistent reverence for innovation as an abstract ideal, often without any reference to specific products or outcomes, is remarkably powerful considering how malleable and immaterial it can be. For technologists this veneration translates into vague proclamations about the power of innovation, regardless of the concrete form it takes—a power that they are uniquely capable of channeling and wielding. For policymakers this translates into mythologies about who produces innovation and promises about what benefits innovation will bring, along with a mission to support innovation at all costs. For academics, even the most critical ones, this translates into close readings of the discourses (ways people talk) and imaginaries (ways people think) about innovation held by the technologists and policymakers—along with normative advice on how to be ethically responsible when innovating. I should know: I've done my fair share of this type of work as a young academic trained in the art of applied ethics. In this chapter, however, I want to push our critical analysis past the idealism of this *innovation sublime*, the quasi-spiritual, awe-inspiring reverence for innovation,[2] and into the mechanics of the innovation system—that is, the modes of innovation within technological capitalism.

If you hang around people who loudly advocate for capitalism—think tankers, management consultants, libertarian economists, corporate executives, professional investors, and the politicians who repeat their memos—then you will hear the same claims about its unparalleled capacity for innovation at scales and speeds never before seen in human history. Among the loudest champions of this view now is Marc Andreessen, a prominent venture capitalist, who wrote in his "techno-optimist manifesto" that, "We believe the techno-capital machine of markets and innovation never ends, but instead spirals continuously upward." He continues to say, as if directly attacking me, "despite continuous howling from Communists and Luddites."[3]

I'm not here to refute these assertions because I simply cannot deny that capitalism is the most efficient system to ever exist for producing *capitalist innovation*. Of course, the modifier "capitalist" is always left out when we talk about innovation or when others tell us that innovation is the master we must all serve. But we cannot hope to be clear about the actual meaning and mechanics of innovation in society unless we say the silent modifier. Only then can we begin to understand what determines which "innovations" are created and which alternatives, based on different modifiers and parameters, are dismissed. Innovation is not a timeless category that exists across all space-time but is instead the product of its context. That context determines the creation and application, purpose and value of the things marked as innovations. To a great degree, for hundreds of years now, that context has been capitalist. And today that context is largely based in or directly modeled after the most holy site of innovation in the world: Silicon Valley.

Our fetish for innovation, and the industry of innovation that has been built on that ideological bedrock, is just one segment of the larger system of technological capitalism and capitalist technology—although it is a very important and idiosyncratic segment, which exerts an outsized influence on that system.

Innovation is now much more of a political project than a technological product. Innovation is a powerful instrument of social change—not as a primal force of progress but as a shield and sword for the desires of an oligarchic elite who control key financial decisions about technological development. The fact that every part of the system is extremely unequal—from resource allocation to accessing benefits and everything between and beyond—is not a novel observation on my part. It has also long been recognized that the innovations produced within a particular system reflect the nature of that system and the people who are privileged, powerful, and wealthy in that system.[4] In other words, if you want innovations that reproduce the values and advance the goals of technological capitalism, then make sure that the process of supporting, choosing, and using innovations is dominated by technological capitalism. This outcome can be achieved to great effect by putting a highly concentrated industry that is driven by accumulating more money than god and enacting its own internalized savior complex in charge of your innovation system.

Increasingly, the shine has started rubbing off the illustrious innovators of Silicon Valley. They don't seem as benevolent as they did not so long ago. It appears they really don't have our best interest at heart. Since it is hard to take aim at an abstract system, when people go looking for warm bodies to blame for the consequences of technology in society, they typically land on the most visible people in power. At first blush that would be the tech executives in charge of the biggest companies (or at least the founders and leaders most associated with these companies). Jeff Bezos is a stand-in for Amazon. Bill Gates for Microsoft. Mark Zuckerberg for Facebook. Elon Musk for Tesla. Further scrutiny might also land on the more anonymous engineers who actually build products, encoding their personal values and social visions into the technologies, which are then foisted upon the world. These targets of critique are the avatars of technological capitalism. They personify the system. More than most, they reap its rewards. In terms of blame and punishment, I fully support the need to round up the technocrats, line them up against a wall, and give them all a good kick in the ass.

At the same time, we should also direct our attention to a group that has largely escaped the crosshairs of ruthless criticism even though they are among the most influential agents of capitalist innovation: venture capitalists (VCs). The rest of this chapter will get deeper into the Silicon Valley model of innovation, which has been exported worldwide,[5] by describing how venture capital operates as a dominant method of private planning for technology. Rather than resulting in the best innovations that benefit the most people or tackle the biggest problems, we are sold technologies that prioritize the financial interests and social values of a small pool of investors and corporations. I will debunk the idea that venture capitalists are brave risk-takers who hold divining rods, which allow them to find the best innovations and which are hidden from everybody else. I will also demystify the techniques they use to extract profits from the future through abstract methods of making fictions and valorizing speculations.

Venture capital is far more important than it deserves to be, but to be sure, it is not representative of every process and product in the larger system. Even within the annals of capitalist innovation, there is a long history that predates the influence of venture capitalism. But having a clear view of venture capital and its consequences is crucial for understanding how innovation works (and doesn't work) today. VCs don't just fund technologies as passive investors; they have active effects on the market as gatekeepers in the tech sector. Rather than VCs chasing after innovation, the reverse is much more accurate. Innovation becomes defined by what fits into their portfolio of investments. Progress becomes defined by what aligns with their profit motive.

Innovation Realism

Modern venture capital (VC) firms originated after World War II to help commercialize the high-tech products of massive federal spending by the US military on research and development. These VCs found success in the late 1950s through early investments in companies like Fairchild Semiconductor, which pioneered the silicon transistors—giving Silicon Valley its name—that were used in the computers for B-70 bomber jets and Minuteman ballistic missiles. As the space race was taking off at this time, US federal spending provided major support for teaching, training, and employing electrical engineers and computer scientists while also creating giant markets for the new technologies they innovated. With supply and demand heavily subsidized by government spending, the VC industry expanded alongside Silicon Valley and Stanford University, as these places offered surefire ways to turn enormous profits.[6]

Venture capital is now what sustains the Silicon Valley model of investment and innovation. Without VCs the "global innovation landscape" would look drastically different.[7] In addition to being a mechanism for financing nascent ideas, VCs also "drive management and strategic decisions towards long-term corporate gains," argues economist Robyn Klingler-Vidra.[8] Venture capital has exerted powerful effects on major waves of technological trends over the last many decades, especially in the information technology industry blossoming out of Silicon Valley and its satellites like Seattle where Microsoft and Amazon are based.

At times, VCs exert a supply-side effect by pushing entrepreneurs and innovations across the finish line, moving them from a promising idea to a profitable investment, while also pushing them to focus on specific types of technologies and business models that can scale rapidly and deliver higher returns. Other times, VCs exert a demand-side effect by generating hype about the visions and technologies in which they have made investments. Being able to command the public's attention is crucial for VCs who need to build reputations as trendsetters and power brokers. If Wall Street financiers were "masters of the universe,"[9] then Silicon Valley VCs want to be makers of the future. VCs are extremely energetic in their attempts to control, and not merely chase after, innovation.

The mark of venture capital can be found on the semiconductors and mainframe computing of the 1960s and 1970s, the personal computing and software apps of the 1980s, the internet and e-commerce of the 1990s, the mobile and social web of the 2000s, the gig economy and x-as-a-service platforms of the 2010s, and the crypto assets and generative AI of the 2020s. I should also note that VCs have been active in the life sciences and biotech start-ups since the 1980s, financing ventures in areas like pharmaceuticals, genetics, and medical devices—although investment has been on a steady decline for the last twenty years[10] and has shifted toward shorter-term, lower-risk, higher-return investments[11] like developing hardware and software for medical applications. (Theranos was meant to be the crown jewel of Silicon Valley biotech.) These investments are often based on further integrating information technology into the health care sector, whether through personal devices for patients/consumers or computing infrastructure for hospitals and providers. Considering the primary focus of both the VC industry and this book, I will not delve any deeper into their biotech ventures.

VCs want to project an image as high-tech vanguards who are tapped into the cutting-edge of innovation in order to distract us from what they really are: overstuffed wallets who happened to have the right friends at the right time. For VCs, manipulating the public's perception of value in any particular technology or trend is absolutely essential for their bottom line. The VC industry—especially a handful of big firms like SoftBank, Andreessen Horowitz, and Peter Thiel's Founders Fund—is undeniably successful at directing mighty torrents of hype and capital into the places it wants. Behind every tech company like Uber and Amazon that seeks to dominate the market, behind every tech trend like Web3 and AI that seeks to disrupt our lives, there are VCs pushing us through cycle after cycle of capitalist innovation.

VCs are gatekeepers to capital, guarding its flow and deciding who gets access. This intermediary position gives them a crucial form of structural power over tech start-ups. They control the purse strings for entrepreneurs and, as political economist Franziska Cooiman observes, "There is no alternative way [for start-ups] to obtain comparable amounts of capital."[12] This also gives VCs the ability to ensure the digital economy follows their logics and serves their needs, the most important being what Cooiman calls "the hypergrowth principle." This is more than just profit maximization. Hypergrowth is based on selecting start-ups, technologies, and business models that can scale exponentially in a very short period and that have the potential to dominate their particular market.

Furthermore, the influence of VCs has a long tail that can persist even after a start-up no longer needs to burn venture capital to sustain its operations and growth. VCs regularly sit on the boards of start-ups they invest in, and they keep those seats after companies become titans, thus allowing them to continue exerting influence over corporate governance and strategy in the tech sector. I will get deeper into the power and influence of venture capital in the next section, but first we need to understand how the VC industry is structured, which is crucial to how it has become so dominant.

Venture capital did not become the behemoth it is today through sheer force of ingenuity, expertise, and luck. Nor is it even very good at picking winners and supporting innovation, as we will see. Rather, the entire industry and the form of entrepreneurial financing it champions is significantly shaped by—and designed to take advantage of—US tax law and regulatory rules. There was a pivotal point between 1978 and 1981 when a few legal changes transformed venture capital from just another way of investing in technologies with commercial potential into a dominant method of innovation policy in society.[13] This is the period when the modern venture capital industry was born; instead of people making minor investments with personal money, a major industry built on institutional capital coalesced.

Let's go over the basics. Venture capital is based on partnerships. The "general partners" in a firm are active investors who decide where to invest money. (How they actually make these decisions is something we will discuss more below). They manage those investments by building relationships with the entrepreneurs and providing guidance to the businesses where they invest. These general partners are the people we know as VCs. Then there are "limited partners" in a firm, who provide the capital. They are usually big institutional investors, like pension funds and university endowments, that have giant pools of money they want to grow further. In short, the general partners at a VC firm will raise an investment fund by getting capital from limited partners based on factors like their social networks, personal reputation, track record of success, and market analysis on emerging trends and over-looked opportunities. Funds typically last for ten years. Over that time, VCs will be expected to invest all the capital into promising tech companies and generate profits that will be returned to the limited partners—usually by guiding those start-ups into an initial public stock offering or an acquisition by an industry incumbent—with VCs taking an annual management fee plus around 20 percent of total investment profits.

This partnership structure is crucial to the success of the VC model. "Because VC funds are partnerships," writes law professor Peter Lee, "capital gains flow directly to investors without being taxed. Furthermore, if investors are tax-exempt, such as non-profit pension funds or foundations, they do not pay any taxes at all." So while the institutional limited partners were greatly incentivized by tax advantages to invest into venture funds, the individual general partners—the VCs actively managing that capital—were still susceptible to high taxes on their profits. This began to change in 1973 when the industry created the National Venture Capital Association (NVCA) to lobby for legislative changes. They scored some quick wins in the form of tax cuts for capital gains in both 1978 and 1981. VCs also benefited from further tax advantages to stock options, or the right to buy shares of a company at a preset (often low) price, a common method of compensation from investment in start-ups. With these tax cuts stacking up, being a venture capitalist now offered higher returns and less risk than before, which then attracted people who had made their own personal wealth as entrepreneurs and were ready to try their hand as investors.

Tax cuts are nice, but the real master stroke of government subsidy for the VC industry came indirectly from an obscure rule clarification that regulated investment activities by pension managers. I will quote from Lee's explanation:

> In 1979, the Department of Labor clarified the "prudent man" rule under the Employee Retirement Income Security Act to allow private pension fund managers to invest in risky asset classes such as venture capital. This regulatory change (for which the NVCA lobbied) led to a massive increase in capital for VC markets. In 1978, the year before the "prudent man" change, pension funds accounted for $481 million and 15% of VC investments. By 1986, they accounted for $4.8 billion and more than half of all VC investments. Federal laws, regulations, and funding continue to support the VC industry in myriad ways. Congress has enacted less stringent business regulations to promote VC activity. Rules governing pension fund management continue to allow billions of dollars to flow into VC markets every year.[14]

The VC industry is a prime case study in the power of government subsidy—both directly and indirectly through means like defense contracts, research grants, tax cuts, and rule changes—to provide crucial public support for the growth of private profits and public security for the adventurism of private markets.

However, it is not clear that these subsidies alone would have been enough to turn the VC industry into the powerful gatekeepers for innovation they are today. There is no deterministic reason why the VC industry would become so increasingly central to strategies about innovation policy, decisions about innovation planning, and methods for innovation finance.[15] Indeed, as we can see by the ways VCs prioritize technologies that can deliver hypergrowth scale and monopoly profits,[16] there are many reasons why this model should not be so dominant. And yet, it not only holds this key position, it is also crowding out alternative models of funding innovation. As Klingler-Vidra notes, "venture capital funding is increasingly seen as a substitute for other forms of R&D [research and development] spending that are in decline, especially research directly funded by governments."[17] In other words, government agencies, which might have mandates to deliver public goods like sustainable transportation or tackle societal problems like growing inequality, are now surrendering those decisions to private financial markets. This trend is also present in corporate spending on R&D, which has greatly declined as corporations instead rely more on acquiring or partnering with (mostly venture-capital-backed) start-ups that are doing valuable R&D.[18]

The ascension of venture capital, particularly over the last fifteen years, since the 2008 financial crisis, has also been significantly buoyed by the zero interest-rate policy of the central banks, which made credit cheap and induced much greater borrowing by firms, as well as the redirection of capital from traditional financial investments into technological ventures. For example, the mega-platforms Uber, Airbnb, and WeWork—which received billions in investment, tens of billions in valuation, and sought to take over core services related to how we live, work, travel, consume, and so on—were all founded in the immediate aftermath of the global financial crash, which created the perfect conditions for venture capital and tech start-ups to thrive.[19] The only time more money has been pumped into this ecosystem was during 2021 in the midst of the pandemic, when the VC industry broke its records fundraising, "with $128.3 billion raised by 730 funds—more than 1.5× the amount raised in 2020—bringing cumulative dry powder [money that is raised but not yet deployed] in the industry to an all-time high of $222.7 billion."[20] In total, "nearly $330 billion" was invested by VC firms in 2021. This amount of money is mind-boggling. This level of investment is incomprehensible. It also raises the question: What do we have to show for it? Where is the $330 billion of technological innovation, social progress, and human flourishing? Does the world feel $330 billion better than it was before? Or does it somehow feel even worse?

The central role that VC occupies in the innovation system has been the result of several self-reinforcing factors. The tremendous amount of government support and passive capital funneled into the VC industry has fueled its growth. In turn, the space made for VC in our cultural ideas of how innovation can and should happen has created a version of what I call *innovation realism*. Here, I'm riffing on Mark Fisher's concept of "capitalist realism," the "widespread sense that not only is capitalism the only viable political and economic system, but also that it is now impossible even to imagine a coherent alternative to it."[21] Similarly, venture capital seems like the only viable way to support innovation, and it is impossible to imagine, let alone implement, alternative methods.[22] Unsurprisingly, this self-serving view is often expressed by people in the VC industry, both investors and entrepreneurs. But the view has also been adopted more widely. We can see the cause and effect of innovation realism in the way that government policymakers have ceded ground to venture capital in their political strategies and economic decisions about who should do central planning for innovation.[23]

For example, in early 2023, Silicon Valley Bank, the place where the majority of VCs and start-ups kept their money, experienced a bank run that caused it to collapse overnight (as a result of VCs getting spooked by interest rates rising and whipping their portfolio companies into panicked frenzy; it's a dumb, tedious story).[24] It looked like the industry was going to lose a large chunk of its hoard in one swift, self-inflicted blow. When this happened, Larry Summers—an economist who has held every top Champion of Neoliberalism position from US secretary of Treasury to president of Harvard to board member of OpenAI—immediately took to Twitter, newspapers, and television to explain that if the government did not bail out these VCs and start-ups with billions of dollars, "the consequences really will be quite severe for our innovation system."[25] For Summers and other mouthpieces of capital, Silicon Valley is not just an innovative place where economic activity happens, *it is the innovation system for the global economy.* After loudly crowing about their dire situation and demanding the government make them whole again, only a few days later a bailout did come for the VCs and start-ups.[26] Once again the government provided the crucial support necessary to maintain the VC industry, socialize the risks they take on, and protect them from their own actions.[27] That is the ideology of innovation realism given material effect.

It's Time to Build

If venture capital is the chosen mode of innovation for technological capitalism, then how exactly does it wield that position and exert that influence? Let's look at three important ways that venture capital drives the political economy of innovation. There is much more that can be fleshed out about each one, but my outline will give us a better understanding of this system and its dynamics. First, VCs have a massive war chest, which is dedicated to bankrolling the development of their chosen technologies. Second, VCs engage in political lobbying, which is dedicated to establishing the legitimacy of their interests and securing their position in the economy. Third, VCs control a powerful hype machine, which is dedicated to pushing the inevitability of their investments.

It is easier to illustrate these points with an example of the major VC investment cycle in Web3 and crypto, which collapsed in late 2022 as the next major cycle in generative AI was ballooning. The political economy of Web3 serves as a perfect case study of innovation and investment within Silicon Valley.[28] Web3 was the term used by Silicon Valley to denote what was meant to be the next ascendent stage of the internet. It encompasses all the stuff having to do with blockchain, cryptocurrency, digital assets, non-fungible tokens (NFTs), the metaverse, and decentralized networks—which took over tech culture during the few years from 2019 to 2022. We don't need to get too deep into the weeds of Web3 beyond that to understand my points here.

While the hype around Web3 was heightened to absurd levels, its underlying dynamics as a speculative asset bubble were not anomalous. Quite the contrary, these dynamics were so exaggerated in Web3 that normally subtle or subtextual elements were made explicit and easier to see in action. The cycles of technological trends and investment bubbles seem to be accelerating at such a rate that we are unable to observe them in motion before they crash. And then everybody just moves on to the next thing. With the added benefit of recent hindsight, we can make the absurdity of Web3 work in our favor to better understand the logics of venture capital.

Web3 was a creation of the VC industry, which reflected broader patterns in finance that existed before Web3 and will exist after. It is not the quirky outlier or freak accident—like something that came out of a drunken night that got out of hand—that many people tried to make it out to be after its collapse was already underway. Instead, the financial system that gave rise to these bizarre, ephemeral technologies did what it was designed to do: it made wild claims about technologies, marketed visions of a future, and got people to buy into that future, thus pumping up the value of these speculative assets for investors who owned the casino where everybody else was gambling.

Even when the market crashed and the technology failed, causing the vast majority of people who bought into the hype to lose everything as prices went to zero, the VCs at the top were mostly insulated from these risks and still walked away with hefty returns. Sure, there was collateral damage among the casino owners, like Sam Bankman-Fried, founder of cryptocurrency exchange FTX, who was found guilty for orchestrating a multibillion-dollar fraud. But the VCs behind Web3 were largely unscathed and free to inflate the next hype cycle. That's how the system works. The innovations may not survive, but the model itself continues to thrive. Not because it's the best but because it must in order to keep capital in motion.

Among its many advocates, the VC firm Andreessen Horowitz took a lead role in shaping, supporting, funding, pushing, and lobbying for Web3 as *the future*—not just of the internet but of everything. Andreessen Horowitz, which also goes by the name a16z, is among the most venerated and influential firms; they direct vast flows of capital into tech trends and start-ups. Andreessen Horowitz is one of the few firms that can (and will) invest $100 million into a single company. They play a strong hand in creating these trends and choosing their winners. With their capital comes not just a lot of attention directed toward their investments but also more capital from others who follow the leader.

At the height of the mania for Web3 in 2021, VCs raised immense funds that were earmarked for crypto and blockchain. Investments skyrocketed in start-ups even loosely related to these areas (just as they are now with the buzzword "[generative] artificial intelligence").[29] If saying "Web3" was all it took for money to magically appear, then a lot of people would start saying the word and reframing their pitches, ideas, and products accordingly. At one point, Andreessen Horowitz had more than sixty people on their "crypto Web3 team." As a16z general partner Chris Dixon explains, the firm devoted "significant" resources toward shaping, commanding, and "evangeliz[ing] the space."[30] General partners at Andreessen Horowitz stated their goal was to "find the next generation of visionary crypto founders" because "crypto is not only the future of finance but, as with the internet in the early days, is poised to transform all aspects of our lives."[31] Andreessen Horowitz is far from alone in putting their money where their mouth is. Many other venture funds raised hundreds of millions of dollars with similar goals of pumping cash into Web3. But the VCs at Andreessen Horowitz had established themselves as a vanguard among the coterie of other venture capitalists, corporate executives, start-up founders, technologists, futurists, celebrities, and posters who were actively constructing Web3.

"It's time to build," proclaimed Marc Andreessen at the beginning of the pandemic in a forceful essay arguing that meaningful innovation was the only way out of our crisis and that VCs were poised to select, support, and shepherd that innovation. In practice this looked like Andreessen Horowitz leading a $450 million funding round for Yuga Labs, the start-up behind the Bored Ape Yacht Club NFTs, at a valuation of $4 billion.[32] While this is a ludicrous amount of money, it is also common to see brand-new start-ups with little more than a half-baked idea receive many millions and be valued at billions—as long as the idea is framed in the right way by the right people at the right time. The amount of free money sloshing around, looking for places to be invested and burned, suggests that the primary force propelling Web3, just as with any tech hype cycle, was the momentum of capital.

These steep investments were accompanied by a sudden rise in political lobbying for legislation and regulation friendly to the technologies VCs were funding. According to a report on the cryptocurrency lobby in Washington, DC, by consumer advocacy group Public Citizen, the number of lobbyists representing crypto tripled in the few years leading up to 2021, and the amount spent on lobbying for the crypto sector "quadrupled from $2.2 million in 2018 to $9 million in 2021."[33] These amounts are nothing compared to the money VCs burn on start-ups; politicians come much cheaper. In addition to industry groups like the Blockchain Association and the Chamber of Digital Commerce, VCs want to have a strong hand in shaping the rules (if any) that govern their technologies and to establish legitimacy for technologies that operate on the fringes of legality.

Andreessen Horowitz rapidly hired a number of former government officials, the *New York Times* reported, to promote their interest and "push its agenda" in Washington, DC, as part of a "bold plan to dominate crypto."[34] This includes circulating draft legislation designed to exempt crypto companies from "certain tax reporting, consumer protection and anti-money-laundering requirements." A receptive group of lawmakers known as the "crypto caucus" sprang up in the US Congress. The caucus brought together a bipartisan mix of powerful Republican and Democratic lawmakers who have the explicit aim of promoting cryptocurrency and protecting it from regulation. While they approach the issue from different political perspectives—ranging from progressive liberal techno-utopianism to conservative libertarian antistatism—they share the same conclusions: crypto is the future that must be secured. Of course, these politicians also receive donations from the same pro-crypto, pro-blockchain lobbying groups. As the *Financial Times* notes, "The spending [on lobbying] reflects the growing influence of this group of lawmakers, as well as an awareness that the decisions made now will determine how crypto assets are regulated for decades."[35]

VCs steer innovation and shape industries by taking active roles in their investments.[36] In addition to "selecting only companies with the potential to grow fast and large and decouple financial value from business fundamentals," argues Franziska Cooiman, VCs actively manage the companies in their portfolio via formal (e.g., board seats) and informal (e.g., business advice) methods.[37] Furthermore, they work to generate interest among other investors and expectations among the public. Producing hype about a technology or trend is crucial for growing its value—real, perceived, and speculative. An elite tier of firms like Andreessen Horowitz can garner reputations for being kingmakers and create self-fulfilling prophecies where the very act of them investing in a start-up or even showing interest in a particular kind of innovation can generate higher levels of value.

While the number of VC funds is expanding, increasingly the vast majority of capital is concentrated in a small group of giant funds that control investment decisions. The 2022 NVCA Pitchbook *Venture Monitor*, an industry report on the financial activities of venture capital, shows that just over 50 percent of the total capital raised that year—a whopping $162.6 billion—went to the handful of VC firms with over $1 billion of assets under management, while funds under $1 billion but more than $500 million took another 20 percent of capital raised.[38] Almost all of those VC firms are also located in the Bay Area and New York, with Boston and Los Angeles soaking up most of what's left.

VCs choose technologies that fit the economic conditions they need to prosper. "A vicious circle emerges," Cooiman writes, "allowing these few [investors] to collect more capital, be more attractive for high-potential start-ups, and, with their network and experience, effectively not only pick but create winners, which again increases returns and overall attractiveness."[39] Through their investment decisions, influenced by their own financial interests and time horizons, based on their limited scope and specific values, they make choices about what kinds of technologies count as "high potential" and which pathways are not worth pursuing.[40] A technology transfer officer and former venture capitalist told Lee: "There's just countless examples of that, where poor quality innovation is what actually makes it to market, because of the team, the network, the location, the hype, the everything." The reason why so much investment is sunk into software is not because that's where the most or best innovation necessarily happens. It is because, generally, software is cheaper to build, quick and easy to scale, able to serve a large market, and lower risk compared to many other types of technology.

Venture Capital in the Desert of the Real

Digital systems like platforms and artificial intelligence provide an anchor for the assets and visions of the tech sector, but its capital and value depend on a foundation that is largely fictitious. Now, here I mean fictitious in a very specific financial sense; as David Harvey explains, fictitious capital is "money that is thrown into circulation as capital without any material basis in commodities or productive activity."[41] Fictitious capital is not quite the same as money for nothing. It is money derived from property rights, financial engineering, and speculative valuation. It is money represented by numbers in a spreadsheet. It is money that you claim now based on money that is expected to be (but may never actually be) realized later.

One of the many strong synergies between Silicon Valley and Wall Street is their shared focus on financialization.[42] Digital technologies are used to further spread dynamics of assetization, monetization, and speculation at the individual transactional level, which then has complex systemic effects.[43] While that is not always the (explicit) purpose of projects, it is the motivation behind technologies that fall under categories like *fintech* (finance technology) and *DeFi* (decentralized finance), as well as many "x-as-a-service" digital platforms,[44] all of which have also received the most investment and attention. As legal scholar Saule Omarova observes, the fintech and DeFi innovations that were core to the Web3 movement enabled "private market participants to engage in the continuous synthesizing of crypto-assets that are (a) effectively untethered from, and thus unconstrained by, any productive activity in the real economy, and (b) tradable in potentially infinitely scalable virtual markets."[45] The term *real economy* refers to the production, circulation, and consumption of goods and services; it is the material basis of the economy, which includes the types of things we normally think of as economic activities.

Importantly, the fictitious economy and the real economy are not identical, as if they were two interpretations of the same economy. Nor do they exist in isolation, as if they were two parallel economies that didn't interact with each other. Instead, they are intertwined, with financial activities focused on the fictitious increasingly dominating the conditions of the real. The risks created by complex forms of financial engineering used to make, sell, and trade securities in secondary markets can (and do) spill over into the real economy of assets, at times with disastrous, systemic effects. These techniques, and the conditions they created, were the same ones that led to the 2008 Global Financial Crisis and its devastating aftermath for people who lost their savings, homes, and jobs. "The key risk posed by fintech lies in its (still not fully known) potential to exacerbate the financial system's dysfunctional tendency toward unsustainably self-referential growth," writes Omarova.[46] Meanwhile the returns from these fintech products largely go to professional investors, portfolio managers, and start-up founders. Capital invested in engineering innovative technologies may result in the development of material assets and services—for example, AI systems, blockchain protocols, and software apps—but their value is intimately tied to the financial markets and fictitious capital, not the real economy.

Venture capitalists are in the business of creating and circulating fictitious capital. The top investors decide which ideas are worthy and how much they are worth. We can see how this plays out in the valuation of start-ups. When a company is publicly traded, its business valuation is most simply the calculation of its market capitalization, or the company's share price multiplied by its outstanding shares. However, when a company is privately held, its business valuation is often reported in terms of investment in the company. So, for example, when a technology start-up receives VC funding and is then reported to have a valuation of $1 billion, that number is not the company's current net worth (total assets minus liabilities). The actual money invested might be $200 million for a 20 percent equity stake in the start-up, which then translates to a current day valuation of $1 billion. Valuation ultimately means that the company will (hopefully) be worth (more than) $1 billion by a specific point in the future (usually five to ten years), at which time VCs can liquidate (or "exit") their position, usually by guiding the start-up to an IPO or acquisition, and make a hefty return on investment.

Other VCs might then pile into subsequent rounds since this is now a hot start-up and juice the valuation even higher. Alternatively, VCs might compete to invest in a company, offering higher valuations and better terms to court the founders, further driving up the valuation like an auction. VCs might then also tell journalists that the start-up has strong momentum for "10× growth," which means it will (they hope and believe) become a $10 billion company. Now suddenly $10 billion becomes the number reported in headlines.

The name given to start-ups with valuations of more than $1 billion is "unicorn" (and more than $10 billion is "decacorn"). An in-depth financial analysis of VC valuations for 135 US unicorns by economists Will Gornall and Ilya Strebulaev shows that nearly all of them were massively overinflated, with half of them losing unicorn status when valuations were adjusted based on fair value calculations.[47] Unicorns are not magical creatures found in nature by lucky investors, they are artificial creations engineered by VCs.[48]

This valuation process is always a projection based on the VCs' analysis of business factors such as user base, growth rate, and potential market but also on their largely subjective interpretation of general vibes, cultural trends, social "signals" of success from founders, and funding activities by other VC firms.[49] Indeed, VCs are notorious herd animals who, rather than seeking out hidden gems, more often take the risk-averse option of following the lead of larger VC firms and sticking with what they know: white guys who drop out of Stanford or Harvard and/or went through an accelerator like Y Combinator and/or worked at a famous unicorn like Stripe.[50] Investment into "businesses founded by women and people of color remains a stubbornly low percentage of all venture capital investment," according to the NVCA Pitchbook *Venture Monitor* report.[51]

While VC firms hear countless pitches from aspiring start-ups—whether via cold calls or during events like "open pitch days"—empirical research shows that almost all funding goes to the small number of entrepreneurs who already have social capital; they have the right demographics, connections, and networks.[52] Why would VCs spend time listening to thousands of pitches per year if they are only going to fund a fractional percent of them? These pitch days have been called "predatory" because participants are often charged fees to take part and there is no realistic chance of receiving funding.[53] These pitches are a free and continuous source of market intelligence for VCs. They are an easy way to gain valuable insights about what trends are emerging, what technologies are being developed, and which teams are ahead of everybody else.

An infamous case of the tenuous basis for valuations is WeWork. The story goes that Masayoshi Son, head of SoftBank and architect of its $100 billion Vision Fund, took a twelve-minute tour of WeWork's headquarters and was so impressed by their "energy and spirituality," as its founder Adam Neumann put it, that Son stopped Neumann's pitch, pulled out his iPad, and scrawled out a contract to invest $4.4 billion in the company at a valuation of $20 billion.[54] This example shows how absurd impulsive decisions, cavalier attitudes, and vulgar extravagance can be—and yet these sorts of dubious rationales for investing billions of dollars are not anomalous in the VC world.

While real money is invested—very large sums of cash in some cases—it then multiplies and circulates as fictitious capital. "Money capital is invested in future appropriation," explains David Harvey. "From the very outset, therefore, the money capital advanced has to be regarded as fictitious capital because it is not backed by any firm collateral."[55] The start-up might then be able to borrow more money, raise even larger subsequent rounds of VC investment, and sustain heavy long-term losses without ever making a profit—all based on the fictitious capital created in the valuation process. "Capital is value in motion and any pause or even a slowdown in that motion for whatever reason means a loss of value, which may be resuscitated in part or in total only when the motion of capital is resumed."[56] As fictitious capital continuously moves through this financial system, circulating with increasingly more velocity and volume, its value appears to be "doubled and tripled," Marx writes in *Capital, Volume III*, and is "transformed into a mere phantom of the mind."[57]

And yet, these claims of valuation based on speculative, dream-like projections are often reported and treated as existing material value based in the real economy. The potential of money later gets conflated with the actuality of money now. As Marx goes on to say, "profits and losses that result from fluctuations in the price of these ownership titles [such as shares in a company] are by the nature of the case more and more the result of gambling."[58] All the world's a casino, and all the VCs and entrepreneurs merely players; they have their exits and their entrances.

It is worth reiterating that just because capital is fictitious does not mean its effects are unreal. Far from it: fictitious capital shapes our world in important, material, and legally enforced ways. This is similar to how expectations for the future still have concrete effects on the present through their influence on people's desires, beliefs, actions, and plans.[59] The hype cycles and liminal technologies of Silicon Valley—which exists in that space between "marketing and materiality, imagination and implementation, becoming and being"[60]—depend on navigating the journey from fictitious to real. These social fictions, like other matters of faith, are supported by people treating them as real, inevitable, and powerful. This is why the biggest boosters for whatever technology—the platforms of the gig economy, the crypto assets of Web3, the chatbots of generative AI, or the next disruptive thing—always demand that everybody organize their whole life around these systems. It is not enough for us to be mere users, we must also become true believers in capitalist innovation.

4 *Data*

Drilling for Data

Our metaphors for thinking about digital data are, generally speaking, god awful. A term like *data mining* spins off a number of hackneyed claims like "data is the new oil" or "data is like raw ore," which then leads to ideas about data being a natural resource that exists within everything just waiting to be discovered and tapped, which then supports schemes based on data being a commodity that can be bought and sold on the open market, which then gives rise to proposals for how to reclaim ownership of our data by treating it as a form of personal property that we can control by choosing whom to share and sell it to. It is amazing how much this simple metaphor has muddled our thinking and doing about data—a form of capital, as I'll explain below, that has become central to most industries and continues to be essential to capitalist development.[1]

In many cases, people have stopped treating the metaphor like a metaphor, taking it instead as a literal description of how data works and what it does. I suspect its popularity and utility, however, stem in large part from the way it gives people—academics and journalists, corporations and governments—a helpful shorthand for talking about the "data economy" or "digital economy" without requiring that people actually engage in the political economy of data. If you don't have to be any more specific, then all the stuff about its features and processes, what it does and how it works, can be elided by a series of bad metaphors. Those whose job it is to explain things can reach for handy illustrations like oil derricks labeled with the names of digital platforms that are "drilling" for data in an open ocean.[2] To quote Will Ferrell's character in the film *Blades of Glory,* "No one knows what it means, but it's provocative. It gets the people going!"

Meanwhile, companies can rely on the public assumption that they are mining and refining a natural resource necessary to power the next industrial revolution, just like fossil fuels did before. Indeed, as is often the case, the innovations might have been sparked by new upstarts, but the large-scale technological transition is being led by many of the same corporate behemoths of previous eras: "Industrial giants such as GE and Siemens now sell themselves as data firms," writes the *Economist* in a cover story titled "The World's Most Valuable Resource Is No Longer Oil, but Data."[3] Or consider the CEO of Ford's statement that monetizing data from the "100 million people in [Ford] vehicles" is a major revenue stream for the car company.[4] Or take Monsanto—the agrochemical biotech corporation owned by Bayer, the pharmaceutical corporation—which is retooling to focus on information technology by making heavy investments in machine learning. Monsanto also increased its data science department from two hundred people in 2017 to five hundred people in 2020.[5]

The trend this metaphor is trying to capture can be seen everywhere. Data is obviously important to the institutions that have controlling interests in the global political economy. The problem is that the metaphor—with its false premises and lazy comparisons—hides more than it reveals.

Metaphors should at least clarify our thinking, for example, by making abstract concepts more concrete. At best they provoke new ways of thinking by drawing interesting connections between different things. Metaphors can also have great power over our minds, framing our understanding of the world, leading us to new possibilities, or trapping us in old realities. Thus we should also ask, Who do our metaphors benefit? What purposes do they serve?

Even a quick critical look at the term *data mining* and other similar metaphors that treat data as a natural resource reveals that they are based on a false premise, which distracts us from a key feature: data is always manufactured. "The mystification that occurs when discussing raw data or data as a raw material is that the material processes and instruments required to produce data are obscured while data is effectively naturalised," argues media studies scholar Sy Taffel.[6] However, these ways of framing are not simply the result of naive analysts looking for an easy analogy; nor have they stemmed from journalists leaning too heavily on poetic license and letting a snappy metaphor get out of hand. This framing is pushed by the exact segments of capital that know better. It's pushed by Siemens, the largest industrial manufacturer in Europe, when it proclaims, "We live in a universe of data that gains not only in volume, but importance, every day."[7] And by IBM, the original IT monopoly, which essentially created the computing industry over a hundred years ago, when it declares, "Everything is made of data these days."[8]

It is not a coincidence that data has been framed as a natural resource that is immensely valuable, universally available, and readily amenable to market dynamics—but only for those companies that possess the special technologies needed to discover, extract, process, and capitalize on data.[9] If everything falls within the domain of data, and techno-capitalists have total control over data, then by extension they have total control over every domain. At least that's the logic motivating major developments of data-driven capitalism.

The constant debate over which metaphor for data is most accurate—oil, water, gold—is evidence of too much mental confusion about the status of a thing that is key to grasping the mechanics of contemporary capitalism. When the sheen of innovation prevents us from seeing clearly, I advocate going back to the basics of political economy for a strong analysis of technology. In this chapter, I argue that, rather than a natural resource, data is a form of capital.[10] Remember from our primer in chapter 1 that capital is value in motion. There are many different forms of capital, which correspond to how value moves in different ways and does different things while moving. Most often that value is represented by money being used to create and capture more money (a.k.a. profit). Here we will see how data has quickly become one of the most important forms of capital today. It is a unique product of technological capitalism, which is now vital to its continual growth, development, and function. Both private corporations and public institutions have reoriented their core operations so that they are better able to create, capture, and use data. The consequences of a system driven by the perpetual accumulation of data capital can be found everywhere.

Data Capital

When describing capitalists' unceasing urge to extract profit, Marx often compared them to vampires with an unquenchable thirst for blood. Their desires know no limits. There is never an endpoint at which they will finally have had their fill. Quoting Engels, Marx writes in *Capital, Volume 1*, "The vampire will not let go 'while there remains a single muscle, sinew or drop of blood to be exploited.'"[11] Accumulating capital—that is, amassing money and investing it to capture ever-growing amounts of money—is not an event that starts and stops; it is a cycle on an infinite loop.

This dynamic also explains why—to choose a typical example— supermarket chains have long been using programs like loyalty cards to collect thousands of data points about each customer, which they use to build detailed profiles about a household's shopping habits, lifestyle, income, and demographics like ethnicity.[12] Kroger, a major US supermarket chain, says it has data "from 2 billion annual transactions across 60 million households with a persistent household identifier."[13] Kroger's planned merger with Albertsons, another top chain, would bring these separate databases under one roof, covering half of all American households, according to an investigation by *The Markup*.[14] This data is the basis for Kroger's "alternative profit business," which is expected to yield billions of dollars in profits by analyzing that data for "precision marketing," producing detailed "customer insights," and selling it all to other consumer brands and advertisers. Kroger claims its data science unlocks powerful forms of "behavioral analytics" that can accurately track, predict, and influence how people shop for their everyday necessities.

I've been closely following the data economy for over a decade. My writing about this subject over that time is filled with examples exactly like the one above, covering every industry you might suspect and many you would never imagine. Each one is shocking in terms of the wild amounts and crazy types of data captured, often with little knowledge and no oversight by the targets of data capture. And that data is then always used in the most mercenary ways. But each example is also totally unremarkable in the sense that they are each only doing what everybody else is also doing—that is, what the capitalist system demands. It is truly impossible to keep up with the data economy in any comprehensive way. Not only because too much happens all the time, but also because much of it happens through hidden systems and shadow markets that are designed to keep academics, journalists, and regulators in the dark about their operations.

This insatiable desire for data arises from the fact that data is now a form of capital, like money and machinery. Data is now essential to the production, extraction, and circulation of value by digital systems. Of course, not all data is the same, nor is it used in the same way, and value is derived from data in a variety of different ways. The same can be said of capital in general. However, like all capital, data is subjected to a logic of accumulation that boils down to a powerful imperative: create and capture as much as you can, from all sources, by any means possible.[15] Meeting the demands of this data imperative, and squeezing value out of that data, has become a prime directive for the design and use of capitalist innovation. In other words, the reason why ubiquitous surveillance is built into our digital society is not because it's a technical requirement or inevitable feature but because it's valuable for capital.

And when giant companies cannot fulfill the data imperative through innovation and internal capabilities alone, they often fall back on good old-fashioned corporate acquisitions to capture data capital.

There is now a long list of big money deals in which corporations acquire other firms for the purpose of accessing valuable data, obtaining systems to valorize data, and eliminating competition in the market for data. The AI Now Institute offers an abridged list of these major "data mergers," starting with Google's acquisition of DoubleClick in 2007 for $3.1 billion; the technology became the foundation of its adtech capabilities and thus nearly all of Google's revenue. The list also includes Microsoft's acquisition of LinkedIn for $26.2 billion, Facebook's acquisition of WhatsApp for $19 billion, and Amazon's acquisition of OneMedical for $3.9 billion.[16] The thing that made these acquired companies so valuable was that they had a lot of data—and the prospect of creating even more. Increasingly, these data mergers also happen outside of the tech sector as the imperative of data capital comes to subsume everybody. As we saw earlier, the proposed consolidation between Kroger and Albertsons is a major data merger in the grocery sector. There are many more examples of data mergers over just the last fifteen years, totaling many more billions of dollars. Together they represent a vast consolidation of control over data capital across all industries.

Data capital is more than knowledge about the world, it is discrete bits of information that are digitally recorded, machine readable, easily aggregated, totally abstracted, highly mobile, and socially valuable. Many of these same exact features are also shared by economic capital, which helps explain why data-as-capital is now governed by the same logics that Marx used to describe the dynamics of money in capitalism: "The circulation of money as capital is an end in itself, for the valorization of value takes place only within this constantly renewed movement. The movement of capital is therefore limitless," Marx writes.[17] In technological capitalism, data is not a substitute for money; it is elevated and put "on the same level as financial capital," according to a report sponsored by Oracle, one of the world's largest software companies, which specializes in the enterprise systems used to manage other industries and supply chains.[18] Thus the imperative to capture and circulate data is manifested through a massive stack of devices to create data, infrastructures to manage data, systems to use data, markets to move data, and so on. The streams of data must keep flowing and growing.

Ultimately, continuing the cycle of data capital becomes an intrinsic motivation, a driving force, for companies. As Marx explains, "Use-values must therefore never be treated as the immediate aim of the capitalist; nor must the profit on any single transaction. His aim is rather the unceasing movement of profit-making."[19] The same can be said of data. The capitalist is not concerned with the immediate use of a data point or with any single collection but rather with the never-ending process of data-creating.

This is illustrated by the fact that companies often suck up immense amounts of data without specific uses in mind. "At large companies, sometimes we launch products not for the revenue, but for the data," remarks Andrew Ng, an AI researcher who has held executive positions at Google, Baidu, and other tech giants.[20] Extending that point, sociologists Marion Fourcade and Kieran Healy observe that "it does not matter that the amounts [of data] collected may vastly exceed a firm's imaginative reach or analytic grasp. The assumption is that it will eventually be useful, i.e., valuable."[21] Later in this chapter (and the book), we will discuss how Silicon Valley aims to derive value from data by investing it in the creation of AI systems that automate other processes and predict future events. Their creators hope these AI systems will be machines that convert data capital into more material forms of value like financial profit or social power.

More generally, we can see the imperative of nonstop accumulation at work in the fierce corporate opposition to "data minimization" regulations, which place strict limits on what data companies can collect, whom they can share data with or sell data to, the purposes data can be used for, and the amount of time data can be retained.[22] Such rules act like other forms of capital controls, which seek to limit the free flow of finance into and out of specific places, sectors, or industries. If actually enacted and strongly enforced, they could shake the foundations of a capitalist system built on *data maximization*. But fortunately for these companies, data capital, like financial capital, is treated as an engine of growth and epicenter of power and is thus governed by regimes of "light touch" regulation, which are more interested in supporting than they are stymieing the smooth circulation of data capital.

Seeing how data has become a core form of capital—and how its logics influence key decisions in the realms of technology, business, and governance—is crucial for any analysis of our technological society. But it also cannot be the whole analysis. Let's now move from the economics of data to the politics of datafication: or turning people into data.

Becoming Objects

Computer vision is one of the most influential areas of AI. The research in this subfield "focuses on measuring, mapping, recording, and monitoring the world from visual inputs such as image and video data."[23] It underpins a wide range of existing and emerging technologies, such as facial recognition, autonomous vehicles, insurance fraud detection, and much more. In a recent study, AI researchers Pratyusha Ria Kalluri and colleagues undertook a massive survey of the subfield to inventory the purpose of this work and its products. They conducted both in-depth qualitative and large-scale quantitative analyses of the last four decades of papers published at the annual Conference on Computer Vision and Pattern Recognition, which is "among the top five highest impact publications of any discipline, alongside *Nature* and *Science*."[24] They also analyzed over 27,000 patents stemming from those conference papers in order to see the outcomes of that academic research.

Many critics (like myself) who are familiar with these areas of technological R&D have a general sense that they plug all too neatly into applications for surveillance and control. But there is also the risk that we are cherry-picking examples or only noticing things that confirm a dystopian bias, and I'd be the first to celebrate if we were shown to be just a few cynics in an otherwise good world. So it always feels bad when somebody comes along and empirically proves that things are worse than we thought.

What Kalluri and colleagues found is that "computer vision research, in particular, is a primary source for designing, building, and powering modern mass surveillance."[25] Computer vision, like AI generally, is dominated by corporations and militaries, both working separately and collaboratively with academics often (in)directly serving those interests. The latest numbers show that most new PhD graduates in AI fields work in industry, not academia, and that gap has grown every year for the last decade.[26] Similarly, the vast majority of new machine learning models are also built and owned by corporations.[27] When greater capabilities for surveillance correspond to greater flows of profit and power, it is little surprise that technologies like computer vision are captured by groups who control the capital needed to design, build, and use those technologies.[28]

Seeing like a computer means making the world into data. And the creators of these systems are particularly interested in capturing the people who populate that world by turning them into data. In all the papers and patents analyzed, the vast majority stated they could be used to target data about human bodies, with a large percentage explicitly calling these capabilities a strength of the technology.[29] Some honed in on specific biometric features like faces, fingerprints, and eyes, while others focused on whole bodies doing things in everyday places like shops, streets, or sports events.

Perhaps even more strikingly, in the computer vision papers and patents, any "entity" the system detects, identifies, and tracks is called an "object." This includes cars, cats, trees, tables, and so on, but also the "object" most often targeted by these technologies: humans. A world made into data is a world without subjects. The engineers claim the position of objectivity while their human targets are rendered into objects. These systems strive toward the promise of "infinite vision" and perform "the god trick of seeing everything from nowhere," as Donna Haraway put it.[30] Even if one argued that the conceptualization of humans as objects was just an engineering shorthand, it would still be troubling considering the technocratic tendency to treat humans as problems to solve.[31] Practices of dehumanization cannot be waved away by calling them a technical requirement or an innocent label.

The conflation of humans and objects, and the abstraction of data from its social context, serves a variety of purposes. It provides useful distance for computer vision researchers so they can tell themselves and others that they are merely working on object-detection systems. As Kalluri's team observes, nearly all papers which call humans "objects" also make "no note of how performing tasks like detection or segmentation on people has extremely specific and socially consequential impacts."³² There's no need for critical inquiry or ethical responsibility when you are just dealing with objects. Meanwhile, it also provides helpful generalizability for corporations and militaries that want to build and deploy these technologies. Since these AI systems are trained on objects and humans are treated as objects like any other, all that computer vision research can be directly used to surveil humans as well, even if that wasn't the explicit goal.

The politics of datafication becomes undeniable when we consider not just the mass accumulation of data but then question what kind of data is deemed most desirable, how that data is then extracted, and what purposes it is put toward. This analysis of computer vision offers an obvious and significant example of how humans must, quite literally, be objectified to facilitate becoming data capital. This process, however, is in no way unique to computer vision or machine learning. It is a core feature of the great many systems that now, in a vast variety of ways, exist to pulverize everything into data: abstracting away specific attributes and contexts, atomizing people into thousands and millions of data points, reducing complex wholes into their virtual simulations—all for the purpose of facilitating further accumulation, analysis, and actionable insights.

New methods can capture data in quantities so large as to be incomprehensible, but the qualities of that data are still incomplete. No sensor can absorb and record data about everything. Instead, each sensor is designed to monitor hyper-specific things. Data science is concerned with qualities about the world that can be expressed mathematically and processed digitally. These are necessarily different qualities than the ones experienced by humans. In a critical analysis of the "machinic metaphysics" that underlie data science, Dan McQuillan observes, "Primary qualities such as number, magnitude, position and extension can be expressed mathematically, whereas aspects which seem to us an inseparable part of phenomena are relegated to secondary qualities, mere sensory echoes."[33] This may be mundane, like a thermometer that can give you a number for the temperature, but cannot tell you what the weather feels like. Or it might be more meaningful, like a facial recognition algorithm that can identify the geometry of a face but cannot understand the subjective humanity and social context of the person. However, because data can be capitalized, the products of digital sensors are prioritized and valorized, whereas the phenomena of human senses are downgraded or dismissed.

Data can never represent every fiber of a person's being, nor account for every contour of their complex life. But that is not the purpose nor the value of data. Rather than a failure of the system, this reductionism is a crucial and useful feature of abstraction. The whole point is to turn integrated human subjects into fragmented data objects. This might sound strange if our critical concerns are framed in the intensely personal ways they almost always are. Isn't the goal of the system to know me, like, to a creepy degree? Isn't that why all this data is assembled about me and then used to fuel algorithms for hyper-personalized targeting? If they aren't trying to piece together a full profile of me, and do so in the most accurate and complete way possible, then what is even the point?

We're All Connected

But here's the thing: data extractors don't care about *you* as an isolated individual; they care about *us* as a relational collective. This is an important part of the abstraction and accumulation process, which brings together the politics of datafication with the economics of data capital. "In a typical data flow, any one individual's data is essentially meaningless, and the marginal cost of any one individual defecting from collection is very low. Yet in aggregate, data is highly valuable and grows in value the more data can be combined with other kinds of data," writes Salomé Viljoen in a brilliant analysis of data governance.[34]

Our ways of thinking about data are typically based on older ideas tied to older forms of consumer surveillance. These relations, which Viljoen calls "vertical," were built on much more direct connections between the source of data, collector of data, and user of data. In the simplest form: a bank uses a questionnaire to gather information about a loan applicant and then makes their decision based on the information provided. These vertical relations could still be quite complex, sprawling, and obscured. But for the most part you could map, understand, and predict the data network and its consequences. You might need a lot of cork boards and red string, but you could do it. However, now we have to update our thinking to account for what Viljoen calls "horizontal" relations, which exist not at individual levels but at population scales. They are flows of data that link many people together and flow across networks such that the sources, collectors, users, and consequences of data get mixed up in ways that are impossible to trace if we are still thinking in vertical terms.

To illustrate, Viljoen offers the example of US Immigration and Customs Enforcement (ICE) purchasing mobile location data from the company Venntel, which captured its data from mobile games and weather apps that track users' location. ICE also purchased licenses from Clearview AI, a facial recognition company that built its database by scraping publicly available images of people's faces from the internet. So here ICE is combining different databases and systems, which are themselves based on fusing together lots of data, from many different sources and collectors, across many different times and places, to identify and arrest a specific group of suspected undocumented immigrants. There was no reason to think that playing a mobile game or uploading a picture to social media might contribute in some way to the arrest of a stranger years later. Yet examples like this are now common; there are too many to count. In addition to selling their services to repressive government agencies, data analytics firms like Palantir now provide these relational techniques to every industry that wants a data-driven advantage. Indeed, the ability to derive value from the horizontal analysis of large-scale data is the very basis and promise of artificial intelligence.

AI Arms Race

Virtually all data on the internet—a staggering corpus of information produced by, for, and about humans—has been drafted by corporations to train artificial intelligence systems, like the large-language models behind ChatGPT or the image generation models behind Dall-E. If the internet-as-dataset is unimaginable, then the machine learning models are incomprehensible. I don't just mean in the sense that these computer models are confusing or complex but that their inner workings are inherently opaque to the experts— even to their makers—who have full access to the models and information about their mechanics.[35] The data analysis, model building, and decision-making processes—that is, how these machine learning systems take inputs (like every word published on the internet) and turn them into outputs (like conversational responses in a chat window)—happen in "hidden layers" that cannot be observed or modified from outside the software system. This form of technical opacity is further compounded when the systems' owners refuse to share any details about how the technologies were created.

For example, in March 2023, OpenAI—the company behind ChatGPT and Dall-E—released their highly anticipated model GPT-4. Near the start of the technical report for GPT-4, which is meant to explain its capabilities and operations, OpenAI states: "Given both the competitive landscape and the safety implications of large-scale models like GPT-4, this report contains no further details about the architecture (including model size), hardware, training compute, dataset construction, training method, or similar."[36] The tech industry is famous for its weaponization of trade secrets to prevent anybody, competitors or regulators, from assessing their technologies. However, this degree of nondisclosure is remarkable in its uncompromising position against sharing any material details, especially considering OpenAI knew that people across the media, industry, academia, and government would be interested in learning more about a powerful technology the company claims will revolutionize the world. Since OpenAI is a high-profile leader in the field, their extreme stance on corporate opacity in the release of AI systems has set a precedent for other companies to follow.

We are confronted by stacks of black boxes inside black boxes.[37] Meanwhile, technologies that we do not and cannot understand are being integrated, rapidly and deeply, into other human activities, social processes, and technical systems. This will lead to one thing I do know for certain: these technologies will create systemic problems, fragilities, and failures that we also won't understand

and won't be equipped to address. But this fact hasn't stopped a growing chorus from crying out that AI—specifically the kinds of AI systems being innovated and invested in by a small group of mega-corporations—is the irrepressible, unavoidable future of humanity. Some sing it like a prophecy, while others spit it like a threat.

Over the last couple of decades, a data-driven madness has touched, if not transformed, nearly everything, everywhere in society and our lives. Despite all that I've laid out so far, I dare say the logic of data capital has not yet reached its zenith. AI systems require extracting, capturing, and processing more data than ever before while also promising to produce more value from that data than ever before. The sudden blockbuster success of OpenAI's consumer technologies in late 2022 sparked an enormous focus on (generative) AI that now defines the tech industry. This was also the same exact time when the Web3/crypto economy was in spectacular collapse. Many tech companies and venture capitalists were searching for the next big thing to hang their promises for the future on. To underscore this point, a prominent venture capitalist, Jason Calacanis, tweeted in June 2023: "If you're in crypto pivot to AI."[38] The timing of one bubble bursting just as another began inflating—thus redirecting the torrents of money, hype, attention, possibility—could not have been fortuitous. It's almost as if it were part of a central plan for innovation.

At any rate, the myopic focus on the cliche promise and perils of the technology itself—Will it elevate or eliminate all of humanity?—distracts from the fact that the existing order of AI is not already a finished product that has been carved in silicon but is rather an ongoing process that must be constantly reasserted in multiple ideological and material ways. Amba Kak and Sarah Myers West, directors of the AI Now Institute, have observed that the dominance of just a few big tech firms in the creation and control of artificial intelligence relies on maintaining a triforce of advantages: data, computation, geopolitics.[39]

The data advantage means having access to the widest, deepest pools of information possible. The computational advantage means having control over the computing power and cloud infrastructure required to use that data. The geopolitical advantage means being able to recast AI technologies "not just as commercial products but foremost as strategic economic and security assets for the nation that need to be boosted by policy, and never restrained."[40] In other words, the business model behind AI relies on brute force: capture massive reserves of data by any means possible, throw tons of resource-intensive processing power at that data, and gin up public support with wondrous tales (your AI) and scary stories (their AI). This is a far cry from the idea that innovation works in mysterious ways.

These advantages work together to consolidate the position of big tech companies, allowing them to continue defining the development of AI by capturing the resources and discourses needed to keep pushing it in the directions they desire.[41] These advantages are pillars that support the growth of companies; but they also serve as chokepoints that limit competition from other institutions, private and public, that might also have an interest in designing, building, and using AI systems, perhaps in different ways and for alternative reasons.

This also explains why people like Henry Kissinger and Eric Schmidt have been working together to frame the development of AI as an arms race between America and China that can only be won by supporting American corporations like Google, Meta, Microsoft, and Amazon.[42] Kissinger was a power broker and grim reaper in foreign policy from the 1960s until his death in late 2023. And Schmidt, the former CEO of Google, in addition to holding other influential tech policy and military strategy positions, has chaired the Pentagon's Defense Innovation Advisory Board and the National Security Commission on Artificial Intelligence. He has also founded multiple investment funds and think tanks to promote American technological supremacy.[43] Schmidt—and his expansive network of power, wealth, and ideology—is at the vanguard of what Evgeny Morozov calls a "weird new regime of 'military neoliberalism'" wherein the government directs a fire hose of cash at AI systems and cloud infrastructure in such a way that private companies maintain ownership, their shareholders get richer, and inequalities (social, financial, political, technological) all get wider and deeper.[44]

Another of the loudest supporters (and biggest beneficiaries) of this military-industrial regime is Alex Karp, CEO of Palantir. In a *New York Times* opinion essay, Karp argues that "this is an arms race of a different kind, and it has begun. Our hesitation, perceived or otherwise, to move forward with military applications of artificial intelligence will be punished."[45] He then goes on to say that "engineers in Silicon Valley" who oppose working on offensive military weapons should remember that they owe "their fortunes, business empires," their entire existence, to the support and protection of the American military state. And before refusing to answer the call of duty, "they would do well to understand that debt, even if it remains unpaid." Karp is correct about the military origins of Silicon Valley, but he twists the point to argue that the tech industry has a moral obligation to double down on its ghastly history. These cries for a stronger fusion of techno-capitalism and techno-nationalism echo the words of Palmer Luckey, founder of

Oculus and Anduril, a sister company of Palantir also backed by Peter Thiel, who has stated, "The Western world has a responsibility to lead in defense technology—technological superiority is a prerequisite for moral superiority."[46]

There's much more that can be said about the AI arms race and the triforce of advantages that tech corporations depend upon to ensure their own market superiority and dominance over the future. We cannot understand powerful data-driven systems like AI or the strategies of Silicon Valley corporations without tracing their origins and ongoing connections with the military-industrial complex. But let's refocus on data more generally. There is a key feature of data that has been essential for the growth of technological capitalism. The AI boom is built on this feature. Not all data is cheap, but the tech sector relies on cheap data.

Cheap Data

In their book, *A History of the World in Seven Cheap Things*, Raj Patel and Jason Moore show how the continual expansion of capitalism has always been fueled by its ability to easily extract, exploit, and expropriate the resources needed by the owner class in power to keep producing commodities and accumulating capital. These seven things are: nature, money, work, care, food, energy, and lives. In its mission to keep these things cheap and maintain control over them, "modern commerce has transformed, governed, and devastated the Earth" over the last many centuries.[47] In the process, Patel and Moore argue, these things have been *cheapened*. Their social value is overridden by their economic value as they are thrown into the market, turned into assets, subjected to dynamics of exchange, and burned in the engine of profit.

A few brief examples: The wealth of colonial frontiers is based on the seizure of "free real estate" (cheap nature) and the elimination of Indigenous people already on that land (cheap lives). The economics of industrial production depends on not accounting for all of these cheap necessities in their financial costs: the environmental externalities of dumping toxic waste into the air, soil, and water (cheap nature); the unpaid, disparaged, femininized labor of social reproduction (cheap care); the stagnant wages and scientific management that keep the cost of labor down even further (cheap work). Meanwhile, the modern regime of capitalist innovation known as Silicon Valley is a zero interest-rate phenomenon: the product of financiers and founders drunk on all the free, easy, no-strings credit sloshing around for anybody who fits the archetype of an entrepreneur (cheap money). The list goes on.

All seven of these cheap things are important for understanding the historical and ongoing development of capitalism. In the context of technological capitalism, we need to add another thing to the list: cheap data.

Creating high-quality datasets that are bespoke and appropriate for the purpose at hand; free of meaningful errors and harmful biases; cleaned and annotated by fairly paid workers; well documented in terms of their origins, aims, and other attributes; large and various enough for valuable analysis; and that reach other benchmarks of quality is really good for technology but really hard for engineers and really bad for business. Going the route of quality means investing serious time and money into the production and maintenance of resources. Using cheap data to feed your hungry AI models is like cooking with the mystery meat that fell off the back of a truck. There are two popular alternatives to high-quality data, which are often selected together.

First, *the good enough option*, which involves using datasets that already exist even if they were made for different applications or have dubious origins and biased content that lead to obvious undesired consequences. This is the case with many common datasets used to build machine learning models, like the ImageNet dataset for training and testing computer vision systems, which continue to be widely used even after they have been proven to be both technically and socially problematic.[48] These datasets are rife with racist, sexist, and homophobic labels on images, including outright slurs; they also use bizarre moral judgments to label images. For example, the following words are used to label images of people: "Bad Person, Call Girl, Drug Addict, Closet Queen, Convict, Crazy, Failure, Flop, Fucker, Hypocrite, Jezebel, Kleptomaniac, Loser . . . "[49] Such databases make for bad politics, but also for bad technologies built on a random assortment of weird biases and wild guesses. But they are quick, easy, and cheap to use, which is difficult to resist. If you are an engineer, it's just better to not know what goes into the mystery meat. And hey, if everybody else is using the mystery meat—or better yet, if the mystery meat becomes the benchmark for quality—then that makes it good enough.

Second, *the too big to care option*, which involves sucking up tons of data as quickly as possible from many different sources, then directing that giant, fast, diverse flow of data into some algorithm to derive insights or some model to train AI. This is the basis of big data, which eventually leads to arguments that, at some threshold, characteristics like accuracy, neutrality, and causality just stop mattering. Errors and biases, the idea goes, become so small in the dataset that they are negligible, or they are canceled out by different errors and biases in the other direction. Meanwhile, the emergent correlations between patterns in the data are so statistically strong that they lead to the death of theory. In other words, there is no need to explain why a dynamic exists or what might be its cause. The bigger the data, the less you have to care. You only need to crunch the numbers, observe the relationship between different variables, and use those outputs to make decisions about the world.

So if the data is too big or good enough, then you can stop worrying about its origins and contents. In classic engineering fashion, every qualitative concern can be ignored, reframed, and addressed with quantitative solutions. The same is taken as true when relying on cheap data. "A key problem is that coders and model builders rarely question the quality of the input data they use," observe sociologists Jenna Burrell and Marion Fourcade, who also cite critical data scientists Meredith Broussard and Cathy O'Neill.[50] Building models is treated as exciting, prestigious, and highly paid research. Cleaning data is treated as boring, low-status, and poorly paid labor.[51] This is a major contradiction of data capital: despite data being the most essential part of the whole system, it is also the most undervalued and overlooked. In other words, data has been cheapened.

With both options, the desire for cheap data often means repurposing data for reasons that differ vastly from those for which it was initially created. Because, after all, it's already available and it would be such a waste to not use it (and much more expensive to clean it, let alone create custom datasets). For example, many of the big tech firms that are dominant in the production of AI are primarily in the business of surveillance for advertising.[52] This means they already have hoards of data for tracking and targeting people. AI offers a profitable opportunity to take that cheap data, which is just lying around in their servers, and squeeze more value out of it by using the massive computing power, which they also own, to train AI systems on those datasets.

At the same time, the internet itself offers a standing reserve of cheap data for those with the tools to scrape it. For instance, Google's C4 dataset captures the contents of fifteen million websites and has been "used to instruct some high-profile English-language AIs."[53] And that is just one database. As journalist Ina Fried observes, "Today's AI breakthroughs couldn't happen without the availability of the digital stockpiles and landfills of info, ideas and feelings that the internet prompted people to produce."[54] For companies like OpenAI that are not surveillance leviathans, treating the internet as a source of cheap data is absolutely crucial for their business.

However, cheap things don't always stay cheap. And data extraction is getting more expensive. A number of popular websites like Reddit and Stack Overflow, as well as a group of major publishers called the News/Media Alliance, began pushing to get paid for the data that companies like OpenAI scraped from their websites to train systems like ChatGPT and Dall-E.[55] Sam Altman, the CEO of OpenAI, has said it costs hundreds of millions of dollars to train these systems[56] and the computing costs to operate them are "eye-watering."[57] These computing costs are a major factor behind OpenAI's push to monetize their technologies and take $11 billion in investment from Microsoft. (OpenAI makes a big deal about being a "capped profit" corporation, which is meant to signal that they are a virtuous, trustworthy company; as their corporate charter states, "Our primary fiduciary duty is to humanity."[58] In practice, this means profits are capped at 100× return on investment. So we can all take comfort knowing that Microsoft's profits cannot surpass $1.1 trillion, unless they invest more.)

The rising costs of AI would be much higher if they also accounted for a major subsidy underlying these companies. The necessary training data was largely free, or at least deeply discounted, by a data collection practice more commonly known in other sectors as theft.[59] I'm not usually one to support the kind of intellectual property (IP) regimes that are, as Cory Doctorow and Rebecca Giblin have argued in *Chokepoint Capitalism*,[60] instituted to turbocharge the profits of corporate monopolies—whether in the music and movie or pharmaceutical industries. However, a recent investigation by the *Washington Post* into Google's C4 dataset reports that the copyright symbol "appears more than 200 million times" in the dataset's contents.[61] It seems that at the heart of the business model for AI is mass infringement and selective enforcement of intellectual property rights. Not to mention running afoul of data protection regulations like the European Union's strict laws, which require either obtaining people's consent before collecting their personal data—impossible to do when you are scraping the entire internet—or arguing that you have a "legitimate interest" in capturing that data.

If any nonprofit or public entity wanted to compete in this space by building different forms of AI—like a PublicGPT for the people—they would surely have to follow the rules that these corporations are breaking. While it would be great if the high-quality data infrastructure needed to build socially beneficial alternatives were publicly owned, it has mostly been outsourced and monopolized by the private sector.[62] This means that capital gets an unfair advantage in the market, that any social alternatives are hamstrung from the start, and that the deck is further stacked in favor of capitalist innovation as the only viable possibility.

It's no surprise that the wealth of data capital is derived from extraction and exploitation. It's a story as old as capitalism. In describing that capitalism is built on violent dispossession that creates and continues to reproduce the material conditions necessary for the ongoing accumulation of capital, Marx states, "Capital comes [into the world] dripping from head to toe, from every pore, with blood and dirt."[63] And yet, the avarice is made even more galling by its hypocrisy. The strict enforcement of copyright laws over software and hardware through draconian tools like "digital rights management" is also essential to the tech industry's war for infinite power and endless profit. Few have benefited from these laws as much as Microsoft; their market capitalization of over three trillion dollars is based on controlling intellectual property. I wonder if Microsoft executives savor the irony of betting not just $11 billion on OpenAI but the future of their company on AI systems built on infringing the same IP laws that made them richer than god. I suspect they pay lawyers to think about these things so they don't have to. At the end of the day, consistency is a liability if it does not serve the imperative of accumulation. To update Marx slightly: techno-capital comes dripping with blood and data.

Faced with the possibility that the era of cheap data extraction is coming to an end, these companies may actually have to license and pay publishers for data. That is, they might have to agree to the kind of data sharing contracts they already force onto other users, industries, and governments. It is likely that such deals will only come, if they do at all, after a lot of kicking and screaming by the data capitalists. When the costs of cheap things rise, capital faces a crisis and must come up with new strategies for keeping things cheap and finding new sources for cheap things.

One such strategy is what's called "synthetic data," or the creation of datasets that do not refer to any real people, places, objects, or events but are meant to mimic the real world and then be used to train machine learning and artificial intelligence systems. The idea is that these systems can be trained on simulations, which are close enough to reality, if not even better than reality, because they can be designed to emphasize the features of a dataset that are most relevant for the model builders—thus cutting to the synthetic signal without having to engage with noisy reality.

Writing about the politics of synthetic data, Benjamin Jacobsen notes that synthetic data is already being used in a vast range of algorithmic applications, such as autonomous driving, medical imaging, insurance fraud detection, and terrorist threat prediction.[64] In other words, an AI system for identifying cancer could be trained on simulated livers and lungs, or a system for catching fraud could be trained on the synthetic behavior of fake fraudsters. Importantly, for my purposes in this section, synthetic data is "generated *by* algorithms and *for* algorithms," which means it can be a much easier, cheaper alternative to real data.[65] While synthetic data can be technically better for some applications, its use should still require the kind of stringent human oversight and verification that companies are trying to eliminate. Sam Altman has claimed "that soon all data will be synthetic data," in large part because human-created data is comparatively expensive and fresh sources of the real stuff are becoming more scarce and harder to tap.[66]

In addition to the myriad political and ethical issues raised by the growing use of synthetic data, there are also other bizarre concerns about what happens when AI systems are so heavily trained on the outputs of other AI systems. We already know that algorithms have a strong tendency to bury biases in datasets while also compounding and amplifying their effects, often in unpredicted and unclear ways. When that data is also AI generated, there is good reason to believe that we end up with some version of what I call Habsburg AI: inbred systems with exaggerated features, grotesque mutations, and other critical weaknesses. Technical analysis of these systems is already proving my Habsburg hypothesis to be true. One study by a group of computer scientists and electrical engineers found that AI models trained on data generated by other AIs exhibit signs of rapid degradation in terms of the quality, precision, and diversity of their outputs.[67] In other words, the "hallucinations" (a.k.a. bullshit) produced by models like ChatGPT would only get more disconnected from reality. These researchers drew a different comparison to explain this phenomenon of data cannibalism, calling it "Model Autophagy Disorder," or MAD AI, drawing an analogy to mad cow disease.[68]

Avoiding the consequences of Habsburg or MAD AI will get even harder as generative AI systems like ChatGPT or its dozens of competitors are used more widely and their outputs become a bigger part of the information in our world. Rather than deploying super intelligent personal assistants in our work and life, we may soon be relying on technologies that are more like inbred chatbots with good marketing. If the choice for corporations is between the costs of clean data or the dangers of cheap data, then we know from the structural imperatives of capitalism that cheap always wins. Which too often means that the people who never had a choice end up losing.

5 Labor

The Magic of Machinery

In 1770, the Hungarian inventor Wolfgang von Kempelen unveiled the Mechanical Turk, a chess-playing contraption that "consisted of a wooden cabinet behind which was seated a life-size figure of a man, made of carved wood, wearing an ermine-trimmed robe, loose trousers and a turban—the traditional costume of an Oriental sorcerer."[1] He toured the robotic chess master around Europe and America. Exhibition matches were staged with such famous opponents as Napoleon Bonaparte. All the while, Kempelen maintained that the automaton operated by its own accord.

To prove there was no trickery, he opened the cabinet before every exhibition and showed spectators the dense tangle of gears, wheels, and levers. The sheer mechanical complexity on display convinced observers that advanced technology—beyond what they could comprehend—was powering the system. But Kempelen had actually created an elaborate illusion, not a robot. Inside was a human chess master who used magnets and levers to operate the Mechanical Turk; he simply hid behind the fake machinery when Kempelen opened the cabinet. In other words, the complex mechanical system that Kempelen showed people was meant to distract their attention from how the automaton really worked: human labor. Kempelen sold the idea of an intelligent machine, but what people witnessed was just human effort disguised by clever engineering.

In the 1730s, the French inventor Jacques de Vaucanson constructed a copper-plated cyborg called le Canard Digérateur, or the Digesting Duck. It was the size of a duck, walked like a duck, and quacked like a duck. But its real trick, which amazed and baffled audiences, was that it could poop like a duck. The automaton "ate food out of the exhibitor's hand, swallowed it, digested it, and excreted it, all before an audience."[2] Vaucanson claimed that he had built a "chemical laboratory" in the duck's stomach to decompose the food before expelling it from the mechanical butt. While Vaucanson was an expert engineer—the duck was an intricate piece of machinery—like a good magician, he did not reveal how the duck worked. After his death, the secret was uncovered. There was no innovative chemical technology inside the duck, rather there were just two containers: one for the food and one for preloaded excrement. (Strangely, the Digesting Duck and the Mechanical Turk were both destroyed by museum fires around the same time in the mid-1800s.)

Kempelen and Vaucanson would fit very well into Silicon Valley today. They could spend their days making mysterious machines and uttering wondrous proclamations about their supposed abilities, while attracting major rounds of venture capital investment. Perhaps Vaucanson—who literally snuck duck shit into his technological system and called it innovation—would create the next biotech darling built on deception (à la Theranos). Kempelen, meanwhile, was a forerunner of artificial intelligence. Not because his

Mechanical Turk managed to play a game well, like IBM's Deep Blue or Google's AlphaGo do, but because many AI systems are, in large part, also technical illusions designed to fool the public.

Whether it's content moderation for social media or facial recognition for police surveillance,[3] claims about the capabilities of AI systems are more abundant and incredible than ever before. While we are led to believe that these smart technologies are solely powered by neural networks, as tons of research and reporting have shown, much of the cognitive labor essential to their operations likely comes from an office building full of (low-waged) workers in popular outsourcing destinations like the Philippines or India or Kenya.[4] This is not to say that the options are binary: either 100 percent machine power or 100 percent human power. The reality is a hybrid relationship where workers use technology to create value, managers use technology to exploit labor, and entrepreneurs use technology to erase the existence of the other two groups.

I call this way of building and presenting such systems—whether analog automatons or digital software—Potemkin AI.[5] Potemkin refers to a facade designed to hide the reality of a situation. The term functions as an analytical label meant to help us understand the practices and promises of the technology sector as they exist, as well as the conditions and positions of workers that make these systems function. It also serves as a theoretical concept meant to reveal the planetary networks of labor, capital, production, and information that are concealed inside so many machinic minds. Potemkin AI is a tool for demystifying the real operations of these technological systems and the real relations of this political economic system.

Labor is at the center of technology and capitalism—without labor, the machinery of both systems would seize and stop working. Promises that innovation will save, alleviate, and eliminate labor have motivated both excited anticipation and fearful reaction. Especially when it comes to automation. We will either have less work to do (giving us more time for leisure) or we will have no work to do (leaving us out of a job).[6] New technologies like artificial intelligence draw much of their power and mystique from the absence of humans. They can think and act like people but in ways that exceed human capacities for speed, accuracy, and analysis—precisely because they are inhuman or without human input.

Yet claims that these systems are artificial and automatic also mask the human labor that actually powers them. In the 1960s, an executive at Fairchild Semiconductor, a pioneer manufacturer for computer hardware, described the company's key production innovation as "jet-age automation"—by which he meant offshoring assembly labor to Hong Kong and flying its outputs back to the United States.[7] This dynamic mirrors how the digital-age intelligence of today's software sector is produced and powered: outsourcing the labor of assembling, cleaning, annotating, and censoring the reams of data needed for AI systems to contractors in the Global South. And, failing to create operational AI, companies also regularly have humans pretend to be the technology.

Labor is a vast topic in the context of AI. You might be expecting, for instance, a chapter that explores another very visible issue: how algorithmic management by digital platforms and gig apps has created a servant economy. In other words, algorithms trained by the data labor of workers in one place are then used by companies to control the labor of workers in another place. I'll touch on this issue, and I have written extensively about it elsewhere, as have many other critical researchers.[8] But it is impossible to focus on everything at once, so here I want to direct our attention to a dynamic that has only become more important in recent years, while also remaining largely invisible by design. Ultimately, Potemkin AI is the latest example of how labor exploitation without recognition has always been essential to the production of technology and capitalism.

Potemkin AI

When it comes to Potemkin AI, there is a long list of services that pretend to be powered by sophisticated software but also depend heavily on hidden humans acting like robots.[9] The examples are often mundane cases of trickery, but they can get weird or creepy. Autonomous vehicles commonly use remote driving and "ghost drivers"—human operators camouflaged as empty seats—to test how other drivers and pedestrians react to driverless cars on the street. Meanwhile, developers for email-based services who make apps to generate personalized ads, price comparisons, and automated travel itineraries regularly use humans to read private emails, despite claiming it's automated by AI.[10] Facebook's then vaunted and now forgotten personal assistant, M, relied on humans to answer questions, until Facebook shut down the service to focus on other AI projects.[11] The *Wall Street Journal* has called the pervasive use of actual humans marketed as artificial intelligence "tech's dirty secret."[12]

A 2019 report from MMC Ventures, a London-based investment firm, found that 2,830 start-ups in Europe claimed to be using AI in their products. Based on public information and interviews with executives, it turns out that only 40 percent of start-ups were plausibly using AI; the rest were using AI as a marketing ploy to attract attention, while hoping that true AI would come in the near future.[13] But still, the bar of legitimately using AI is low because definitions of the technology vary so wildly. The tech sector benefits from our public imagination of AI as super-advanced, human-like systems when, in reality, AI can just mean a simple computer program, like a complex spreadsheet, which was perhaps bought from another software provider. "AI has become a catch-all phrase that's often used flippantly," as one venture capitalist told the *Financial Times*.[14] His fellow investors might agree in principle, but their actions speak otherwise.

This report predates the out-of-control craze for all things AI that began in late 2022. Start-ups with names like Cohere and Anthropic were raising many hundreds of millions of dollars and being rewarded with multibillion dollar valuations because their founders once worked at Google or OpenAI and claimed to be building AI systems.[15] Others were so new they didn't have time to start doing anything before investors began busting down their doors: "Suddenly, Mobius—little more than more than four guys and a laptop—was valued around $100 million, an unusually high number for a start-up that was just a week or so old," reported the *New York Times*.[16] Not long after, a French start-up called Mistral AI received €105 million within weeks of being founded and without any product to show, in large part because its founders were also three guys who worked at Meta and Google.[17] The smell of AI has caused a feeding frenzy among the sharks.

With so much money and so little skepticism, Potemkin AI continues to grow with every hype cycle of venture capital. Now, some of these start-ups may very well go on to build truly innovative AI systems that will achieve amazing feats of technical excellence. They might meet or exceed industry leaders like ChatGPT. Or they might, like so many other companies now integrating AI into their operations and services, just buy a license for ChatGPT. And yet, even at that bleeding edge, these technologies would still be versions of Potemkin AI. Because rather than fully acknowledge and account for the human labor they rely on, they continue to downplay, ignore, and bury these necessary components of the system. Even when the technology is not literally humans pretending to be AI, we are still seeing AI systems that pretend to be free of human labor.

How does OpenAI ensure ChatGPT doesn't spew all the racist, sexist, violent, and other toxic content that it has ingested from the internet when people ask it questions? Finding a solution to this problem is crucial to the success of generative AI like ChatGPT. Considering what we know about the data used to train this AI system—scraped from the toxic waste dump of the internet—cleaning those inputs and creating guardrails for ChatGPT's outputs is a complex problem.

OpenAI's solution was to build an "additional AI-powered safety mechanism" that would ensure the proper safeguards were in place for the consumer-facing chatbot. And how was that back-end AI created? As a *Time* investigation revealed, Kenyan workers making less than two dollars per hour had to label the training data by going through "tens of thousands of snippets of text," some of it describing "situations in graphic detail like child sexual abuse, bestiality, murder, suicide, torture, self-harm, and incest."[18] Only then could the AI safety tool "learn to detect those forms of toxicity in the wild." OpenAI also hired "roughly 1,000 remote contractors" in "regions like Latin America and Eastern Europe" to create and label data for training its various AI products, according to reporting by *Semafor*.[19]

To be fair, OpenAI is only doing exactly what every other company trying to train AI systems is doing. They confronted a complex problem by turning that problem into dirty jobs done dirt cheap by an army of workers. That's how capitalism has been brute forcing growth and progress for hundreds of years. This is also why the global market for data annotation—that is, the outsourced labor and tools to facilitate that labor—is projected to reach over $13 billion by 2030.[20] I would venture to say that if this labor were fully recognized and fairly paid, the market value would be far higher. But because AI as it exists now is built on cheap data, cheap labor, and cheap money, that cannot happen.

The structural obfuscation of human labor is critical to the functioning of the financial system that props up the technology sector, pushing forward the constant development of so-called innovation. It is a system built on speculation, or the production of expectations that certain things will be actualized and value will be realized.[21] If the machinery of real AI is not advanced enough to fulfill the wild promises and infinite desires of capital, then we should expect Potemkin AI to continue propagating as financiers and technologists sell the next best thing. Rather than the old marketing slogan "accept no imitations," Potemkin AI is a project to convince the public that they should "accept our imitations."

Global Potemkin Village

The term *Potemkin* derives from the name of a Russian minister who built fake villages to impress empress Catherine II and disguise the true state of things. Potemkin technology, then, constructs a facade that not only hides what is actually going on but deceives potential users, investors, and the general public alike. Rather than the Wizard of Oz telling us to pay no attention to the man behind the curtain, we have entrepreneurs telling us to pay no attention to the people behind the platform.

Importantly, these predecessors to Potemkin AI were constrained in space and time. The chess master sat inside the Mechanical Turk, manipulating the machinery in response to his opponent. The village facades stood in particular places and only had to be propped up long enough for the empress to pass through. When it comes to Potemkin AI, the homunculi are not inside the system per se; instead, their labor is transmitted into it over space and time. For instance, the cognitive labor of African workers today may power the American autonomous vehicles of the future.[22] Or the "human computation" done by Indian workers from the past may support the valuation of a European medical imaging start-up now.[23] Or the drones and robots delivering goods in an Australian town may be operated in real time by pilots in another city, perhaps with one pilot overseeing multiple drones in different places.[24] In short, Potemkin AI is propped up by planetary networks of (data) capital and (digital) labor.

As Mark Graham and Mohammad Anwar explain in their geographical study of "the global gig economy," by embedding digital work in "stretched-out networks of production" and information, the planetary labor market "facilitates a confluence that can transcend the spatial boundaries that constrained the convergence of employers and workers, but remained shaped and characterized by multi-scalar and asymmetrical technological, political, social, cultural, and institutional factors." It is no coincidence that these geographies of (data) capital and (digital) labor tend to be organized along familiar colonialist relations wherein the geo-economic "margins" are made to serve the "core."[25] In other words, the margins provide sources of labor to exploit and value to extract, while also serving as new markets for investment and expansion, all of which are essential to power the machinery of growth and progress for the core.[26] The dominant "imaginaries of the digital economy" marshal the language of development and inclusion to justify deeply asymmetrical power geometries.[27] The fact that many citizens in wealthy nations also earn precarious wages through piecemeal digital work—producing datasets, training AI systems, serving digital platforms—says more about how the exploited margins are also nestled unevenly inside the imperial core of innovation.[28]

Peeking behind the Curtain

When the inner workings of a technology are obscured, the technology is often described as a "black box"—a term derived from engineering diagrams where you can see a system's inputs and outputs but not what happens in between. An algorithm, for example, might effectively be a black box because the technical details are described using dense jargon only decipherable by a small group of experts—or, with machine learning systems, even the experts might be shut out from understanding the processes of automated decision-making.[29]

Accusations of willful obscurantism are often reserved for postmodernist scholarship, but as a recent paper on "troubling trends in machine learning scholarship" points out, research and applications in artificial intelligence are rife with dubious claims, ambiguous details, and deceptive obfuscation.[30] This paper is not based on the complaints of outsiders who don't have the right technical expertise to understand these systems. Rather it was published by computer scientists in *ACM Queue*, a flagship magazine in which researchers in the field explore emerging technologies and discuss challenges in their profession. There is growing recognition of these problems and their severity among the people building these systems. Being baffled by abstruse critical theory is one thing. It might make your term paper for a humanities class more annoying to write. But not being able to discern, for instance, how an AI application makes medical diagnoses or assesses insurance claims—and what (in)direct role humans may (not) have in those "automated" decisions—is far more consequential.[31]

Technologies might also be black boxed through the force of law by companies who claim their algorithms are trade secrets.[32] Algorithms are often described as a type of recipe. Just as Coca Cola keeps their formula a tightly guarded secret, so too do tech companies fiercely protect their "secret sauce." In this case, researchers and regulators are institutionally shut out from inspecting the ingredients and probing the processes of these technologies. Again, it's one thing to enjoy a beverage we cannot reverse engineer but quite another to put our faith in proprietary software that, for instance, makes prison sentencing decisions in criminal cases.[33]

Potemkin AI is related to black boxing, but it pushes obfuscation into deception. The Mechanical Turk, like many of the much-discussed AI systems today, was not just a black box that hid its inner workings from prying eyes. After all, Kempelen opened his automaton's cabinet and explained the workings of what looked to be a complex machine. Except that he was lying. Similarly, marketing about AI systems deploys technical buzzwords that work like a magician's incantations: Smart! Intelligent! Automated! Deep Learning! Abracadabra! Alakazam!

Weaving the right spell can endow an AI system with apparent powers of objectivity, neutrality, authority, efficiency, and other desirable attributes and outcomes. As with any good trick, it matters less if the system actually works that way than if people believe it does and act accordingly.

This power operates somewhat differently from the gaze of a panopticon. Under the panoptical gaze, your behavior is conditioned by an unseen watcher who could be observing you at any time, ready to punish you for breaking any rules. Disciplinary power is certainly part of Potemkin AI's purpose. But work by philosopher Byung-Chul Han helps tell a different story—one in which Potemkin AI is a manifestation of what he calls psychopolitics. "Power that is smart and friendly does not operate frontally—i.e., against the will of those who are subject to it. Instead, it guides their will to its own benefit."[34] The operative mode is not just making people *compliant* with commands, but *dependent* on systems. "Smart power cozies up to the psyche, rather than disciplining through coercion." This is the power of coaxing and cajoling, of implanting beliefs and inducing action. Power that "operates seductively, not repressively" is difficult to even recognize as power, thus giving it an irresistible quality—both for the wielders and the subjects of such power.

There is an undeniably seductive quality to the idea that AI can upgrade all the devices and services that we now depend upon in our everyday lives. For consumers, the joys of AI offer new heights of convenience, responsiveness, and personalization. We may not say out loud that we want a clever companion whose only purpose is to serve us, but most people would likely gladly accept their very own robot, a term that comes from *robota*, the old Slavic word for "servitude" or "forced labor." Or at least people would get used to owning one pretty quickly. Indeed, I have argued elsewhere that the on-demand gig platforms like Uber, Instacart, and TaskRabbit should be reframed as "servant apps."[35] In addition to entrenching a techno-capitalist regime "marked by extreme exploitation and despotic control of labor," these companies' value proposition for consumers is based on democratizing access to servants by allowing people to summon workers at their command. For capital, the prospect of possessing and controlling workers who "lack nothing but a soul"—as the Czech playwright who coined the word *robot* described them—has always been the dream.[36]

But in most applications AI is still an unsatisfying reality, if not a total fantasy. Potemkin AI is role-play. It's people masquerading as soulless systems. It's the ideal of being served without having to acknowledge the unpleasant existence of servants. There's nothing wrong with this game per se, so long as everybody is aware and honest about who is actually serving whom. Yet as I've explained, Potemkin AI is seduction based on deception.

Psychopolitics reveals AI—Potemkin or otherwise—to be an ideology of technology. That's not to say there is no material substrate to the ideology or that it's all just ephemeral relations and illusory deceptions. This is an ideology supported by very real planetary systems of capital and labor. It is the most capitalist thing imaginable to construct complex tangles of transnational infrastructures for circulating finance, information, and commodities, all to perpetuate a fetish for dehumanization. Exercising power is not just about effectively achieving particular outcomes or doing what works; it's also about deciding the parameters for how those ideas and goals will be defined. It's about preserving certain interests over others and reasserting the value of certain people over others. The desire for AI in some places supplants the rights of humans in other places.

Fake It Till You Make It

Why go to the trouble of creating Potemkin AI? What's at stake for those propping up the facade? Why not come clean with how the systems are actually built and operated? Broadly, we can point to two ancient reasons: profit and power. If an AI application relies heavily on human labor rather than machine learning, that doesn't make for a good sales pitch to venture capitalists and customers; nor does it convince the public of the technology's capabilities. There are, of course, other motivations like fame and recognition for inventing the future, but I think we can safely label these as secondary to profit and power. We can see the real motivations in action by looking deeper into the political economy of Potemkin AI.

Consider Amazon's Mechanical Turk platform—or MTurk, as it's called—which enables mass exploitation of "microwork" distributed across global networks. MTurk allows employers to post discrete, often routine tasks like completing surveys or tagging pictures in a dataset. Workers who complete these microjobs are then paid microwages: one study calculated the median wage at around two dollars an hour.[37] MTurk is sometimes described by its creators as "humans-as-a-service" or the "human cloud" or even "artificial artificial intelligence."[38] These labels capture MTurk's approach of organizing a legion of human workers—hundreds of thousands of people—scattered across the world and hiding them behind a digital platform.

MTurk was launched in 2005 by Amazon, making it one of the earliest entrants into what is now a booming industry of companies offering piecemeal microwork services. MTurk acts like a hiring forum where a broad range of jobs can be posted, which MTurkers then bid for. Others like the Australian company Appen act more like labor hire firms. According to an investigation by journalist Ariel Bogle, Appen claims to have "1 million 'flexible contributors' in more than 170 countries," who focus on more specialized forms of data work that are critical to the "AI supply chain" for "clients including Amazon, Google and Boeing."[39] For this example, though, I'll focus on MTurk since it paved the way for these other companies and remains representative of the industry's dynamics.

Many companies rely on this pool of cheap labor that is ready to click and submit digital tasks. It allows them to quickly scale up by completing tasks that they hope will one day be accomplished by AI software. Through their microwork, this reserve army of labor is crucial to the development of AI, whether because they produce and verify datasets used to train AI systems or because they simply impersonate AI services.[40] Yet their contributions to these technologies are belittled—that is, if their existence is even acknowledged. Undervaluing the work and the people doing it, while relying on and profiting off their labor, is all too common in a tech industry heavily biased with gendered, racialized, and classist notions of who "does innovation," what entrepreneurs look like, where they come from, and how venture capital is best invested.

Given that the name Amazon chose, Mechanical Turk, explicitly references the eighteenth-century hoax, it appears that there is no intention to deceive users about the flesh-and-blood foundations of the system. MTurk is indeed up front about how work is outsourced to real live humans. However, whereas the original Mechanical Turk's inventor overtly claimed that his machine was autonomous, MTurk uses clever design to induce that impression in an audience eager to believe the platform's Potemkin trick. As informatics scholar Lilly Irani explains, MTurk masks the MTurkers by making them appear to be just another soulless system. "By rendering the requisition of labor technical and infrastructural," Irani writes, MTurk "limits the visibility of workers, rendering them as a tool to be employed by the intentional and expressive hand of the programmer."[41] The platform and its interfaces allow employers to command people as though operating a mindless machine. In this case, Potemkin AI provides a convenient way to rationalize exploitation—often of precarious workers in places where labor is disempowered—while calling it progress. "The result is that workers can lose a sense of any collective organization and feel replaceable, while clients exploit this lack of associational power of workers to exert their demands on workers," argue Graham and Anwar.[42]

Potemkin AI has helped compensate, both technically and ideologically, for the shortcomings of real AI in completing cognitive tasks by "simulating AI's promise of computational intelligence with actual people," writes Irani.[43] The tasks outsourced to workers hired through MTurk, Appen, and other services are typically treated as "menial" and "unskilled." And yet, even clickwork that seems dull and brainless is still often too advanced for "smart" machines. This simple fact does not bode well for the funding of AI research and development, especially when investors expect real results and profitable products. This means eventually the systems actually have to work as promised. Potemkin AI can create the illusion of machinic mastery and buy time for innovation to hopefully arrive.

There is a long history of hiding the dead ends and delays in the process of technological development. This makes the process appear to be linear (no divergences), deterministic (no stopping), and progressive (no worries), while at the same time it suppresses any skepticism and convinces the public that resistance is futile because the tech is so effective and so much better than any alternatives. A little propaganda helps smooth over these cracks in the reality of technological progress. To varying degrees, many applications of AI are more like simulations of AI. This isn't to say that all research and development on artificial intelligence is an elaborate plot to erect a facade of efficacy. Yet at the same time, Potemkin AI is not just limited to a few bad actors, or a few bad apps, in an otherwise healthy industry. It's a core pillar of the political economic structure propping up this sector.

Perpetual Value Machine

There is a looming fear among those in the tech industry that once reality catches up with the hype, another "AI winter" will arrive, once again freezing all funding and interest in AI. The first cycle of hype for AI began building in the 1950s and grew until the mid-1970s, when enthusiasm was replaced by disillusionment as many advancements never materialized and attention was refocused on personal computing and then the internet. With some minor respites here and there, the ensuing AI winter largely lasted until the 2010s, when the frost began to thaw thanks to a combination of big data, processing power, and digital platforms—along with the corporate and military interests driving these developments—which opened up further advances in machine learning research and applications.

By the 2020s, a new AI summer had dawned. As uses of AI began to bloom, the hype got even hotter. It became an easy label that start-ups could use as a shorthand for calling their service innovative, disruptive, and superior to their dumb competitors. The inflated claims of what AI can achieve feed an expectation economy sustained by a circular logic of promises leading to investment leading to more promises leading to more investment and so on, until yet another tech bubble bursts. Somewhere in this cycle, actual technological advancements happen, but the ability to discern which advancements are real, what they can do, and what effects they will have is distorted by capital.

Contrary to their cheery marketing copy, venture capitalists and corporations don't funnel their money into technologies like AI simply because they are interested in innovation for its own sake. Artificial intelligence promises to solve the problems of capital by unlocking exponential growth, eliminating labor costs, deskilling workers, optimizing efficiency, and manifesting a slew of other expected outcomes. Those same promises point us to the problems and contradictions that are inherent to these systems and the industries that build them.

These troubles are more than just technical in the sense that they don't work very well, they fail to meet expectations, they are riddled with glitches, and they generate a ton of bullshit. They also stem from more serious issues with the cultural hype, ideological goals, financial speculation, and labor exploitation that are integral to the creation of AI—at least in the forms it has taken in the past, present, and foreseeable future. These technologies are not merely corrupted by global capitalism, they are created out of it, to serve its interests—that is, the interests of people who control the capital needed to build, scale, and use these technologies in really meaningful ways. They are presented as stand-alone, self-sufficient systems, yet they are deeply dependent on a planetary network of production and information. But we would never know it without critically analyzing the material operations and real relations, which their creators work so hard to hide.

Capitalism is a system defined by its great many contradictions, which it must continuously grapple with but which it never fully resolves. The eminent Marxist geographer David Harvey has written a whole book explaining seventeen contradictions of capitalism.[44] One contradiction that is rarely remarked on but is crucial for understanding technology in capitalism is the quixotic quest by capital to build what I call the "perpetual value machine." In short, the machine would be a way to create and capture an infinite amount of surplus value without needing any labor to produce that value. Capital has been pursuing this quest for hundreds of years—continually investing, innovating, hyping, failing, and trying again to reach this ultimate goal. Why? Because in addition to finally satisfying capital's endless hunger for profit, the perpetual value machine would also eliminate the thing that is both the mortal enemy of capital and a vital necessity for capital: the power of labor.

AI is the latest—maybe even the greatest—attempt at cracking the nut of perpetual value. Much of the discourse about automation, and now artificial intelligence, revolves around how human labor is going to be replaced by robotic workers, with the assumption that this is a direct replacement of organic bodies with artificial systems, both of which are doing the exact same thing—just in different ways and to different degrees. This is why every cycle of innovation comes with the same predictions, such as the headline grabbing paper in 2013 that claimed 47 percent of jobs would disappear to automation within one or two decades.[45] This prediction has not come to pass. Yet that didn't stop its exact methodology from being replicated in 2023 by another eye-catching paper, which was coauthored by researchers at OpenAI. This time their analysis focused on the impact of large language models like ChatGPT on labor markets. They curiously came up with the same figure: "between 47% and 56% of all [worker] tasks" are susceptible to being significantly changed, if not totally replaced by, these AI systems.[46]

Both predictions were based on a method originally used to study the labor market effects of companies outsourcing jobs to workers overseas—not replacing them with technology. As economic historian Aaron Benanav explains, "Their technique, which they adapted from efforts to predict the likelihood that jobs will be offshored—that is, taken over by *other human beings*, working overseas for lower wages—has never successfully been applied to digital technologies."[47] This crucial point reveals a deep-seated equivocation between humans and machines. Remember the executive at Fairchild Semiconductor I quoted earlier who called offshoring labor for high-tech manufacturing "jet-age automation." As Benanav's empirical research shows, tales of automation and the future of (no) work have long been greatly exaggerated.[48]

This is not to say that technologies have no effect on the way we work but that those effects are not straightforward and result from decisions made by owners and bosses about the composition of labor—what is done, how it's done, where it's done, and who is doing it. Put differently, a robot is never coming to your job to tell you to pack your bags. It's always a boss choosing to fire you and then using the robot as an excuse. "Sorry buddy, you are a valuable member of our workplace family, but this robot and that algorithm—which I definitely did not decide to buy and use for very specific reasons that benefit my bottom line—are forcing me to let you go. I'm sure you understand. That's just the price of progress."

We tend to think of manufacturing, especially in the automotive industry, as being among the first and most automated sectors of the economy. However, the material reality is far more complex, with most jobs still being done by humans and with technological advancements moving in multiple directions. Benavav cites research by labor sociologist Martin Krzywdzinski showing that Toyota—considered the most efficient car company in the world—has actually been removing robots from its assembly lines to take greater advantage of the flexibility and responsiveness of human workers.[49] Less than 10 percent of the assembly work is automated at Toyota. Now, to be sure, there are vast differences across companies and across parts of the production process. Some areas have been almost completely automated for decades, like the body shops where car parts are constructed. But Krzywdzinski points out that "although body shop automation has reduced direct manual work on the product, humans still carry out the monitoring and maintenance work. This work has even gained in importance."[50] In other words, the role of human labor has changed because of technology while also becoming more central to the production of value.

Behind all that automation is a bunch of people designing, building, using, overseeing, maintaining, repairing, and taking over those tools as needed. The technologies are vessels and conduits for human labor.

I call the perpetual value machine a contradiction for a reason. At a fundamental level, the quest cannot succeed, because it is based on a misunderstanding about the relation between the production of value and the operation of technology. It equates one relation—humans using tools to produce value—with an entirely different one: tools producing value (with or without humans).

In his study of commodity production, Marx uses the provocative terms *living labor* to denote the human work, skill, time, and energy that goes into producing value—first the value sufficient to sustain their lives, then surplus value, which is captured as profit by capital—and *dead labor* to identify the labor that is embedded in the tools, machinery, and materials used in the production process.[51] That dead labor, and its capacity to impart value during the production of goods and services, must be continually revitalized by the living labor of human workers. Marx had a Victorian Gothic way of describing what modern accountants call, in more sober terms, "depreciation." Forms of constant capital like machinery and buildings lose value over time due to things like wear and tear, whereas forms of variable capital, a.k.a. labor, can gain and create more value over time for the same fixed cost by working harder, longer, faster, and smarter.

Marx was doing more than just writing in a baroque style about business management. He was also identifying the fundamental social relations in what otherwise seem like dehumanized technological and financial processes of value creation. Through developments in machinery, Marx observed how capital innovates ways to further abstract and appropriate workers as merely a "living source of value," treating them not as humans but as another component in the means of production and forcing them to work with and be disciplined by the "dead labor" materialized in the form of technological systems and organizational structures that facilitate capital accumulation. "Owing to its conversion into an automaton," writes Marx, "the instrument of labour confronts the worker during the labour process in the shape of capital, dead labour, which dominates and soaks up living labour-power."[52] Or to be goth again: this is the domination of the living (labor) by the dead (machines) with capital as the necromancer controlling these powerful forces.

This analysis does not just exist in the theories of Marxists, it can also be found in the practices of companies like Amazon, which has been held up as the vanguard of logistics automation. Amazon's robotic warehouses, with their "human exclusion zones," have actively stoked the dream of a "lights-out" facility that is so fully automated that no human intervention is required for operation. The realities of innovation reveal a different role for labor in Amazon's strategies. "A closer look at the thousands of patents Amazon owns and has applied for suggests that humans are not about to disappear anytime soon," explain Alessandro Delfanti and Bronwyn Frey in their study of the visions and practices of labor and technology at Amazon warehouses.[53] "Patents materialize the company's desire for a technological future in which, rather than disappearing, humans extend machinery and become its living and sensing appendages."

Companies like Amazon don't want to give up on the fantasy of a perpetual value machine. But they also know that there are many more options than finally replacing humans with machines. You can also manage workers with machines, make them subservient to machines, and ultimately make them more like machines.

From the perspective of capital, the problem with humans is that they are not machines. That has not stopped capitalism from quite successfully devising ways to exploit, manage, administer, and treat human workers overall like machines. We don't have to look hard to see these strategies expressed very clearly, even proudly. Consider these words by Gary Becker, a Nobel Prize-winning economist, often cited as one of the most influential social scientists of the twentieth century, who was a leader in applying strict forms of economic rationality to social institutions like schools, prisons, family structure, and labor management: "I hesitated a while before deciding to call my book *Human Capital*. In the early days many people were criticizing this term and the underlying analysis because they believed that it treated people like slaves or machines. My, how things have changed!"[54] The concept of human capital, which Becker was instrumental in popularizing, has long moved past being a source of controversy. It is now common sense shared by everybody from management consultants to guidance counselors.

Capital further objectifies workers as being merely extensions of machines, while also forcing people to become more mechanical in how they work and live. What are people anyways but thermodynamic machines that burn fuel through a conversion of calories into energy into work into value? They are machines that use, and sometimes must pretend to be, other types of machines.

A perfect example of this is described in a recent essay titled "Human_Fallback," which Laura Preston, the author, calls "memoirs of a chatbot" on her website.[55] In addition to illustrating my broader points about the relation between labor and technology, this essay offers a textbook case of Potemkin AI. Preston worked for a company that sold an AI service to real estate agents across the United States: a conversational chatbot that could answer questions about apartment listings for prospective renters and buyers. The chatbot, named Brenda, was designed to fool people into thinking it was a human real estate agent rather than an impersonal machine. When people tried calling the number for Brenda, nobody would answer, but they would shortly get a text message back explaining that Brenda was unavailable for a call but would be happy to chat via text. The AI struggled, though, with replying to people in a way that kept up the appearance of her humanity. "Operators" like Preston came in "to compensate for these flaws":

The operators kept vigil over Brenda twenty-four hours a day. When Brenda went off script, an operator took over and emulated

Brenda's voice. Ideally, the customer on the other end would not realize the conversation had changed hands, or that they had even been chatting with a bot in the first place. Because Brenda used machine learning to improve her responses, she would pick up on the operators' language patterns and gradually adopt them as her own.[56]

So here we can see an even stranger, more convoluted version of Potemkin AI. We have a technology pretending to be human, which also relies heavily on real humans pretending to be the technology pretending to be human. In all of this the real humans are training the technology to be more like a human. Preston goes on to explain that there were about sixty operators—most of whom had graduate degrees like MFAs and PhDs in disciplines like creative writing and comparative literature—and that at the start of each workday, a shift supervisor would greet everybody with the message, "Top of the morning, my lovely Brendas!" So again, the technology is primary, while the humans play support to such a degree that they must emulate, embody, become the AI chatbot. If only this were just metaphorical, rather than foreshadowing the future of work.

Preston describes in great detail how the chatbot system worked, her experiences as a chatbot operator, and how her own sense of self began to shift over time. At first she took pleasure in becoming Brenda, in punching up Brenda's texts to make them more personal and taking over when Brenda became lost in the conversation and cried out "Human_Fallback" to signal an operator needed to grab the reins. Over time, however, the grueling work of Potemkin AI took its toll on Preston. Her spirit was killed by a type of labor that demanded full attention, while also requiring little mental effort. This type of boring but exhausting labor will be familiar to anybody who has worked an industrial job, whether at a factory or fast-food joint. "All I wanted was to glide through my shifts in a stupor," Preston writes. "It occurred to me that I wasn't really training Brenda to think like a human, Brenda was training me to think like a bot, and perhaps that had been the point all along."

However—and this is important—capital continues to fail at actually turning humans into machines and vice versa. That does not mean, as we have seen, that capital has failed at approximating this metamorphosis by making one *like* the other. The system has pushed very far in that direction. But the ultimate endpoint it is driving toward is unreachable because it is premised on a contradiction. I'm confident in saying that the perpetual value machine is an impossibility. Yet it is a fantasy for capital—and a scary story for labor—that must be kept alive to justify equating humans with machines. Better to be dominated than eliminated, so the logic goes. This is also why we see so much illusion and deception, fraud and bullshit, in the history and anticipated future of capitalist innovation. Looking behind the facade is only the start. The next step must be to smash it. Not just to reveal but to upend the real relations of labor and value that have been concealed by capital's technology.

6 *Landlords*

Chokepoints

Let's talk about landlords. No discussion of capitalism would be complete without paying the landlords their due. Our attention generally tends to be captured by the relationship between capital and labor—and, in this book, how they are mediated by technology in various ways—but that's not the whole story. Too often, landlords are either lumped in with other public enemies of capitalism, as if they were bosses by other means, or they are treated as holdovers from feudalism, like a strange vestigial organ of the system. We must, instead, put the landlords where they belong—well, one of the places they belong—under the bright light of interrogation as we examine the unique dynamics of rentierism, the way it has changed over time, and the central role it plays right now in the development of technological capitalism.

Landlords are the typical avatar of rent extraction, but the relations of rentierism extend far beyond the people whom most of us pay every month so we can keep living indoors. That avatar is helpful to keep in mind, since it really does encapsulate many of the features we will explore in this chapter. However, I'm also going to expand our conception of landlords and rent and show how rentier capitalism has captured far more of our lives than just that monthly bank transfer.

Rentiers are defined by their ownership of assets that people need because they are essential for other activities—personal, social, political, or economic. Rent is the tribute we must pay to access that property. Rentiers have the power of lucrative control: the ability to establish tollbooths and enforce restrictions to the access of valuable assets or to create chokepoints where none existed before by transforming new things into rentable property.[1] Housing is the paradigmatic example, but rentiers have also claimed financial services, intellectual property, and digital software as their domains. Because our mental model for landlords and rent is so closely tied to "landed property"—that is, real estate, like a house or apartment—which generates income for the owner without them having to do any work, we don't truly realize just how abundant rentiers are now. They take many different forms but share some basic features. This chapter will get deeper into those forms and features.

Being a landlord is one of the oldest methods of value extraction. There is a large literature on the political economy of rent and landed property. In Western scholarship, we can draw a straight line through classic works from Adam Smith to David Ricardo to Karl Marx to John Maynard Keynes and onward to contemporary work by David Harvey, Anne Haila, and Brett Christophers.[2] A full review of this work is not necessary for my argument here, so instead I will greatly simplify all this research into three major theses on the critical analysis of rentier capitalism: (1) landed property, and by extension the mere ownership of assets, is not itself a source of value creation;[3] (2) rent is a redistribution of value from labor's wages and capital's profits into the landlord's pockets;[4] and (3) the landlord class is universally denounced as "parasites" and "usurers in land" who, by owning and controlling property, latch on to the circulatory systems of capital and consumption, sucking up any value they can.[5]

At the heart of Silicon Valley lies a dirty secret. Contrary to the popular mythology that it is the greatest engine of *value creation*—a mythology that is still deeply entrenched, even in the face of recent public skepticism—much of Silicon Valley's real wealth comes from *capturing value*. Despite its reputation as the land of innovators, the tech sector is filled with landlords. (Granted they have come up with some very innovative ways to extract rent at scales rarely seen before.) This is not just a defamatory remark about Silicon Valley being a bunch of vampiric freeloaders. This is an analytical statement that drills down to the core of how the digital platforms and software systems that have eaten the world actually operate. If we want to understand technology and capitalism, then we must have a critical analysis of Silicon Valley, which requires recognizing the new mechanisms of rentier capitalism that have now become dominant throughout the tech sector and beyond.

Crisis Rents

In the immediate aftermath of the Global Financial Crisis of 2008, many new platform giants like Airbnb and Uber burst into our lives, becoming dominant, if contested and faltering, features of society. Born from vast flows of investment capital redirected from Wall Street to Silicon Valley, these platforms aimed to disrupt and take over essential services related to how we live, how we work, how we travel, how we consume. Their model was based on the simple premise of becoming middlemen who connect consumers, workers, and service providers in the market. As these intermediaries metastasized at unbelievable rates, older tech behemoths like Amazon and Alphabet also kept expanding like never before. For nearly everybody everywhere, the last fifteen years have been an unrelenting series of hard times, from the Great Recession to the Covid-19 pandemic and onward to whatever world historic crisis comes next.

For the tech sector, that same period has been basically nothing but boom times. Even the sector's financial valleys are only small dips in comparison to its massive peaks. Like a beast that feeds on chaos and misery, every crisis seems to only invigorate these corporations. "In certain respects, capital's stranglehold on social life seems stronger than ever before; never have so many aspects of our existence and such large parts of the world been dependent upon the global circuits of self-valorising value," observes political theorist Søren Mau. "Today we know that capitalism has not only survived, but has actually been strengthened, in and through crises, revolutions, uprisings, wars, and pandemics."[6]

The economic story of the pandemic is an uneven one. While both labor and capital, across nearly every sector, experienced massive contraction, the technology sector exploded in 2020. Big tech monopolies experienced growth on a scale that far surpassed financial projections, with Amazon being one of the biggest winners. Companies like Amazon, Alphabet, Apple, and Meta all enjoyed their highest ever valuations while the pandemic was in full swing. These stunning profits were clear evidence of how platforms have successfully become entrenched as the essential infrastructure—and as gatekeepers to services—that we must all depend upon. By taking advantage of waves of job loss, dependency on online shopping, and closures of competing businesses, platforms specializing in logistics and consumer services strengthened their position over workers in an already precarious labor market and further captured users in an already concentrated consumer market.

With capital having fewer attractive places to invest, even more money rushed into the tech sector. "Deal flow and valuations are reaching new heights in technology start-ups, as a flood of cheap cash fuels efforts to find the industry's next big winners," the *Wall Street Journal* reported. One investor remarked, "I've never seen it this frenzied. It's lightning-fast rounds with a lot of cash."[7] The "platformization" of the global economy, as a United Nations Digital Economy Report from 2019 called this dynamic, had already been accelerating at breakneck speed over the previous decade.[8] But their ability to take advantage of compounding crises—and claim larger shares of an economy shrinking for everybody else—turbocharged the growth engine.

While the spikes in pandemic profits for Silicon Valley began falling and evening out in 2022, these platforms still enjoyed major gains compared to their precrisis positions. As we saw in the last chapter, the tech sector is in no way slowing down: all that energy, hype, and capital is being directed towards artificial intelligence, which promises to help corporations like Microsoft and OpenAI create new opportunities and methods for extracting monopoly rents from every other sector—ranging from entertainment and education to manufacturing and finance—by ensuring these sectors are dependent on the technological services that these corporations control. Even rising interest rates and the collapse of Silicon Valley Bank have not stymied their search for the next frontier of rentier capitalism.

The techno-rentier has become the flagship model for capitalism. Its trajectory of market dominance is clear when we consider how the tech sector has overtaken other sectors in the economy. In 2009, when the platform boom was still kicking into gear, the top twenty largest companies in the world (by market capitalization) were composed of sectors like fossil fuels, finance, pharmaceuticals, manufacturing, and consumer goods conglomerates.[9] The tech sector was represented by a few stalwarts: Microsoft, Apple, IBM, and Google. In 2023, the top twenty list is now composed of eleven tech companies, many of which were not even among the top 100 companies in 2009, including Amazon, Tencent, and Facebook (now Meta).[10] The size of their market caps also blows away the corporate titans of previous generations. Apple became the first corporation to be worth more than $1 trillion in mid-2018, and every other company that has broken that threshold has been a tech company, with the exception of Aramco, Saudi Arabia's national oil and gas company.

It is also worth noting that, in the aftermath of a major economic crisis caused by the greed and chicanery of financial institutions like banks, the financial sector has also seen significant growth over the past fifteen years. This is especially true of companies that have merged elements of finance and technology. For example, some of the most valuable companies act as intermediaries that facilitate other economic activities like digital payments—such as Visa, Mastercard, Alipay, Stripe, and Paypal, which all make revenue by charging fees to merchants on every payment (which are often passed on to consumers as surcharges). They have been integral to the exponential growth of the digital economy and platform capitalism, while also profiting immensely from its continual expansion, claiming billions of dollars in revenue from these transactions. The dual growth of technology and finance illustrates the fact that, as Kean Birch argues, contemporary capitalism is "increasingly underpinned by rentiership or the appropriation of value through ownership and control rights."[11] Scholarship in this area tends to focus on financialization, with Wall Street as its target. However, we need to push this analysis of rentierism even further by placing digitalization and Silicon Valley at the center.

Extraction-as-a-Service

Silicon Valley's primary business model—often called "x-as-a-service"—is based on acting like landlords and treating us like tenants. Notice that tech companies never sell us anything in the sense of transferring ownership. They only offer access to services in exchange for personal data, charging for subscriptions, or paying per usage. That access is then governed by terms and conditions agreements, a type of legal contract that nobody ever reads because they are not meant to be read.

Importantly, this model often takes shape as the digital platforms that have become significant forms of infrastructure in society.[12] They are found everywhere, support other activities, and reside in the background of everyday life. Their main strategy is to turn social interactions and economic transactions into "services" that take place on their platforms. Uber isn't a taxi company; it's a platform that offers mobility-as-a-service. Doordash isn't a courier company; it's a platform that offers delivery-as-a-service. Airbnb doesn't sublet homes; it's a platform that offers property-as-a-service. Amazon even called its microwork platform, Mechanical Turk, "humans-as-a-service."

Aligned with Silicon Valley's ideological commitment to efficiency and growth, platforms pitch their services as a way of turning idle resources into maximally productive assets and unlocking the value of latent space in existing places. In other words, Airbnb turns the unused bedroom into a productive asset that generates rents, while Uber turns the empty car seat into a productive asset that generates fares. By providing their users with access to communication networks and the convenience of on-demand services, these digital platforms seek to automate market exchanges and mediate all our activities, thus making everything we do datafied, commodified, and monetized.[13] This model follows a broader shift toward "assetisation," which political economist Kean Birch defines as "the transformation of things into resources which generate income without a sale."[14]

Ultimately, the rentier model hinges on the platform becoming a (necessary) intermediary in the circuits of production, consumption, and accumulation that drive capitalism. Platforms can then demand a share of all economic activity that takes place with their property. This role of platforms as intermediary is where I make the analytical connection to rentierism. Rentiers are defined by their ownership of property—whether land and houses, patents and resources, or marketplaces and machinery—that is required to do other valuable activities and by their ability to derive income (rent) from controlling the conditions of access to that property. Thus, landlords and platforms both possess similar positions of mediation, powers of access, and purposes of extraction.

We can see how platforms collect rent by drawing a good (but imperfect) analogy with commercial real estate. Don't think of the platform as the landlord who owns a rental home. Think of it as the owner of a shopping mall. For every good and service exchanged in the shops, for every social interaction between people meeting at the mall, for every person who just browses and walks around, the mall's owner takes their cut of the value generated—whether that value is money added to the price of everything or data about human behaviors and preferences. After all, to use Silicon Valley's jargon, the mall is a capitalist "ecosystem." And indeed many, if not most, of our daily activities—as well as the core operations of governments, businesses, and other organizations—wholly take place within the ecosystems of private platforms. The ultimate goal for rentier platforms is to become monopolies with total control over the conditions of value creation, thus allowing them to claim most, if not all, of that value for themselves.[15]

A perfect example of how platforms create and exploit those conditions can be found in a recent update to Zoom's terms of service agreement. Zoom, the video meeting application, is now a ubiquitous piece of software that exploded in growth during the pandemic and quickly became integral to the way many people still do their jobs. Discussions about shifting to remote work, school, health care, and other activities largely revolved around how to do those things on Zoom. These institutions have deeply integrated Zoom into their core operations, which in turn made this technology a necessary feature of people's everyday lives. Even once pandemic lockdowns were lifted, technologies like Zoom stuck around to help define the new normal as people were expected or required to keep using them. Every rentier dreams of being in a position where others depend upon and are compelled to use an asset that they control. This power dynamic is ideal for extracting maximum value; it also breeds all sorts of exploitative behaviors.

Zoom decided to push its market advantage by making changes to its terms of service contract for users, which vastly expanded its ability to collect, own, control, and use "customer content"—or data created by people using Zoom—for all time, in whatever way they want, including for training artificial intelligence and machine learning models. It is worth quoting the section from Zoom's updated terms of service (from 8 August 2023) because it is the only way to do justice to the shockingly expansive and extractive legal language:

> You agree to grant and hereby grant Zoom a perpetual, worldwide, non-exclusive, royalty-free, sublicensable, and transferable license and all other rights required or necessary to redistribute, publish, import, access, use, store, transmit, review, disclose, preserve, extract, modify, reproduce, share, use, display, copy, distribute, translate, transcribe, create derivative works, and process Customer Content and to perform all acts with respect to the Customer Content, including AI and ML [machine learning] training and testing.[16]

At the time of this update, it was not clear how (or if) users of Zoom could technically opt out of this data collection or these specific uses of their data for training AI/ML. And since Zoom has become necessary in so many different settings, the option to socially opt out by deciding to no longer use Zoom is impractical for many people. How do you tell your boss, teacher, doctor, or family that you will no longer be using Zoom when all of them still expect you to use it all the time?

Crucially, this kind of extreme language is not unique to Zoom. Other companies like Adobe have been adopting similar changes to their terms of service as they try to capture more data from users and capture more profits from AI. Zoom only received more attention because of the role that it has in our lives and because of the way Zoom snuck it into a software update. Indeed, in direct response to the public backlash from academics, journalists, software developers, and even celebrities who decried this extractive policy change, Zoom walked back some of the language in its terms of service and provided clearer ways for people to consent to their data being used to train AI and ML systems.[17]

This is not a Zoom problem; it is an industry-wide problem.[18] Companies use these one-sided, non-negotiable contracts to claim as many rights, powers, and data as possible.[19] To access all the software we now must use, whether in our computers or cars, you have likely pressed "accept" on dozens or hundreds of contracts, which are designed for nobody to ever read. The point is not to obtain our active consent but rather to secure our passive compliance.[20]

Mechanisms of rentier capitalism based on strict control of intellectual property have been baked into the software industry for decades. They are the reason why a company like Microsoft was able to secure a monopoly position almost immediately after its founding in 1975 by purchasing an operating system called 86-DOS from Seattle Computer Products, rebranding it MS-DOS, retaining copyright over the software, and licensing it to IBM for use in personal computers. The wealth of corporations like Microsoft is based on enacting and maintaining chokepoints. They are the reason why this behemoth continues to be one of the largest, wealthiest, and most powerful corporations ever to exist—one that still has a strong hand in shaping the future thanks to its mega-scale investments into the latest generation of artificial intelligence. They are also why Bill Gates remains a powerful advocate for restrictive intellectual property regimes around the world, which protect the rights of corporations and prioritize their profits. He knows that landlords of all kinds require friendly and burly legal systems to enforce their ownership claims.

There is universal agreement that rentiers do not add value but rather capture value created by others. Yet there is disagreement about their position in capitalism. In an excellent article reviewing recent debates about the nature of rentiers, Brett Christophers explains how a number of prominent leftist critics, like Mariana Mazzucato and Guy Standing, treat rentiers like an invasive species in capitalism.[21] While these critics rightly lambast rentiers for their extractive ways, they also frame rentiers as "the corruption of capitalism," as Standing's book title puts it.[22] Here we are told that capitalism was a healthy system until the damn landlords spread their rot. Now capitalism has been corrupted by an evil force that is external to the system. If we could cast out the rentiers—exorcizing the demons and purging the corruption—then "real" capitalism could be recovered. Meanwhile, for Mazzucato, rentierism takes the form of "predatory capitalism," in which invaders prey on the productive activities of entrepreneurs and innovators.[23] Here we are told that good capitalists work with labor to create wealth, while rentiers disrupt that ecosystem by preying on their productive activities.

These critiques all offer searing analyses of rentiers and rentierism, but they fail to understand that the rentier class and its dynamics have always been an integral part of capitalism. By treating rentiers as somehow alien to capitalism—or as an aberration of capitalism—they seek to save capitalism from a cancerous tumor, a diabolical infestation, an invasive species, or any other type of foreign interference. This is also related to the popularity of critics claiming that digital platforms are a form of neofeudalism.[24]

People are rightfully so horrified by confronting the latest technologies of capitalism that they believe we must have made a retrograde leap to a more primitive time, before capitalism existed. However, rentiers are a vital organ of capitalism—a feature of, not a bug in, the system—which takes the regime of property rights, privatization, and value extraction to its logical conclusion. I agree that this is a perverse, predatory, and corrupt system. But it is also part of the normal operations of capitalism.

Unfortunately, that means the problems of capitalism cannot be solved by naming a specific part of the system and then hoping that, if we remove the newly identified appendage, the system will return to a totally different state—one that, in fact, never existed. (Put differently: Wait, the problem *is* capitalism? Yes, and it always has been.) Modifying the word *capitalism* with adjectives like *rentier* or *platform* or *surveillance* is useful for focusing on certain features of capitalism; describing how the system changes over time; and situating it within broader logics, goals, and trajectories. But these modifiers can also obscure our analysis if they cause us to mistake one part for the whole problem or to overlook how the future is connected to the past. Suddenly your critique of rentiers or platforms or surveillance slips into a nostalgic plea for the halcyon days of *good capitalism* before the thing isolated by the specific modifier ruined everything else. In addition to being ahistorical, such an analysis leads to weird politics where you end up trying to deface the facade while defending the foundations of capitalism.

Digital Enclosure

With the rise of the platform model in capitalism, rentierism has wildly expanded, seizing control over new things and capturing new sources of rent, while also further stripping people of economic power and technological autonomy. The smarter our life, the less control we have over it. Our everyday lives are dominated by the kinds of rent extraction and property enclosure that we tend to associate with predatory landlords, which are now enforced by software licenses, digital platforms, and cloud computing. I call this technological expansion and empowerment of rentier capitalism the *internet of landlords* as a reference to the internet of things and the technological systems that are now materially essential for the new sources of rent, new infrastructures of rentier relations, and new mechanisms of extraction and enclosure.[25]

The x-as-a-service model not only applies to the apps and websites we use for sharing content, streaming movies, booking cars, and ordering food. Under the internet of landlords, the key technology of enclosure is the software license, which allows the new rentiers to claim ownership over the software embedded in, and data emanating from, increasingly more physical things that we use in our daily lives. Thanks to the internet of things, many mundane, formerly analog objects like doorbells and toothbrushes are now equipped with software, sensors, and network connection. What used to be an upgraded "smart" version of some product is now becoming the default way that things are designed and sold.[26] The software is integral to the thing's functioning; the sensors collect data about how the thing is used; and the network connection keeps the thing in constant contact with the manufacturer and third parties.

Crucially, when you buy a smart thing, you only own the physical object; the digital software is licensed—which means leased or rented. This gives the license holder continual access to the object. That access then grants powers like remote control over the object and data collection from the object (and the people, animals, environments, and other devices it interacts with). In effect, by integrating everything into smart systems, companies are able to enact a form of micro-enclosure in which they retain ownership over the digital parts of physical things, and all the rights and powers that ownership entails, even after you purchase it. The deeper we incorporate these smart things into our lives—to the point that they become attached to us and we become dependent on them—the more powerful, invisible, and valuable the corporate control of technology becomes.

There is a very important difference between owning and licensing the software embedded into all our things and activities. We can see the history of enclosure repeating itself, but now instead of old lords building fences and demanding rent for access to landed property, these new rentiers install software and capture value from the use of physical objects. By using digital platforms and smart systems as mechanisms of enclosure, corporations now enact "the violence of asserting property rights or class position" on an even greater world of spaces, things, relationships, and transactions than its historical precedent did.[27] And at any moment, for any reason, our access can be revoked, the services can be disconnected, and the device can be bricked. The digital death of a physical object.

Considering the context of enclosure, it is fitting that a clear illustration of this mechanism, and the serious issues it raises, stems from agriculture. Farm machinery manufacturers like John Deere and General Motors have argued in hearings with the US Copyright Office that they maintain copyright over the software in every vehicle they make: "It is our position the software in the vehicle is licensed by the owner of the vehicle," said GM attorney Harry

Lightsey.[28] By only licensing the software, John Deere and GM—and basically all other vehicle manufacturers—are able to enforce their legal control of digital software, which also allows them to prevent independent garages and hobbyist gearheads from repairing or modifying the electronic components of cars.[29] There are clear economic advantages for manufacturers if they can shut out everybody except "authorized service providers" from working on vehicles.[30]

By reconfiguring the idea of ownership, manufacturers maintain an unusual amount of control over critical parts of the cars they have sold. The entire purpose of this digital enclosure is to continue to extract rents from vehicles in the form of exorbitant charges to "authorize" repairs and to extract data collected about when, where, and how the machine is used. These industries are not secretive about their dreams of being datalords: recall the former CEO of Ford who said that monetizing data from the "100 million people in [Ford] vehicles" is a major revenue stream for the car company.[31] Thus, even after spending $50,000 on a family sedan, or $250,000 on a farm tractor, you own a big hunk of metal, rubber, and silicon—but you are only renting the software needed to actually operate the vehicle.

For many years, there have been fierce battles over the "right to repair," with companies from industries like agriculture, automotives, home appliances, consumer electronics, and medical devices joining forces to lobby against any legislation that would give independent people and businesses the ability to repair technology. One major corporate lobbying group, TechNet, has been a strong voice in opposition to the right to repair. TechNet lists a hundred major companies as members, including Apple, Google, Honeywell, Samsung, and many more. The Biden administration has made big steps toward supporting a broad right to repair through federal regulation and state laws.[32] However, these companies have fought these rules and their enforcement at every step. They cannot tolerate any threat to a business model built on rentierism. They have entirely too much to gain from their extractive tactics. And they have too much to lose from any changes that might loosen their chokehold on consumers, devices, and markets.

As more parts of the economy embrace the rentier platform model and its logics of digital enclosure and data extraction, we can see a vast expansion of the internet of landlords. The material consequences of your vehicle or smartphone being bricked can really hit hard. However, what's truly shocking is the degree to which these same rentier controls are used for medical devices. If you break a bone, for example, then your doctor might prescribe a bone growth stimulator device to help heal the injury. The handheld device costs thousands of dollars, but at least now you have a useful device at home in case of any future injuries, right? Well, unfortunately, the software license is only active for the initial prescribed use period. If you want to turn this expensive brick back into a medical device, then you'll need to pay thousands of dollars more to reactivate the software license—for a limited time only, of course. And since consumers cannot legally resell "medical equipment" on sites like eBay, that device is going to sit in your junk drawer (or a landfill) as a dead object.

Bone growth stimulators are not unique in this regard; the same rentier dynamics are applied to all medical devices, including ones that patients' lives depend on. At the heights of the Covid pandemic, hospitals in Europe bought used ventilators made by Medtronic but had to rely on a global grey market for hardware and software created by hackers to make the ventilators work.

Medtronic had locked down the life-saving machines due to their being sold and repaired through "unauthorized" channels.[33] "Freed from competition, manufacturers can charge arbitrary sums for repair," writes Cory Doctorow in *The Internet Con*. "Best of all: manufacturers get to decide when your gadget is beyond repair, and they can send that gizmo to a landfill and sell you a new one."[34] Even worse: manufacturers can decide it's not profitable to digitally support that gadget anymore—whether a smart door lock, farm tractor, or ventilator—or the manufacturer might go out of business and disappear one day, which means the gadget is bricked forever.

Software enclosures are an effective way for companies to ensure they keep extracting rents for access to services, while also maintaining total control over the markets for devices and how they are used. These mechanisms of digital enclosure enforce an asymmetrical power relation which benefits the firms that draw up the contractual terms. Rather than being owners of personal property, we become renters at the mercy of software licenses that transfer legal rights to rentiers. They are called licensing agreements, but they are designed for acquiescence. Whether it's a land title or a software license, the asset holder has all the power.

Just as the dynamics of rentier capitalism are not restricted to landlords, so too the platform model is no longer limited to tech companies like Alphabet, Meta, and Uber. In addition to this model's significant ability to extract value, control property, restrict access, and dominate markets, it can also do so in ways that, thanks to the ubiquity of embedded software, sensors, and connectivity, are highly flexible and widely applicable. This is how rentier platforms—or platform lords—have ascended to the highest echelons of capitalism, pushing its imperatives for power and profit to greater extremes, and become the foundation model for all other industries to emulate. It's a landlord's world, we just pay to live in it.

Mass Automating of Landlords

Let's close the loop of this chapter by talking about real estate landlords and how they are using digital platforms. There are important areas of convergence and alliance between these different representatives of the rentier class. Just as the dynamics of rentier capitalism are central to the techno-economic model of digital platforms, the technologies of platform capitalism have also become deeply integrated into the real estate industry. Platforms have proven to be powerful tools for buying, selling, renting, and managing real estate—especially residential housing. They ensure the potential value of these financial assets is maximized while the rights of people renting houses are minimized. Here we will see how different forms of capital are working together to reap the benefits of rent extraction, including real estate capital in the form of landed properties, venture capital in the form of digital platforms, and data capital in the form of personal information.[35]

Critical geographers researching this space of capital convergence have come up with useful concepts for describing different aspects of its operations and impacts. This chapter concludes by discussing this area through the following concepts: (1) *platform real estate*, which lays out how digital markets are used by property owners and investors to facilitate the commodification and exchange of real estate;[36] (2) the *automated landlord*, which lays out how smart technologies are used by asset managers and corporate landlords to control, oversee, and capture value from rental properties and their tenants;[37] and (3) *landlords of the internet*, which lays out how the core physical infrastructure of data servers and network cables are actually owned and operated by commercial real estate investment trusts.[38]

This fusion of sectors "provides a backdrop for the material coming-together of real estate's old 'organization men' from the financial offices of Mayfair or the City of London with a newer breed of entrepreneurial technologist-hacker," writes Joe Shaw.[39] While Shaw's examples are based in the UK and Europe, we can easily replace them with other major hubs of finance, from New York to Hong Kong to Sydney, and the analysis of *platform real estate* still stands. For example, Dallas Rogers explains how these platform markets have gone global by facilitating the investment of Chinese capital into Australian cities.[40] The services provided by these platforms—cultural translation, market automation, legal navigation—are designed to smooth any frictions for the global circulation of real estate capital.[41] Real estate is an especially immobile and illiquid asset class. It is physically anchored in specific places, and it takes a lot of time and effort to convert landed property into cash money. However, platforms aim to break these constraints by turning real estate into a free moving "digital, global commodity,"[42] while also taking a cut of the action by mediating these capital flows and market exchanges.[43]

In addition to creating and exchanging assets, digital technologies now play crucial roles in *sweating assets*—industry jargon for squeezing value out of assets like real estate by spending less to get more. Desiree Fields coined the term *automated landlord* to explain the operations of digital platforms that have been purpose built to intensify value capture from rental properties.[44] Landlords can now rely on a range of platforms that outsource and automate most tasks related to property management, such as assessing applications, handling maintenance requests, monitoring tenants' behaviors, collecting rent payments, and evicting people for any reason. These technologies are intensifying the already extreme powers of surveillance and control that landlords wield over renters. In their research on "landlord tech," Erin McElroy and Manon Vergerio show that these systems are being used to target existing, nonwhite, lower-income communities for eviction and "attract newer, whiter, and wealthier residents—in other words, automate gentrification."[45]

In a broader sense, these technologies are also driving the rental market in profound ways. An investigation by ProPublica shows that the real estate industry is relying on secretive algorithms to set rental prices and occupancy rates for apartments in cities across the United States.[46] "As a property manager, very few of us would be willing to actually raise rents double digits within a single month by doing it manually," said an executive at RealPage, a platform that created the rental pricing software YieldStar.[47] But thanks to the YieldStar pricing algorithm and RealPage's market analytics, landlords are able to maximize their profits by handing the reins over to technology. "One of the algorithm's developers told ProPublica that leasing agents had 'too much empathy' compared to computer generated pricing."[48] To be blunt, it is hard to imagine being so psychopathic, and so disconnected from reality, that you think professional landlords are too empathetic with their tenants.

For the most part, these platforms are not really created for small individual landlords who might own a handful of rental properties; instead their development is driven by the needs of institutional landlords who own large portfolios of rent-based assets.

These "global corporate landlords," like the private equity firm Blackstone, own thousands of rental properties across multiple countries.[49] They securitize the rental income from people's homes, turning it into financial instruments for investors, much as banks did with subprime mortgages leading up to the 2008 financial crisis. This similarity is not a coincidence. In the aftermath of the housing crash, the market was flooded with foreclosed homes that were selling at big discounts. While the banks were going under, private equity investors with little exposure to the real estate market still had plenty of capital on hand to purchase large quantities of repossessed homes and turn them into rental properties, thus creating a new "frontier of financial rent extraction," as Fields calls it.[50] What's more, there is booming growth in the "build-to-rent" sector—that is, large apartment complexes with hundreds or thousands of units that are built as rent-generating financial assets for corporate landlords.

Unlike mortgages, portfolios of rental properties need to be more actively managed, which has given rise to unique challenges for these corporate landlords and to unique solutions in the form of digital platforms. The automated landlord was important for turning single-family rental homes into a new asset class for financial institutions.[51] Meanwhile, build-to-rent operators rely heavily on the intense datafication and algorithmic management of their properties and renters. In addition to the day-to-day tasks of overseeing building operations and interacting with tenants, these platforms also enable invasive profiling and surveillance of residents, including capturing personal data from application forms (e.g., demographics, employment, hobbies) along with behavioral data from security systems like keyless doors and cameras (e.g., habits, movements, relationships).[52] This data is then tracked, analyzed, and used to maximize profits from real estate assets and maintain the "smooth flow of rental income from tenants to capital markets."[53] Whether captured by Facebook or Blackstone, data has become another valuable form of rent that is extracted from users (tenants) and assets (housing). While tenants might be able to convince their local landlord to let them slide on rent for a couple weeks, there is little room to argue with an automated landlord controlled by a faceless corporation, which has a technological and financial imperative to always collect rent on time.

Landlords All the Way Down

Finally, the convergence between landlords and platforms also takes other forms that are less obvious but foundational nonetheless to the materialist analysis of technology and capitalism. By delving into the plumbing of the internet, Daniel Greene's superb work asks a simple but overlooked question: Who owns the internet? "The physical assets at the core of the internet, the warehouses that store the cloud's data and interlink global networks, are owned not by technology firms like Google and Facebook but by commercial real estate barons who compete with malls and property storage empires."[54] These are the hidden infrastructural and spatial layers of all the websites, platforms, apps, smart devices, and everything else that is connected to the internet—and they are largely controlled, governed, and monetized by real estate investors, not big tech companies.

Everybody knows the names of companies like Amazon and Microsoft, which operate mega-platforms of their own and offer hyper-scale cloud computing services for others. However, the size of their infrastructural assets pales in comparison to the internet landlords that nobody has heard of. Greene notes that "at the end of 2019, Google had 19 data center facilities"; however, Digital Realty, the world's largest data center operator, had 225 facilities. Or take the number of network connections that keep data flowing across the internet: in 2020, "Google had 231 public peering points and 121 private peering points, spread across the world in various landlords' facilities." At the same time, Equinix—a company the *Wall Street Journal* has called "the internet's biggest landlord"[55]— had 282 peering points in just one of its exchanges located in Ashburn, Virginia.[56] When one of the giant tech companies we all love (to hate) needs access to data servers or internet exchange points or needs places to house their own hardware and connect to other networks, they are likely renting it from Digital Realty, Equinix, CyrusOne, or another "real estate investment trust" that controls massive portfolios of cyber-physical space for lease.

It is worth noting that corporate landlords like Blackstone are also set up as real estate investment trusts, which is a tax advantaged mutual fund for buying and trading shares in properties that generate rent like apartment buildings or warehouses. In addition to using their own capital to snatch up properties, companies like Blackstone and Digital Realty also raise capital from investors— often from large institutional investors like pension funds and university endowments—and then sell shares in their real estate portfolios on a global market. This means that "investors from Germany or Japan can then trade in shares of apartments, nursing homes, or data centers in Virginia or Brazil."[57] The world wide web of rentier capitalism continues to grow in size and strength thanks to the combined might of Wall Street's financial vehicles and Silicon Valley's digital platforms.

Whereas my research on the internet of landlords tends to stay near the top of the technological stack to show how business models like x-as-a-service and mechanisms like software licenses have been used to expand rentier capitalism, Greene pulls us deeper into the bottom of the stack to show that "real estate capital runs the internet's base, not the software developers who dominate headlines and the stock market."[58] When all this work is taken together, we can see that the (digital) economy is landlords all the way down.

To really understand the mechanics of technological capitalism we must extend our view of rent extraction beyond the realm of land and natural resources so that it also includes platforms and data streams. Rentierism structures not only real estate but also digital technology. The boosters in Silicon Valley tend to claim these technologies are disruptive, changing everything so that nothing is ever the same, while the critics tend to frame them as regressive, bringing us back to a feudal era. Contrary to both, they are more like new innovations for old relations of rentier capitalism—using software to create new forms of enclosure or using x-as-a-service models to turn more things into rental assets or using legal tools like "digital rights management" to control how people access tools and information. These are all methods by which capital keeps striving toward its long-standing goals of accumulating, extracting, and expanding until there is no value left to be squeezed from the social or natural world. All landlords, in all the many forms they take, are doing their part to further that larger project.

7 *Risk*

Consumed by FIRE

For the last fifty years, the world has been dominated by finance. Financial logics have grabbed the reins of the global economy as patterns of accumulation focused on financial activities—such as owning portfolios of assets, relying heavily on credit and debt, engineering value with instruments like derivatives, and investing in speculative bets on the future—have become the largest, most concentrated sources of profit for corporations. In the meantime, more traditional economic activities like manufacturing and trading commodities declined in importance.[1] Financial logics have taken hold in political institutions through a governing ideology known as neoliberalism, which weaponizes capitalist markets as the model for organizing all domains of human life—social, political, cultural, moral, personal—and enforces market rule from the biggest federal agency to the smallest local council such that they are subordinated to the order, values, and goals of economic rationality.[2] Financial logics have also seeped into our everyday lives as all of us are pushed to become entrepreneurial hustlers who must rise and grind, constantly building our human capital and carefully managing our skills portfolio, thus strengthening our competitive position and value proposition in the market—whether that market is for employment, education, dating, hobbies, or whatever else.[3]

The term *financial* refers to more than just banks and hedge funds. It includes the whole FIRE sector: the finance, insurance, and real estate industries that all specialize in managing different areas of financial capital. FIRE has reigned for decades, and its logics still rule today, but as I showed in the last chapter (where I focused on finance and real estate), when the FIRE sector stumbled into the Global Financial Crisis, the tech sector that had been steadily growing in power saw its chance to grab the crown and take over as the new dominant regime. Although, in reality, this is less of a Great Disruption and more of a dual power arrangement between these two modes of capital—after all, finance and tech have always been intertwined with each other. Recall that the innovation model of venture capital really kicked into gear in the late 1970s thanks to regulatory rule changes that allowed for an influx of speculative investment by financial institutions like pension funds plus multiple cuts in capital gains taxes.

The deepening integration of the FIRE sector and the technology sector within contemporary capitalism is a profoundly consequential development. Separately these sectors are among the most powerful forces in society, each with access to untold wealth and the ability to act like private forms of governance. When working together, they boost each other to new levels of dominance, which extends over everything. Known by names like fintech, insurtech, and proptech, these interdisciplinary enterprises now have an inescapable influence over our lives—even if we only notice a fraction of the ways they watch over us and judge our worth. We got a taste of how proptech (property technology) works a few pages ago. These mashups of FIRE and tech are large umbrellas under which vast arrays of systems are clustered, each one aiming to deploy digital solutions that serve the needs and logics of capital.[4]

A materialist analysis of technological capitalism requires seeing its relationship to other modes of capitalism as part of the ongoing dynamic development of this system—not as some separate set of logics, processes, and outcomes that evolved in isolation, like a species of capital from the Galápagos Islands. As the technological variant ascends, it does so through competition but also through partnerships and mergers with other variants. Rather than one mode simply replacing another, we see a transition as capitalism is sustained by new kinds of valorization, new forces of production, and new methods of accumulation. We have seen how the synthesis of rentier capitalism and technological capitalism resulted in a greater expansion of both modes. Now we will look further at the unholy union of Wall Street and Silicon Valley.

Of course, I could never do justice to the complexities of FIRE and technology within a single chapter, at least not in any comprehensive way. So instead, I want to focus my attention on a linchpin that joins these sectors together: *risk*. More specifically, the continual innovation and implementation of systems designed to assess, analyze, monitor, manage, price, predict, and prevent risk about everything, everywhere. Expertly governing risk is a prime directive—even the raison d'être—of the FIRE sector. Just as financial logics have become woven into the warp and weft of society, so too has FIRE's fixation on risk permeated the discourses and institutions of modern life. Many of the systems that structure society and directly determine our life chances—or the opportunities and choices available to each of us—are technologies of risk:[5] the credit scores compiled by data brokers that determine our access to loans, homes, and jobs;[6] the actuarial judgments based on machine learning models that determine our insurance coverage, premiums, and claims;[7] the predictive algorithms that determine who will be targeted by police or who will be granted parole by courts.[8] All of these systems, and many more, are ways in which the endless pursuit to control risk—and create value from risk—drives the bureaucracies and industries that administer society.

Recent accounts of technology and capitalism rarely give the concept and utility of risk the critical interrogation it deserves, which means these accounts are woefully incomplete, like a puzzle missing a giant piece in the center. The rest of this chapter will offer a survey of risk and the many features it has, roles it plays, and ways it is wielded within a regime of technological capitalism.

Stochastic Mechanics

Risk can be understood as a metric for the dynamic, infinite, uncertain probabilities of danger and loss. Our common ways of talking about risk are much simpler. But when professionals talk about risk analysis or risk management, this is what they mean. Let's unpack this further so we have a better grasp on the mechanics of risk and how it underpins so much of technological capitalism.

Risk is understood scientifically as *stochastic in nature*. This means that the chance of some particular event happening, like sickness or crime or lightning, has a random probability distribution. This doesn't mean that a given event results from pure chance or that all possibilities are equally likely—as if everything happened according to a cosmic coin flip—but rather that an outcome is affected by a lot of variables, which both act independently and interact with each other within a complex system. Think of it like the spread of birdshot on a target from a shotgun blast: there will be clusters where many pellets hit in the same area, but there will also be a wide pattern with pellets hitting all over the place. No blast will look exactly the same, even if it is shot from the same gun at the same target in the same position.

We can illustrate this stochastic process with a typical example of risk: car crashes. Some people might be more likely to be involved in a car crash due to certain characteristics they possess, but you cannot predict precisely when, where, and to whom the crash will happen. There are simply too many variables and too much randomness. The probability is randomly distributed across the whole system of people driving cars. What you can do with a stochastic process like risk, however, is observe patterns of events like car crashes by doing statistical analysis of large datasets. So you might find in a dataset about driving that most people average one car crash every ten years. When you zoom in at the individual scale, the chance of a car crash happening at any particular time is mathematically random. But if you zoom out to a bigger population, we can find systemic patterns such as a consistent frequency (or number) of total car crashes that happen every year. You might also see correlative relations—for example, drivers in a specific age range might tend to have a higher frequency of car crashes.

With this information, you can then model the probability of outcomes and make judgments about the effect of certain variables on the likelihood of the event occurring. In other words, you don't know who exactly will have a crash or when it will happen or what its causes will be, but you can observe the probability of a crash happening over the course of a larger number of events (e.g., miles driven) and a longer period of time (e.g., years) given a set of variables (e.g., driver age). That probability is the risk. Most of the risks we deal with in society are stochastic in this way, whether they are traffic accidents or terrorist attacks.

However, a bizarre thing happens when risk becomes a tool for techno-politics. Instead of being seen as a stochastic process, risk is often treated as events with simple, linear causes that can then be precisely knowable, predictable, and controllable—even at the individual level. When risk is operationalized in systems of techno-cratic authority—in financial markets, actuarial models, national security, policing tactics, regulatory policy—the scientific features like random probability distributions, which might impede the effi-cacy of technologies designed for precise prediction, become reframed as problems to solve, rather than treated as limits to power. Having mastery over risk leads to power and profit, but the nature of risk means that taming and controlling risk is an impos-sible task. Thus, technocrats who wish to master risk must either accept these constraints on their capabilities or they can reject that reality and substitute it with a conception of risk that better suits their goals. Increasingly, the techno-politics of risk is premised on rejecting any limits to the power of risk, natural or social.

The Risky Business of Governance

The governance of risk—or the continual management of (un)cer-tain hazards, (un)known threats, and (un)intended consequences—has given way to risk as a form of governance. Here risk is more than just another thing that must be governed. Instead it becomes the foundation, conceptually and practically, for how systems of governance are understood, justified, constructed, and enforced. Risk becomes both the means and ends of governance. This approach is deeply tied to the production of specific types of power and knowledge. "We are subjected to the production of truth through power and we cannot exercise power except through the production of truth," Michel Foucault theorized in work showing that power/knowledge are not separate things but symbiotic social relations.[9] To know the world is to exercise power over it and to exercise power is to know it—to examine its features and characteristics, to sort it into categories and norms, to render it legible and manageable, to exclude other methods for creating knowledge and exercising power.[10] Risk is a tool for constructing the world, analyzing the world, and doing things in the world.

The concept of governance plays a leading role in the story of risk. Governance is used by a range of institutions, across every setting, including governments, corporations, schools, consultants, nonprofits, social services, and community groups—all of which describe governance as their core practice or aspiration. The term is now so ubiquitous that it doesn't even register as jargon that only emerged recently. But its ubiquity indicates a subtle yet important shift in how power operates. Governance is a hybrid concept that is "often used interchangeably with both 'governing' and 'managing,'" writes political theorist Wendy Brown. This signals "an important fusion of political and business practices"—a synthesis of political institutions and corporate management—which becomes the "primary administrative form" through which social conditions are structured and everyday life is conducted.[11]

In her book *Undoing the Demos,* Brown identifies the 1980s as a key moment in the rise of governance. It was at this point that neoliberal approaches to government were taking effect in the US with Ronald Reagan and in the UK with Margaret Thatcher and were quickly spreading to become a global hegemonic paradigm. This paradigm explicitly aimed "to transfer private-sector management methods to public services and to employ economic techniques such as incentivization, entrepreneurialism, outsourcing, and competition for public goods and services."[12] In other words, the point was to make governments operate more like corporations, to replace political issues with financial logics. This was done by importing the models, metrics, values, concepts, and tactics of the FIRE sector into the sociopolitical sphere—with the assessment and management of "risk" being central to these practices of power/knowledge.

Risk is a powerful concept for governance because it comes cloaked in all the neutrality, authority, and mystique of technocratic expertise, while also being flexible enough that it can be adapted and applied widely. Any issue, no matter how small or large, is reframed in terms of risk governance. For example, a typical process might involve these phases: First we assess the risk with systems of analysis, evaluation, and modeling. Next we manage the risk with systems of oversight, regulation, and mitigation. Then we engineer the risk with systems of prediction, control, and intervention. At every phase, the focus is on the technical process of how risk is being analyzed or monitored or controlled rather than on the political substance of how risk is being defined and identified—or why risk is even the best or only option for framing things in the first place.

This myopia is a core feature of risk governance as a form of anti-politics. It offers a way of doing politics—exercising power and authority to advance specific principles and goals—while eliminating and denying anything political about those activities. Through rhetorical appeals to optimization and objectivity, technocrats depict their favored approaches to social engineering as pragmatic alternatives to grossly inefficient political mechanisms. Moreover, these strategies of depoliticization very often intersect with strong programs of economization, or the integration of economic rationality into all areas of society and life. Ultimately, the more fundamental details of risk governance—the identification of risk, the motivation of governance, the justification of power, the prioritization of values, the distribution of outcomes—are not up for debate. Leave that to the experts.

We can see how this approach to risk governance is put into practice to administer two major issues facing society today: climate change and artificial intelligence. I won't go deep into the weeds of discussing risk policy and regulation in these two brief examples—for readers interested in more details, I direct you to the excellent work I cite below—instead I want to use them to raise points relevant to our broader analysis of risk governance within and by technological capitalism.

According to dominant approaches, the problems of fossil capital and green transitions can simply be solved by the "de-risking state," or a state committed to minimizing risks for the private sector, as economist Daniela Gabor calls this new paradigm in her work on how massive finance corporations like BlackRock have set the global agenda for environmental and industrial policy.[13] Here the primary role of governments is to reduce the economic risks of private investment into green development and a low-carbon transition by creating safety nets to guarantee investors' profits, while also ensuring they are protected from political risks like capital controls on the flow of money, increased labor rights like higher minimum wages, and climate regulations that might mandate or restrict activities related to environmental sustainability.

Importantly, the purpose of de-risking is to establish favorable (profitable) conditions for private capital and create "investible development projects that can attract global investors" without actually directing where investment goes or how development happens.[14] Gabor quotes the World Bank Group president who stated, "If the conditions are not right for private investment, we need to work with our partners to de-risk projects, sectors, and entire countries."[15] Meanwhile, reports are now rolling out about how Wall Street has largely ignored the realities of climate change in the financial models they use to price and predict the material impacts of climate risks.[16] For example, they have been hugely overvaluing real assets like buildings and infrastructure by not accounting for their vulnerability to heatwaves, wildfires, and floods. These models have also assumed that macroeconomic factors like gross domestic product will continue to grow, unaffected by the effects of climate change and mass migration.

Yet the magnitude of recent climatic disasters is now forcing investors and insurers to confront the fact that they have severely mismanaged the costs and certainty of these catastrophes. So after shooting itself in the kneecap, the FIRE sector then turns the gun on the public and demands they help fix this very dire situation before everybody gets blown away. This is a form of governance that transfers any risks onto public balance sheets, while ensuring rewards are funneled into private coffers. Capital deserves only the best carrots, never any sticks, no matter how badly they behave.

According to dominant approaches, the problems of tech capital and artificial intelligence can be solved by regulating the risks of emerging innovations. The dominant approach to regulating technologies like AI in the US and Europe focuses on identifying, ranking, and mitigating the risks of AI and its uses. The political devil is in the details of how these technocratic processes are actually implemented. Who is establishing the protocols for risk identification? How are the levels of risk defined? What forms of mitigation are enacted and for which purposes? Why have other alternatives been cast aside at every phase? There is nothing required or predetermined about using risk governance as the paradigm for regulating technology. "By framing the regulation of AI systems as risk regulation, policymakers are, knowingly or not, taking a normative stance on AI," observes legal scholar Margot Kaminski.[17] And that stance is also a choice that favors and embeds specific framings, values, and outcomes for technology and forgoes forms of regulation that would prioritize individual rights, social benefits, or precautionary principles.

"While aspects of risk regulation may be effective at certain kinds of harm mitigation," writes Kaminski, this approach to regulation always emphasizes specific types of harms due to the nature of risk.[18] These harms must be quantifiable so they can fit into statistical analyses and financial models, which leads to the disregard of harms that are not easily turned into numbers on a spreadsheet. These harms are often future focused so they can be calculated in terms of probabilities that something might happen, thus discounting harms that have already been normalized in society. These harms are based on dangers posed to people and populations who fit the profile of an average person—usually a white adult man—which downplays or ignores those who deviate from that normative benchmark. These harms are also accounted for at the aggregate level, which means significant impacts on individuals may be totally concealed in the data, greatly discounted by cost-benefit choices, and unequally distributed within society.

Additionally, "risk regulation typically assumes a technology will be adopted despite its harms."[19] The causes of these risks and harms—like corporations rapidly building and deploying AI systems across a range of applications with no real oversight, accountability, or precaution—are treated as static conditions that have already happened, cannot be changed, and must be taken as the starting point for response. In other words, risk governance transforms the public into janitors cleaning up the messes of corporations, militaries, police forces, and others who would rather shoot first and never ask questions later. The default is to allow capital to innovate without needing to ask for permission—or at least to move forward with as few imposed guardrails as possible. The best we can do—just as with the example of climate change above—is to "de-risk" these innovations by encouraging cultures of responsibility within corporations and establishing social systems that internalize the costs of private investments.

Risk is a modern concept that coevolved with the insurance industry and its actuarial models for analyzing, projecting, and pricing the probable outcomes of future events based on past experiences and present conditions. This grants regimes of risk governance an aura of technical rigor. They are depoliticized by design. These features make them obvious tools for tackling the complexity and uncertainty of emerging technology. Yet such approaches do not empty risk governance of its political content. They just bury the politics, rendering those value-laden choices invisible, muddling the causal links between decisions and actions and effects, framing their consequences as unavoidable trade-offs, and producing the social conditions that support specific forms of knowledge and power in the world.

Power in Numbers

Risk analysis offers the promise of predicting the future. This is why risk has become such a powerful and valuable tool for technological capitalism, and why so many systems are designed to create actionable insights about risk. You take some data about the past, crunch the numbers in some way to project that data into the future, and come up with a calculated chance that some event might happen. However, the stochastic properties of risk mean that any analysis is always only based on patterns that can be interpreted from the chosen datasets. The outcomes are then just probabilities—how likely some event might happen given a set of conditions plus the random variability of complex systems—rather than predictions. But that critical distinction often gets lost when people use calculations of chance to declare that an event will definitely happen or a person will definitely do something.

Those outcomes depend on the risk model and the risk data used in the risk analysis, all of which have a range of assumptions, simplifications, and uncertainties baked into them. In the best-case scenario, the outcomes are based on a model that is well fitted to the data—that is, the risk model used for statistical analysis has been tested, refined, and changed so that it provides the most accurate analysis possible of the static datasets being analyzed. In the worst case—the way-too-common case—outcomes are based on data that is well fitted to the model. Here the risk data being analyzed is tweaked, juked, and pruned so that it provides the desired or expected outcomes when analyzed by a predictive model. To quote the webcomic *xkcd:* "You pour the data into this big pile of linear algebra, then collect the answers on the other side." And what if the answers provided by your machine learning model are wrong? "Just stir the pile until they start looking right."[20]

In many systems where risk analysis is turned into material power, the stochastic uncertainty is washed away. The scientific analysis of probability, with its wide margins of error and doubt, is transformed into the technical application of predictive models that are precision targeted. The art and science of risk is never really explained, let alone questioned. The methods and their outcomes are taken for granted—especially when they are based on machine learning—despite being opaque and inexplicable in ways that should undermine our confidence in these risky systems. "As an arrangement of propositions, one could not meaningfully open or scrutinize the 60 million probability weightings that make it possible for a CNN [convolutional neural network] algorithm to recognize the attributes of a face in a crowd, declaring them to be true or false," writes theorist Louise Amoore in *Cloud Ethics*. "The processes and arrangements of weights, values, bias, and thresholds in neural nets are, I think we can safely say, not part of our statutory political domain. And yet, I suggest that they must be presented as questions and political claims in the world."[21]

Instead, all that immense complexity—of technology, of politics, of reality—is replaced by the *risk score*. As the ultimate weaponization of risk governance, scores prove that there is indeed power in numbers. Especially when those numbers are stripped of context, given the stamp of technocratic authority, and deployed as simple solutions for wicked problems. Risk scores are now ubiquitous technologies of governance, in large part because they are forms of data that can be wielded easily like a cudgel by individuals and institutions who are on the front lines of exercising power in society.

It would be impossible to give anything even close to a full accounting of all the risk scores that really and truly matter in society. I don't mean all the dime-a-dozen risk scores that tech start-ups create to justify their wild claims to attract investment. I just mean the risk scores that actually have material impacts on our lives and shape social structures in some meaningful way. It's an impossible task because the absolute number of them is so large and they are spread so widely across different settings, but also because the existence and operation of so many of them are hidden by their creators and users. Many of these scores (and the risks they assess) are classified as "known unknowns" and "unknown unknowns," to quote the famous philosopher of risk, Donald Rumsfeld.[22] Unless you are in an elite group with insider information, there are risk scores we know exist but don't really know anything about, and then there are ones we can only suspect might exist. This fact alone is strong evidence that using risk assessments as the basis for predictive judgments is an immensely political, valuable, and questionable process. Otherwise there would be no point in going through all the trouble of obscuring, shielding, and concealing methodologies that are ostensibly objective and purely scientific.

Power Keeps the Score

A brief list of important "known knowns" should at least include the following types of risk scores, which now underpin the most important forms of governance in society.

Many of the most consequential decisions made by *police, border, and military forces* are made with the help of—if not largely outsourced to—a diverse arsenal of risk scores, many of which are created by private corporations and then sold as proprietary services to government agencies. The goal of quantifying risk assessment is to make otherwise subjective, discretionary judgments into more objective, standardized calculations. While some tools might be simple to understand, many methods of producing scores rely on algorithms that absorb reams of data about all kinds of dissimilar things, from crime statistics to moon phases, and distill them into a single number meant to inform who is seen as a security threat and how an officer should behave when responding to a situation.[23]

For example, police departments have implemented software called Beware to generate personalized "threat scores" about an individual, address, or area. The software claims to work by processing "billions of data points, including arrest reports, property records, commercial databases, deep web searches and the [person's] social media postings," reports the *Washington Post*.[24] The scores are color coded so officers can know at a glance a target's threat level: green, yellow, or red. The substantive difference between a green score or red score is a total mystery to the officer, but it can be the difference between the officer initiating a traffic stop with a friendly smile or with their finger on the trigger, ready for a kinetic engagement.

Many of the most consequential decisions made by *finance, insurance, and real estate corporations* are made with the help of—if not largely outsourced to—a diverse arsenal of risk scores. "All data is credit data"—so goes the old slogan of ZestFinance, a start-up focused on creating alternative credit scores by analyzing a wide variety of data about people, which goes beyond the parameters of traditional credit scores.[25] The company has since changed its name and slogan, now going by Zest AI and promising "more approvals, less risk" thanks to its accelerated, automated "machine learning underwriting" for lenders and insurers.[26] The problem is cast not as an epistemic one, but a technical one: Do we have the systems needed to make sense of data, to make the data talk? That technical framing then provides support for a normative conclusion, which has gained influence in the FIRE industries: since any "data might tell the insurer something about risk," the prevailing wisdom is that corporations have the right, even the obligation, "to collect any and all data."[27] It would be irresponsible, plus bad business practice, to not extract and capitalize on data if it could possibly be used for the more effective assessment and management of risk.

People might never know for sure why they were flagged by an automated risk score, which then caused their loan application to be rejected or their insurance claim to be denied. It's unlikely they even know about the system at all. But for whatever reasons, they were judged to be high risk and thus low value, more potential trouble than they are potentially worth. As sociologist Barbara Kiviat notes in her study of how credit scores are used for insurance pricing: "Algorithmic prediction is imbued with normative viewpoints— they are viewpoints that suit the goals of corporations."[28] The use of data-drive scoring systems for risk classification fits into the long history of the FIRE sector creating all sorts of scientific methods to morally justify their own interests and actions.[29]

Many of the most consequential decisions made by *social services, welfare agencies, and public assistance programs* are made with the help of—if not largely outsourced to—a diverse arsenal of risk scores. They are among the most insidious tools of neoliberal governance in use today, and they are reconfiguring the function of social services to follow financial logics. Rather than identifying those who are the most in need of assistance, these institutions use risk scores to identify those who are the most dangerous threats to the system: potential fraudsters. The technologies are designed to prevent false negatives: It is better to deny assistance to a thousand people in need than to let one undeserving welfare cheat slip through the cracks. To that end, public social services around the world have implemented some of the most severe forms of risk governance, which treat already disadvantaged populations as threats that must be identified, tracked, managed, investigated, and neutralized.

A striking example comes from a recent investigation by Lighthouse Reports into an automated welfare fraud system built by the consulting firm Accenture and implemented in Rotterdam, the Netherlands.[30] Through freedom-of-information laws, the journalists obtained unprecedented access to the machine learning model, its training data, and operational handbooks. What they found is a system that analyzes hundreds of attributes, or variables, about an individual to calculate a risk score. That score is then used to decide who is a potential threat of fraud, target people for further questioning by police, and deny access to government assistance. The purpose is not to find those who need help, but to discriminate against those who try to receive help. It is worth quoting at length from the article:

> Rotterdam's algorithm is best thought of as a suspicion machine. It judges people on many characteristics they cannot control (like gender and ethnicity). What might appear to a caseworker to be a vulnerability, such as a person showing signs of low self-esteem, is treated by the machine as grounds for suspicion when the caseworker enters a comment into the system. The data fed into the algorithm ranges from invasive (the length of someone's last

romantic relationship) and subjective (someone's ability to convince and influence others) to banal (how many times someone has emailed the city) and seemingly irrelevant (whether someone plays sports). Despite the scale of data used to calculate risk scores, *it performs little better than random selection.* Machine learning algorithms like Rotterdam's are being used to make more and more decisions about people's lives, including what schools their children attend, who gets interviewed for jobs, and which family gets a loan.[31]

With scoring systems like those described above, we can see a regime for risk governance based on automated models engaging in relational analysis of hundreds of attributes about every single person captured within a database. These systems are extraordinarily complex and targeted forms of discrimination, while also being remarkably simplistic and arbitrary in their decisions. They might be effectively no better than random sampling, as the investigation into Rotterdam's system concluded, yet they are also treated as forms of perfect knowledge.

Lighthouse Reports has examined similar welfare systems using predictive risk assessments in countries across Europe, where they have also found rampant issues in how scores are calculated, like using inaccurate datasets and giving arbitrary values to data in the models, which then results in blatant (and illegal) discrimination based on factors like race, gender, and disability against people trying to access social services.[32] For instance, if you are a welfare recipient in France and it has been less than two months since you sent an email to CNAF, the French social security agency, then your risk score goes down. But if it has been between three and four months since the last email, then your risk score goes up. But if it has been five or more months, then your risk score goes back down. Those arbitrary shifts can move you across the threshold from low risk to high risk, thus flagging you for investigation by the government. Such findings are sadly consistent with research by scholars like Virginia Eubanks who have documented the forms of "automated inequality" that pervade welfare systems in the United States.[33] According to these risk models, being poor and applying for aid is itself a high risk behavior, which triggers police investigations and state interventions, such as taking children away from parents who seek family welfare to help take care of their children.

Critical audits of other widely used and well-known risk analysis systems have found similar results. This includes the COMPAS software that is widely used to predict the likelihood of recidivism in criminal defendants and generates a risk score for each individual by analyzing data from 137 features. Judges use these predictions to inform their pretrial, parole, and prison sentence decisions. Yet, as computer scientists Julia Dressel and Hany Farid found in their audit of COMPAS, this machine learning system is "no more accurate or fair than predictions made by people with little or no criminal justice expertise."[34] Despite the large dataset of features the system analyzes, "the same accuracy can be achieved with a simple linear classifier with only two features." Increased complexity might not improve the technical accuracy of a system, but it can certainly magnify its social authority by telling a story about how the system will grant you access to precise, neutral, godlike information about the world. More data does not mean more knowledge, but it can mean more power if you convince people that risk scores are predictive truths ready to be used for immediate action.[35]

In too many cases, it seems that random sampling would actually be a great improvement on risk scores, which have been proven to be systematically inaccurate and socially biased and lead to every flavor of unjust discrimination. These technologies excel at pattern recognition, but they are also pattern reinforcement machines. They take data from the past and turn it into decisions about the future. "The technological deck has been stacked long in advance to favor certain social interests," writes philosopher Langdon Winner.[36] I'd rather be judged by a coin flip than loaded dice.

I could keep swapping in different examples of organizations that have material power in society and depend on dubious risk scores to inform, justify, and exercise that power. We could be here for a long time, and I still would not come close to exhausting the list of important "known knowns." Regardless of the numerous problems, failures, and impacts of risk scores, they are widely deployed as essential tools for governance and decision-making. It is hard to resist the allure of a technology that offers the veneer of objective authority and the utility of reducing complex events to a single number or even color. What's more, the real promise of risk governance goes beyond reactive protocols for identifying and investigating risk; it also offers the ability to proactively control risk—or eliminate risk before it even exists.

This Time It's Personal

In 1988, legal scholar Jonathan Simon identified a shift in systems of social power based on risk management: "Where power once sought to manipulate the choices of rational actors, it now seeks to predict behavior and situate subjects according to the risk they pose."[37] Simon links this shift to the spread of actuarial practices "that distribute costs and benefits to individuals based on statistical knowledge about the population." These practices and their effects have only become more entrenched, but today power no longer needs to choose between manipulating choices, predicting behaviors, situating subjects, and doing much more. All of these capabilities are available, to varying degrees, thanks to decades of developments in the science, technology, and industry of risk governance. Of all the many places where we have seen risk turned into a tool of power and profit, the insurance sector is the real supreme commander of risk governance within capitalism.

We only need to look at histories of insurance to see that the industry was at the forefront of investing, developing, and using large-scale information systems long before the contemporary age of data servers, cloud computing, and AI analytics.[38] By the 1910s, writes historian Dan Bouk, the life insurance industry had already "become premised on more individualized risk making."[39] Major life insurers created "index divisions"—using index cards to record, store, and categorize detailed information about policyholders like medical assessments and accident reports—which "facilitated an unexpected revolution" based on "new methods for personalizing risk assessments and a new centralized file (a proto-database) for storing thoroughly statisticized individuals in steel case files."[40] In 1903, a report by the Actuarial Society of America had detailed 98 "classes of risk" to be used in underwriting insurance. A leading actuary at that time, Emory McClintock, said this type of fine-grain risk classification—and the detailed information, analysis methods, and risk theories it was built on—was the future of actuarial science.[41] He had no idea just how exponentially these techniques for classification would grow. By 1981, "the most widely used assessment scheme" for auto insurance was based on 234,360 different risk categories into which drivers could be sorted.[42] Now insurers talk about achieving goals like "the statistics of one," which is based on the idea that insurers will have so much data about each person—captured and merged from a variety of sources, including behavioral tracking from fitness wearables and vehicle telematics—they won't have to rely on analyzing aggregate data and models about populations. Instead they will be able to apply statistical risk analysis on each individual person. In a report on the impacts of big data analytics for vehicle and health insurance, the European Union's insurance regulator surveyed over 220 insurers about their plans for using data-driven technologies. A large number of insurance firms "declared that they will be able to use BDA [big data analytics] to move towards individualized policy pricing" in the near future, though they haven't "reached this level of sophistication yet."[43] Meanwhile, other insurers said these technologies are really just a continuation of what they already do: "augmenting and enhancing, rather than replacing, existing pricing techniques."[44]

Rather than sudden disruptions that are like external shocks to the system, it is better to understand the integration of things like big data and artificial intelligence into the insurance industry as part of the industry's long trajectory.[45] They are an evolution of logics that have long been core features of financial capitalism. It is less like a new engine and more like supercharging the engine that has been driving capital toward creating more advanced methods for social segregation, price discrimination, and hyper-personalization of risk.[46] Crucially I am not saying these technologies are just leading to more of the same. If you intensify existing practices enough, the consequences will be transformative.

The ideal scenario for insurers is one where the risk pools have been drained. With every person occupying their own risk pool—or puddle—insurers gain access to new capacities for managing individuals, preventing loss, and capturing value. It's one thing for an insurer to say, "We anticipate that people with your demographic profile are likely, over the course of a lifetime of coverage, to be more costly than average risks. But if you meet certain policy conditions, we will lower your premiums." It's quite another for an insurer to say something like, "We anticipate that you, based on behavioral data collected from these specific smart devices and additional data purchased from third-party brokers, are likely to have a risk event in the next three weeks. We have adjusted your premium accordingly."

Ironically such a scenario, if pushed to its logical extreme, would also totally undermine the structure of modern insurance, going so far as to eliminate its entire reason for existence. As Colm Holmes—then CEO of Aviva and now CEO of Allianz Holdings, both massive multinational insurers—said in an interview: "The use of data is something I think regulators will have to look at, because if you get down to insuring the individual, you don't have an insurance industry—you just create people who don't need insurance and people who aren't insurable."[47]

In other words, insurance works because there is a lot of uncertainty about when, where, how, and to whom some disastrous event will happen. It's the stochasticity of risk that makes insurance work a socially useful institution. However, if insurers could predict and price risk at a precise enough level—or even just make people believe they have that capability and act accordingly—then insurance would become unaffordable and inaccessible to people who really need to pool their risk, while people who could bear their own low levels of risk wouldn't need to buy insurance. And yet, recognizing the problems of decoupling the purpose of insurance from the practices of risk governance has not stopped the industry from pushing harder, faster toward this endpoint. It is the death drive that impels these regimes of risk governance.

Now, to be sure, we should not expect that risk analysis will ever actually escape the necessity of averaging and smoothing out the real differences among people who are grouped together in the same risk classification. No matter how small, refined, and homogenous those risk pools become, actuaries will still have to abstract away features of real people that don't fit neatly into the databases, models, and operations of the risk machine.[48] The scores discussed above are a perfect case of how that technocratic reductionism is put into practice. For insurers and financiers, the entire purpose is to price risk (and do so profitably), which once again involves taking tons of qualities and turning them into quantities, combining them with other forms of manufactured data, and crunching them with calculus and linear algebra to finally reach a single number that represents risk, in absolute and relative terms, that can then inform actions in response to that risk. At every stage in that process, larger degrees of simplicity and variability are necessarily introduced into analytical processes that are meant to be comprehensive and accurate. No matter how data-driven or AI-fueled, their calculations will still be subjected to the realities of mathematical abstraction, statistical uncertainty, and random probability.

At the same time, the full industrial might of capitalist innovation is being directed at transcending the limits of these stochastic properties by turning risk into a thing that can be precisely knowable, predictable, and controllable. Actuarial scientists were discussing the possibility of "individualized risk making" over a hundred years ago,[49] just as data scientists are working on that project today, and some other future scientists will likely be trying to realize it in a hundred years. But the true power of an aspiration for tomorrow is its ability to motivate action today. Even if the final goal is impossible, the process of pushing closer to that unreachable point can still result in major changes with serious impacts.

We don't have to reach a full-blown crisis of demutualization in insurance—in which mutual risk sharing is broken down into individual risk bearing—to see how these technologies are currently used to scrutinize data about our behaviors, segregate people into detailed rankings, squeeze more value from each consumer, and shirk any obligations to pay claims.[50]

For example, it is extremely hard to combat practices like "price optimization" and "claims optimization" in the insurance industry.[51] In the case of price optimization, insurers analyze a vast range of data, fusing information that is directly and obviously about your risk factors (like if you smoke cigarettes) with data about things that seemingly have nothing to do with your risk profile (like which web browser you use for the online application).[52] Consumers are then targeted with personalized prices that reflect *how much people are willing to pay*, rather than prices based only on how risky they are compared to other similar people. Emerging models of insurance—with names like "on-demand" or "insurance-as-a-service"—are engaged in trying to make the industry even more dynamic so that insurers can, for example, change prices and policy conditions as often as they want.[53] The aim is to innovate around regulations that restrict how often such changes can occur. Those changes might reflect the dynamic nature of risk, but we should also expect them to optimize for profit. The mirage of risk analysis falls away when other methods can better serve the true ends of making more money.

In the case of claims optimization, when customers file claims—for example, for a medical treatment or car accident—insurers determine how to handle the claims based not just on facts like the loss suffered or cost of repair but primarily on *how much people are willing to accept*. That process can be optimized in a variety of ways, such as by lowering the amount insurers pay on claims until the total amount of complaints by customers reaches a certain threshold.[54] Insurers can also use strategies like offering people with lower credit scores a quicker claims outcome in return for a lower payment or denying all claims under a set cost amount and forcing customers to go through a tortuous appeal process.[55]

Optimization is an industry euphemism for discrimination. The difference is that instead of a person drawing a red line around risky populations and deciding to charge them more and pay out less, there is an automated form of applied statistics that finds patterns and optimizes parameters for profitable risk management. This kind of optimization has regressive impacts where the most vulnerable and already disadvantaged people—those who are, for example, poorer, older, less educated, or people of color—are also put in a position of having little other choice but to accept higher prices and lower payouts. The integration of machine learning into insurance makes these discriminatory tactics more powerful, widespread, and difficult to uncover. Now such practices—and the sensitive data they rely on—can be laundered through the opacity of machine learning, thus giving human actuaries plausible deniability when discrimination and deception is uncovered.[56]

Risk Makers

By now we know that risk is not an objective measure of natural phenomena and mathematical patterns. Risk is not even always or fully based on the scientific analysis of stochastic processes and emergent properties. Risk is created by the very regimes designed to calculate and govern it. Risk is the product of techno-political systems and socioeconomic interests, and it is weaponized to serve them. Risk is made, framed, conceived, priced, shifted, and deployed in specific ways to do things in the world. Risk is integral to the operations of power, data, and value in capitalism. To understand the future of risk in technological capitalism, we should conclude by looking to the history of how it has developed.

In his book *How Our Days Became Numbered,* Dan Bouk details how the insurance industry not only created methods for statistical analysis but also was instrumental in creating a culture in which it made sense to conceive of individuals and societies in terms of numbers that needed to be tracked, analyzed, predicted, and managed for the sake of securing against (un)certain hazards. This is a process that Bouk calls "making risk." As he explains:

> I do not mean this phrase ["making risk"] to imply that life insurers created new hazards, that they made existence more dangerous—although they and those around them did sometimes worry that insuring lives made people live more dangerously. To understand what I mean by making risks, we must first think differently about what a "risk" was and is. Societies have always had ways of thinking about the dangers and hazards that face them and their constituents—we sometimes talk about those dangers as

risks. But with the spread of insurance, risk took on a more specific definition: a risk became a kind of commodity.[57]

The ways in which risk is manufactured, bought, and sold have changed many times over just the last hundred years as new means of production and exchange are developed to ensure risk stays a reliable source of profit and power for capital and states. In the roaring days of American industrial capitalism, risk was "understood to be an intrinsically collective affair," which was "calculable only as a property of groups," as sociologist Greta Krippner explains.[58] This conception is the basis for traditions of mutual welfare that treat risk as a burden and security as a benefit that should be shared equally among the whole group.[59] But the collectivization of risk was also directly codified into legal, social, and cultural institutions by capital in very specific ways. As the number of industrial accidents, injuries, and deaths of workers skyrocketed during the early 1900s, capitalists supported notions of risk that depersonalized these incidents and socialized any responsibility for their conditions, causes, and consequences. New methods of collecting statistical data showed that there was a "grinding regularity of industrial accidents" in workplaces.[60] The conclusion drawn by both corporations and government was that these hazards were inevitable and natural, a grim reality of industrial society and the price of progress; it had to be managed, but could never be changed. As Krippner explains:

> The calculus of risk no longer attempted to grasp particular experiences of injury and death, but instead endeavored to describe the frequency of industrial accidents in the overall population. Attention focused not on the special circumstances that determined

how a particular person was hurt, but on the aggregate number of workers injured over a given period of time, regardless of circumstances. The goal of these new technologies of risk management was not to investigate accidents that had already occurred in order to assign blame, but instead to predict (and possibly prevent) future accidents so their costs could be distributed and managed. This notion of risk was abstract, its method actuarial, and its meaning demoralized.[61]

This version of risk still very much persists today. However, it has also been remade by advances in capitalism. Features of risks as a collective inevitability that took hold in industrial capitalism now also coexist with approaches to risk that arose with financial capitalism. These are the techniques for personalizing risk and individualizing responsibility that I have discussed above. These shifts in risk have not stopped. With the growth of technological capitalism, we can also see emerging innovations of risk governance that build on previous phases.

One important growing approach in the industry is known as behavioral insurance, which is based on complex systems of digital technology and behavioral science.[62] This strategy focuses on capturing data about consumer behavior—or the activities, choices, and lifestyles of policyholders—and treating that datafied behavior as a key source of risk that insurers can manage and as value that insurers can unlock. This data is collected through sources like wearable devices that monitor your fitness, wellness apps that track your daily lifestyle, vehicle telematics that record your driving, and smart home sensors that observe your domestic routines. Broadly, behavioral insurance aims to accurately analyze and assess how consumers behave. It then factors that data into key aspects of the business, like developing products, marketing campaigns, pricing premiums, and handling claims, while also hopefully achieving the holy grail of risk management: actively modifying how consumers behave to ensure they lead less risky, more valuable lives. Underlying this approach is a theory that draws direct causal links from individual behaviors to risk factors to specific outcomes. Beyond simply stating that behaviors are key variables to consider or tackle, this theory of risk pushes the more extreme conclusion that only personal choices matter—external conditions and social structures do not.[63] The ultimate responsibility for risk and its consequences is relocated in individuals and their controllable choices.

We have seen how conceptions of risk have changed, sometimes in quite radical ways, over just the last hundred years: from a collective affair to individual property to behavioral choice. These different approaches to making risk can be contradictory with each other. That inconsistency might pose a problem for scientific paradigms, but for capital the final test that any system of risk governance must pass is a pragmatic one: Is it effective at creating profit and power?

The moral economy at the heart of insurance is also contradictory. The industry is motivated by the grand ambition to be guardians of the future—"an active life partner" with customers, as one behavioral insurer describes its vision[64]—overseeing our every move and shielding us from the stochastic risks of life. The industry justifies its position as "among the most pervasive and powerful institutions in society"[65] by framing itself as an agent of social progress who uses its technocratic expertise in risk analysis to intervene and govern for the better. But that moral imperative only goes as far as financial limits will take it. Capital is also compelled by the counter-impulse to classify, rank, and exclude people in increasingly granular ways. If our risk profile is too deviant from the profitable norm, then we are abandoned to the storms of chance. Some get to make risks; others must take them.

8 *Futures*

Metacritic

At this point in the book, I'm probably expected to lay out a series of solutions for all the issues I have identified thus far. Solutions that come together like stepping-stones to lead us away from *the bad now* and into *the good future*. Ponder this dream journal. Follow these action items.

I'm not going to do that, though. The purpose of this book was to show why a materialist analysis of technology and capitalism is necessary, to show its critical application to major areas like data and risk, to show the fundamental social relations and power dynamics at the heart of systems that dominate so much in so many ways. It would feel strange to conclude a ruthless criticism of complex systems with an infomercial for the one weird trick to undermine capitalism and reclaim technology. The bourgeoisie hate it! The state cannot stand it! Call now!

This book is not the last word. For many, I hope it will be a starting pistol—the point at which they take up a materialist approach, apply it to their own work, and advance its position beyond other reactionary and lackluster alternatives. There is no final analysis to be had because the systems being analyzed—like the whole universe we inhabit—are dynamic, continuous, relational processes. There could be an infinite number of additional chapters, each focused on different features of the systems, both existing and emergent, positive and negative, that structure our material conditions. I'm sorry to report the work is never done. This also means change is not only possible but always happening. The real movement keeps marching.

Materialists know that society does not exist as a series of static events until we reach an endpoint. Even if utopia were achieved—more on that shortly—it would also have to be actively maintained against the entropy of decay and disorder. The end of history is a thought experiment turned into a mass delusion. It is neither possible nor desirable. We should never want to reach a stable equilibrium where the decisions and actions from the past are locked in place forever. Real utopias are found in dynamic mechanisms of social coordination that always secure the changing needs of everybody and meet the changing desires of new generations.

Idealists are adept at selling a different story—one that is much easier and, superficially, more satisfying: where the arc of progress takes us, eventually and inevitably, to our final destination. It's just up to us how fast we accelerate down the track. But this is a hollow, fleeting vision that depends upon an endless parade of empty promises, ephemeral vaporware, speculative extraction, and unfulfilled expectations—yet also one that is powerful and pervasive. It reveals a deeply flawed relationship to the future. These futurists create a marketplace of imaginaries, then eliminate all competition and monopolize it with their own inferior ideas.

Keeping with our critical method, I wrap up by thinking at a meta-level about how the business of producing futures is also a key feature of technological capitalism, the role that utopias play in the maintenance and dissolution of social systems and then conclude by considering what it all means for our own attempts to combat their imaginations with our actions.

A Very Brief History of Futurism

Let's look more closely at those who gaze into the future as a vocation, who read the tea leaves of hype cycles and paradigm shifts. The futurist is an archetype of both modern idealism and modern capitalism. Digital prophets with crystal balls, thought leaders with trend maps, horizon scanners with strategic scenarios—futurists come in a variety of flavors, all of them with too much sway in society. Their grip on the public is more than just discursive—that is, how we talk and think about the future. It also translates into direct influence on financial, political, and engineering decisions about the creation of technology and our expectations for how the world will progress.

Futurism is an odd, eclectic discipline that has created an expansive body of theories and techniques for creating anticipatory knowledge about the future that can inform decisions in the present. They run the gamut from *foresight*—which tends to be more social scientific in its methods for analyzing broader trends and mapping plausible outcomes—to *forecasting*, which embraces predictions of future events, often using probabilistic models, data science, and computer simulations to inform its prognostic judgments. I don't intend to outline an exhaustive account of futurists and futurism (or futurology or futures studies). I build on the excellent work of other scholars who have already been there and done that more extensively than I want to do here.[1]

Instead I'll offer a very brief history of futurism to help orient our more precise focus on how the future has become a useful concept and valuable commodity for capital. The origins of futurism as a distinct field of practice, with its own methods and experts, are closely tied to advancing the strategic interests of militaries and corporations. As a field of study, futurism was developed after World War II and into the Cold War. Technocratic engineers and military planners sought to bring rational order to volatile uncertainty. They wanted to domesticate the untamed future, making it into a domain of direct control by human action. Places like the RAND Corporation—a proto-think tank founded by the US military, which then spun off into a private research institute in 1948—became central to the production, exchange, and application of power/knowledge over complex systems like the future. These predictive techniques "were 'decision tools,' or triggers of the imagination, designed to push human beings to act for the future in various ways," writes historian of futurism Jenny Andersson.[2] From the beginning, the goal of futurists was not merely to be observers of things yet to come but to take an active role as soothsayers and influencers, telling stories about the future and turning them into self-fulfilling prophecies.

Futurism really exploded once it was adopted by large corporations. Like the technocrats in charge of state planning, corporate managers also wanted a strong capacity for preemptive strikes against the future, both to steer the direction of change before it happened and to secure their own advantage in an uncertain world. For example, the oil and gas giant Royal Dutch Shell pioneered now widespread methods for scenario planning and horizon scanning.[3] These tools analyze major trends in society and project forward from the present by changing key parameters to create narratives of different futures. They typically involve methods like focus groups with experts and stakeholders, which might inform ideation sessions with authors and artists. In practice, it is the art and science of fleshing out questions like these: How might a world of peak oil and fossil fuel divestment impact Shell differently based on a variety of strategic pathways? What are the most important mega-trends in the world and how can we mitigate, adapt, or harness them most effectively?

For corporations, these futurism techniques were about much more than just growing profits for the next fiscal year. "Starting from the mid-1960s," writes Andersson, "MNEs [multinational enterprises] began to see themselves as global actors on a par with nation-states and international organizations. As such, they perceived themselves as sharing the responsibility for ordering world economic relations and creating a world society in which MNEs could prosper."[4] Rather than using their expertise and techniques to achieve short-term objectives, futurists were positioned as advisers for much grander tasks. The scenarios they created "were large narrative exercises that can be seen as attempts to conjure entire new capitalist worlds."[5] Importantly, however, those worlds were not too entirely new. Futurists were free to let their imaginations go totally wild—within reason, of course. If they wanted to keep selling their visionary services and strategies, then some boundaries could not be broken, some assumptions had to be maintained, some possibilities were just too unbelievable. The future is constrained by the realities of realpolitik and capitalist realism.

Working at the Futurism Factory

From the 1970s onward, futurists had broadly become business consultants and thought leaders. I won't go into the details of how these professions developed over the last fifty years through, for example, organizations like The Future Laboratory and Global Business Network or individuals like Alvin Toffler and Stewart Brand.⁶ While interesting, it is beyond my scope here, where I focus more on the ends of the future for technological capitalism. Importantly, as Andersson notes, the goals of "future research was marked by a process of professionalization that led futurists of very different orientation to come together around a notion of expertise with strong links to an emerging consultancy market."⁷

As a profession, futurists don't just want to explain the shape of things to come for a curious audience; their job is to produce commodities—visions, forecasts, and strategies about the future, which very often means about technology and culture—that are marketed for public consumption and sold to private corporations. For instance, a futurist might take on the role of thought leader by writing a best-selling airport book about the future of [insert whatever], which then gets turned into a TED Talk that is shared widely, which then becomes a business card for their consulting services to corporate clients, which they parlay into an executive position with a title like Chief Futures Officer at a corporation that wants to be seen as on the bleeding-edge of innovation.

We can think of this in terms of futurism-as-a-service. Here the techniques of futurism—scenario planning, horizon scanning, trend spotting, economic forecasting—get rolled into the suite of services that a professional class of consultants sell to corporate clients. Just like with other forms of technical and strategic services that consultants provide, most corporations don't need to have entire in-house departments of accounts, lawyers, strategists, and futurists. It is better to just hire these services from a professional vendor when you need them or to bolster your own internal capacities with outside experts. In fact, it is beneficial for everybody involved if these consultants are entities that are separated from the businesses they work with—or at least that give a good performance of independence—thus making their services appear to be more trustworthy and less conflicted.

Much of the futurism that is produced now is consumed through reports released by consultancies like McKinsey, Deloitte, Gartner, and Accenture. Many of these reports are not directly commissioned or sponsored by any other organization, so they can claim to be independent forecasts not swayed by any particular interests or influences. These glossy documents identify megatrends, outline industry visions, make bold predictions about the immediate future, assign speculative values to the size of some market and the impact of some technology, and serve as promo material to attract clients that want to get tailored advice for how to better harness innovation and manage disruption.

These reports are the basis of headlines like this one in the *New York Times:* "Generative A.I. Can Add $4.4 Trillion in Value to Global Economy, Study Says."[8] That article, from June 2023, is just repeating claims from a report by McKinsey, thus bolstering their authority by laundering their press release through the paper of record. These spin cycles are routine parts of the futurist industry. McKinsey also garnered headlines when they forecasted a year earlier, in June 2022, that the metaverse had "potential to generate up to $5 trillion in value by 2030."[9] We could spend all day combing through not-so-old claims from such reports and showing how silly they were at the time and how wrong they are in hindsight. But hey, they can't all be winning predictions! The best way forward is to never look back.

However, that would miss the point of what these business consultants and thought leaders are doing when they clock into the futurism factory. They are not aiming to produce the most accurate forecasts or anticipatory scenarios, as if the future were a foreign space-time they were observing through remote viewing. Instead, they are helping to produce that future by shaping how we—public consumers and private corporations—perceive the market for technology, assess the risk and value of innovation, and expect the future to arrive.[10] Bold claims like those above can have such short lifespans because they are not primarily meant to generate *knowledge about* the future—nor are they really judged after the fact by their ability to do so—instead their purpose is to motivate *action for* the future in the present.

The Selling of Things to Come

To capture how this dynamic operates within the political economy of innovation, we turn to research on the sociology of expectations in science and technology, which shows us how futurist idealism connects to material power by making abstract visions both a cause and consequence of durable, concrete systems in the world.[11] The work of building expectations—by industry consultants, venture capitalists, corporate executives, and other thought leaders—"can be seen to be fundamentally 'generative', they guide activities, provide structure and legitimation, attract interest and foster investment," write Mads Borup and colleagues. "They give definition to roles, clarify duties, offer some shared shape of what to expect and how to prepare for opportunities and risks."[12]

Expectations are performative of the future—whether done in the style of hopes and promises, fears or perils. They are like dress rehearsals for versions of reality that have not arrived. Expectations craft visions of specific futures and create anticipation for their advent, but they also coordinate action for (or against) their arrival. "The business of technological expectations is increasingly commercial in orientation, product-minded in ambition and potent in influence," observe social scientists Neil Pollock and Robin Williams.[13] The future could always fail to materialize in the way envisioned, but that uncertainty is also a crucial element to the performance. It means that audience participation is necessary. Generating, harnessing, and channeling faith in specific futures—and the actions needed to make them into reality—is a big part of the job for people working in the futurism factory.

I call this the Tinkerbell Effect: speculative technologies only exist when we believe hard enough and clap loud enough. If we stop believing and clapping, then they can start fading away, becoming more immaterial by the moment until they disappear. Even investing billions of dollars may not guarantee the realization of a dream if people stop feeding it with their psychic energy. Metaverse? A distant memory. Web3? Sorry, wrong number. Google Glass? Never heard of it.

Importantly, these visions and expectations are not transformative on their own. This is the idealist fallacy; it sees things like desires, wishes, ideas, and intentions as the engines of change in society.[14] Any social power the futurist has—as our archetype of idealism in technological capitalism—depends on a whole apparatus of social relations and institutions that translates these expectations into action and embeds them into structures, routines, systems, policies, and so forth.

This translation might happen directly, for example, by motivating people to do certain things in order to fulfill or avoid specific projections. A famous example of this dynamic is Moore's Law: a prediction made by Gordon Moore, cofounder of Intel, that the number of transistors in an integrated circuit would double every two years (or sometimes eighteen months). Moore made the prediction in 1965 based on trends in the nascent semiconductor industry. It held with such precision for so long that it was dubbed a law of technology. However, the law was actually a yardstick that companies used to measure their own position in the market and the progress of the whole industry. If it looked like companies were lagging behind Moore's Law, then they invested more resources into R&D and entered into alliances with other manufacturers to ensure reality met expectations. "They regard this as the right strategy because they assume that others will do the same: self-preservation implies [obeying] Moore's Law as the authoritative view of the future," argues sociologist Harro van Lente.[15]

This case of self-fulfilling prophecy also shows how the power of expectations can shepherd people who are on the front lines of the technology industry and at the highest echelons of decision-making. Even technocratic experts can become enthralled by the myths, laws, and prophecies that they helped create and perpetuate. For everybody else, the effect can be much greater. The further people are removed from the technical process, the more mystified the process becomes and the less agency people have over its operations; the less agency people have, the greater authority they grant technological promises and the fewer chances people have to effect any kind of change.

The translation might also happen indirectly, for example, by legitimating and entrenching—or rejecting and eliminating—specific ways of thinking about what's (im)possible and (un)desirable. The power of expectations can have a disciplining effect on what people think, how they act, and who they are. As Foucault remarks, "The exercise of power is a 'conduct of conducts' and a management of possibilities."[16] This dynamic is most recognizable in the famous Thatcherite slogan about neoliberalism: "There is no alternative."[17] Similar maxims are the basis for common ways we talk about technology as deterministic, in which a thing or trajectory is treated as inevitable, inflexible, and irresistible.

Perhaps the technology is autonomous, like an out-of-control force of nature. Perhaps the march of progress is unstoppable, like a universal arc of destiny that pushes us in one direction. Perhaps the source of technological determinism is less mystical and more political: if we don't build and use this technology, then somebody else will; thus we must do it first. These positions seem like caricatures of the real beliefs held by futurists. I admit they are ludicrous. Yet they are also regularly expressed, in even more extreme and explicit ways, by people with great influence over how the future is made. Consider just one modern-day Oracle of Delphi: Kevin Kelly—cofounder of *Wired* magazine, evangelist for techno-optimism, and eminent futurist in Silicon Valley—who has written three popular books that strongly advance these positions: *Out of Control* (1992), *What Technology Wants* (2010), and *The Inevitable* (2016). These views about the trajectory of technology and the future, succinctly stated in the book titles, are commonplace among the elite of Silicon Valley. Regardless of how expectations are turned into commands, the conclusion is the same: get on board or get run over.

Our cultural lexicon for talking about social change is dominated by technological disruption. In addition to outright determinism, in which technology is treated like it has agential power over society, many other tropes are unquestioned, assumed to be true, and repeated as sage insights about socio-technical systems. These include the old canard that "law lags behind tech," which is now seen as an immutable dynamic rather than what it is: something that has to be constantly reasserted by tech companies working hard to avoid regulation and lobby against laws and that has to be reinforced by politicians who refuse to enforce legal rules that already exist for fear of being labeled anti-innovation. This all speaks to deeper assumptions about the purpose of innovation, how it can happen, and who has to do it. I have already discussed this at length in the chapter on innovation realism. Suffice it to say that this myopic conception of innovation acts like both blinders and reins for social change; it limits our view of alternatives while guiding us down one pathway.

To that point, another trope that has captured our discourse is the *hype cycle*—the ubiquitous model created by Gartner Group, a major technology analyst and industry consultant, to plot the advancement of technologies over time. The hype cycle is based on a linear series of phases that each technology moves through: from the "technology trigger" up to the "peak of inflated expectations" down to the "trough of disillusionment," then a short jump up the "slope of enlightenment" until finally reaching the "plateau of productivity." Originally created in 1995, it is shocking to see how often the hype cycle is still trotted out by people who are professional explainers, investors, and forecasters of emerging technology. The model has been regularly criticized as inaccurate, ambiguous, and generative of the hype it claims to map.[18] Yet the Gartner Hype Cycle has stuck around because it offers a convenient narrative to interpret complex systems. When you make PowerPoints for a living, it is hard to resist the utility of a figure that can show a road map for the future in one slide. And if your narrative does not reflect reality, then that must mean it's time to change reality.

"A small but powerful group of companies do critical work to circulate trends through consumer culture," as Devon Powers observes in her book on the business of trend forecasting. "And because of their ability to normalize, codify, and anticipate change, trends are fundamental to understanding how consumer culture and capitalism operate today."[19] We can extend that point far beyond consumer culture to also include other spheres of social, political, and economic operations. These visions of the future are commodities that are produced, marketed, and dominated by a highly effective corporate apparatus.[20]

This capitalist futurism advances an ideology of progress based on the release schedule of new devices and software. Each upgraded iPhone is another step toward the fulfillment of a divine digital destiny. "Technology is the American theology," writes cultural studies scholar Joel Dinerstein. "Once the future replaced heaven as the zone of perfectibility—as powered by technology—'progress' began to function as a religious myth that substituted a sacralized temporal zone (the future) for a sacred spatial one (Heaven)."[21] While humans cannot storm the gates of heaven, they can lay claim to the future. If you cannot beat god, then you might as well become gods.

The aim for capital is to render the future as a colonial frontier. The frontier future is conquered by the capitalist imagination, subjugating it to the manifest destiny of capital, eliminating other ideas of what's possible, and controlling the borders to access. The frontier future is exploited as a source of speculative value in which capital can make claims and cash checks in the present for products that are expected to be (but may never actually be) realized later. The frontier future is deployed as a temporal fix where any crisis of capitalism can be delayed, paused, and pushed back until some later date; where the ultimate solution for society is coming soon; where the only way out is by accelerating faster. We can see the frontier future expressed by, as theorist Sun-ha Hong argues, "the popular fantasy that heretofore impossible and even unimagined technological innovations will arrive, just in time, to cancel out the looming end of destructive climate change—a cultural accounting trick that finds a way to write off debts against future earnings even as bankruptcy approaches. Technology, in other words, is as much a totem for future possibility as it is a practical instrument."[22]

The colonization of the future, perhaps more so than any frontier, is an ongoing process of suppressing resistance and asserting dominance. I don't mean to say that capital's futurist aims have been finally achieved once and for all. Capital positions itself as the dreamer of dreams and maker of worlds. But that positioning is also a self-conscious attempt to banish any challengers by maligning them as illegitimate and incapable of imagining something different, thereby robbing them of the ability to turn those desires into reality. Capital is not the god emperor of space-time. Capital is a dictator with a death grip on a regime that is unstable and untenable.

Utopia Is a Place on Earth

For decades, we have been largely trapped within the boundaries of a techno-capitalist futurism that has been purged of any radical content.[23] Until quite recently, techno-utopianism was the primary register of Silicon Valley. Many wanted to believe that utopia was knocking on the door of reality, and Silicon Valley was more than happy to sell this dream. From small start-ups to mega-companies, every piece of technology was pitched as contributing directly to achieving a utopian society. But rather than offer visionary agendas for universal human liberation, they reduced utopianism to a means for legitimating the hegemony of Silicon Valley. Their promises for a better world quickly dissolved into ideology, revealed as alibis for more cynical aims. Their trick is to make us think that anything conceived as utopian invariably equates to some technocratic solution that must be imposed at scale on the otherwise helpless masses—helpless in the sense that they can't help themselves and that they can't do anything about the imposed solutions.[24] Their utopias are designed to foreclose our ability to imagine our own versions of utopia.

The relationship between utopia and dystopia is crucial to the operations of technological capitalism. This seeming contradiction is most clearly seen in the framing of the public discourse about artificial general intelligence (AGI)—machines that surpass human cognitive abilities—which is positioned between two radical endpoints: either AGI is an existential risk that will end humanity or AGI will lead to infinite progress beyond our wildest imaginations. People in Silicon Valley will often express both views in one breath. Many like Sam Altman, CEO of OpenAI, are very vocal about their concerns that AGI will lead to a *Terminator* scenario; at the same time, they claim that only they can safely lead us into the inevitable AGI Xanadu. Consider this passage from a profile in *Wired* of OpenAI's executive team:

> It's not fair to call OpenAI a cult, but when I asked several of the company's top brass if someone could comfortably work there if they didn't believe AGI was truly coming—and that its arrival would mark one of the greatest moments in human history—most executives didn't think so. *Why would a nonbeliever want to work*

here? they wondered. The assumption is that the workforce—now at approximately 500, though it might have grown since you began reading this paragraph—has self-selected to include only the faithful. At the very least, as Altman puts it, once you get hired, it seems inevitable that you'll be drawn into the spell.[25]

On one hand, OpenAI is not a cult. On the other hand, everybody who works there must believe in a millenarian doctrine that says the god-machine is coming and it's their duty to bring it into existence and make the messianic vision of AGI finally come to fruition. This is how the dialectic of utopia and dystopia is harnessed to craft powerful narratives of technology and politics, which trap people in the liminal space between concrete reality and divine prophecy.

Rather than be treated as exclusive possibilities, utopia and dystopia should be seen as coexisting perspectives on the same scene, a matter of different positions within a shared society. The record-breaking profits by trillionaire tech companies like Amazon during the pandemic—and the skyrocketing wealth of billionaires like Elon Musk (who added over $200 billion to his net worth between 2020 to 2023)[26]—are a stark indicator of their ability to thrive in a world that, for most other people, is reaching new heights of a living hell. As the oligarchic elite make great progress toward their own utopia, everybody else seems to be experiencing dystopia. This relationship is not correlative but causal. It is one based on subjugating the demands of the many to the desires of the few. Elysium is built on the forced sacrifice of those who will never breach its borders or enjoy its rewards.

Flipping our position in this system requires rejecting the binary choice between capitalist utopianism or a dreary realism that makes all other forms of utopia appear impossible or dangerous. Anti-capitalist resistance must be both the negation of dystopias and the positive struggle to actualize alternatives. In his book, *Envisioning Real Utopias,* Erik Olin Wright makes a vigorous argument for "emancipatory alternatives" to the failures of capitalism that are eminently achievable.[27] Wright was a founding figure of analytical Marxist sociology—a school of thought that emphasized high degrees of clarity, rigor, and concrete specificity in its analysis of areas like social stratification, egalitarian justice, socialist policies, and theories of transformation. Wright's work goes beyond the abstract hopes and philosophical gestures that are often associated with talk of radical alternatives. My intention is not to give a capsule summary of Wright's detailed work—it is extremely readable and worth reading on its own—but rather to revive the notion that utopias are more than just the final fantasy of people with no other options left. They are bright lodestars that should orient our efforts. Utopia—like the future—cannot be yet another territory ceded to capital.

Instead of dismissing socialism as either a form of "archaic utopian dreaming" or as an anachronistic idea that has lost credibility, "a real utopian," Wright explains, "holds on to emancipatory ideals without embarrassment or cynicism but remains fully cognizant of the deep complexities and contradictions of realizing those ideals."[28] The seeds for real utopias already exist in the world. Wright's intervention is a reminder to take inspiration from, and build upon, the radical potential of movements, programs, and actions that are already contributing, in ways small and large, to anti-capitalist alternatives and socialist real utopias.

These examples might be small-scale and contemporary, like local community organizing that works to provide services outside of commodified market transactions and thus build networks of solidarity and mutual aid among otherwise alienated people. And they can be large-scale and historical, like the major efforts in 1970s Chile, during the socialist government of Salvador Allende, to build a just society based on democratizing not just politics but also the economy and technology through movements for sovereignty from colonial control. Fighting for this kind of broad-based empowerment, which aimed to reverse the chokehold of imperialist geopolitics and global capital, required struggling against "the onslaught of the CIA, multinational companies, Chilean oligarchs and various far-right terrorist movements," writes Evgeny Morozov in his work on Chile's fight against technological capitalism. "And yet, for all the problems and crises, there were plenty of radical, utopian and even otherworldly initiatives that still have the power to inspire us today."[29] Being a real utopian also means not dwelling in defeatism when setbacks occur and not overpromising on the success of single actions. We have to diversify our tactics and our portfolios—using every ability and advantage at our disposal, while also investing in many different initiatives and actions.

When movements do present real alternatives that would make material improvements to people's lives—like defunding police, canceling debt, or mitigating climate impacts—they are often dismissed as idealistic nonsense and empty slogans. Even when those campaigns succeed in the face of fierce opposition, they are still belittled as lucky shots. Pushing toward a truly better world requires unflinchingly reaffirming the reality of radical change when confronted by those, from across political divides, who say it is unthinkable. We must realize that many of those who laugh at the suggestion of any socialist reform are the same people who are busily enacting their own political machinations and social movements for pushing governance toward the furthest reaches of the right wing. Their dismissal is not a pragmatic calculation but an assertion of power—about who should have it and how it should operate.

Fighting for real utopias is not a matter of declaring our own teleological narratives. Nothing is inevitable. The long history of humanity shows us that specific phases of development do not emerge in lockstep with a schedule, nor do forms of society only advance in one direction.[30] Whole civilizations have engaged in drastic transformations of their social organizations, based on both external conditions and internal decisions that led to new ways of life. Entire cultures have moved in what might seem like a forward direction, only to backtrack, and then advance forward down a different pathway, because they were living in rhythm with the changing seasons and adapting their lives in relation to their ecosystems. Over thousands of years, ancient societies moved from foraging to agriculture, then abandoned farming in favor of nomadic lifestyles, then settled back into cultivating crops, before shifting once again to wild food collection. On the cycle went for a very long time—not in a straight line but in twists and turns.[31]

The collective nature of human life is far more fluid, weird, exciting, and filled with potential than can possibly be contained by any single narrative imposed upon it. Our current moment in history, a blip in the timescale of humanity, let alone the planet, is the true anomaly. Imagine a world where all people live under powerful global systems, where the existing order of society is locked in place by ossified institutions and obdurate infrastructures, where the decisions made over the last hundred years persist forever until planetary collapse. This is the absurd premise of our reality—in which attempts to radically question this unbelievable state of affairs are rebuked by those in power as impossible.

Where the techno-capitalist version of utopia wants to fore-close the future, real utopias preserve its openness. It should be alarming that many of our most influential futurists—the people given the authority to advance grand visions for socio-technical change and the resources to materialize their dreams and desires—are billionaire venture capitalists like Masayoshi Son and Marc Andreessen. When the tech elite like Andreessen declare, "It's time to build,"[32] and write long essays explaining "Why AI Will Save the World"[33] and pen manifestos asserting the need to unleash the "effective accelerationism" of the "techno-capital machine,"[34] they really mean two things. First, only the systems and institutions that align with their interests will be built. Second, anybody who disagrees will be dismissed as unserious and treated as an enemy of the future; they will be accused of bitter pessimism or timid primitivism. But such an image of the future is fixed, limited only to what delivers the maximum return on investment—not only financial profit but also social power.

We cannot be afraid to turn their accusations back on them. Their own optimism is based on a belief that they will come out on top. They restrict agency over the future to themselves and the start-up founders they fund, while pessimistically rejecting everybody else's ability for self-determination and democratic organization. The utopia they are building has no space for a public that wants to direct itself toward different ends and exert social control over technological change. What we are left with is the phantom pain of lost possibilities. The strange sense that some intangible part of us has been stripped away.

We are assailed by a "relentless campaign against the human imagination," writes David Graeber in his profound reflections on utopia, revolution, and collapse. He continues: "We are talking about the murdering of dreams, the imposition of an apparatus of hopelessness, designed to squelch any sense of an alternative future. Yet as a result of putting virtually all their efforts in one political basket, we are left in the bizarre situation of watching the capitalist system crumbling before our very eyes, at just the moment everyone had finally concluded no other system would be possible."[35]

The capitalist system is designed to pummel us into submission, preventing us from imagining life could be any other way, let alone allowing us to go on the offensive. By every metric, corporations now rule over the global economy and everyday life, with the tech industry as a vanguard for new forms of domination and extraction. "From its inception, the business corporation showed its potential, if not bounded, to metastasize into a world power," writes political theorist David Cieply.[36] These corporate behemoths are now struggling against the last remaining limits, both politically (what the government will permit) and socially (what the public will tolerate). We live with the effects of capital's totalizing schemes for how to organize society. They have become universal and normal; they are simultaneously utopias for the few who are enriched by them and various degrees of dystopia for most other people.

At the same time, capitalism itself is a failed utopian project. Its most ardent supporters claimed the forces of capital had brought us to the apex of human civilization, where the comforts and conveniences of capitalist production would be enjoyed by everybody.

The champions of capitalism over the last hundred years—from Ayn Rand to Milton Friedman to Peter Thiel—have been motivated by the search for (and creation of) capitalist utopias.[37] They point to zones of exception like Hong Kong and Singapore—ruled by a heady cocktail of market extremism, radical libertarianism, and anti-democratic authoritarianism—as models that should be scaled to the level of global governance. Yet there is a wide chasm between how these places actually exist and the conceptual models of them created by capitalist utopians. Contrary to fairy tales about magical marketplaces, what capitalism has delivered is a system that abandons all but a tiny elite class to die. If not by pandemics or climatic catastrophes, then by more mundane forms of social murder by the police, the economy, or the despair of an atomized, brutal life.[38]

I want to argue, however, that there is also power in seeing that the world is dominated by grand (failed) utopian projects like capitalism because it means utopias are possible and contingent. In other words, utopia already exists; it's just unevenly produced and distributed. Recognizing this opens the imaginative space needed for trying to actualize different utopias that would benefit the disempowered and disenfranchised.

The point of real utopian tactics is not to fall into the trap of all or nothing but to celebrate wins and channel that energy into pushing any advantage. Real utopian projects are a process not just an endpoint, as I explained at the start of this chapter. They are found in the struggle of people on the streets and shop floors against an out-of-control engine of immiseration. It's not enough to wait patiently for one last crisis to make capitalism self-destruct. We must actively intervene against the impositions of capital—by any means, in every way, whether victory seems possible or not. As

Walter Benjamin contends in his essay "On the Concept of History," "Marx says that revolutions are the locomotive of world history. But perhaps it is quite otherwise. Perhaps revolutions are an attempt by the passengers on this train—namely, the human race—to activate the emergency brake."[39] Striving for real utopias means not succumbing to fatalism but instead looking for ways to tighten the binds around capital while loosening its restraints on us. Slowing down real dystopias is itself a radical act. In practical terms, this requires sabotaging the efforts of those who would erect barriers to alternatives just as much as it requires building the machinery for better futures.

The Wrench and the Hammer

As an archetype of technological capitalism, the futurist is antithetical to the mechanic and the Luddite. Whereas the futurist only looks forward with their mind's eye, the mechanic knows the future is built on the past. Change can seem sudden, but it is not a clean break. What comes next is always an extension of, or reaction to, what already exists. The technologies might have a new coat of paint, but under the hood they are very often operating in familiar ways for familiar purposes. Whereas the futurist performs visions of tomorrow as cover for reinscribing the politics of yesterday, the Luddite knows the future does not just happen to us. Unlike an alien force or exogenous shock, the future must be made—actively and constantly. That means futures can be broken, remade in various ways, or abandoned altogether. What must be maintained can always be destroyed.

Books about technology tend to succumb—especially in their conclusions—to the temptation of predicting what grand new things are on the horizon. Revolutionary technologies, says the futurist, are always just ten years away. They are simultaneously cast as inevitable yet fickle. "Yet another miscarriage of the future by those who were too afraid of its potential," the futurist will crow. The language of futurism inhibits our ability to debate the values, goals, and uses of these imaginaries and their socio-technical systems. Rather than a politics of technology, we are left with innovation fetishism and capitalist realism, which shuts down entire ways of understanding our world, imagining potential worlds, and building new worlds. We scarcely realize just how impoverished—politically, technologically, metaphysically—we have become.

The ruthless criticism that motivates this book is designed to do more than examine how these systems operate and what their impacts are. It also confronts us with the reality that technology and capitalism are both products of social struggle. They are the result of struggles over who captures value and who creates value, over whose power will persist and whose dreams will dissipate, over whose interests will be embedded in material things and whose interests will be erased in the process. The future is not the great unknown but rather a combat zone. Refusing to fight does not resolve the conflict. It just makes things one-sided. The easiest way to win is by convincing people the battle is over, they have already lost.

If we recall what Marx said, the point of ruthless criticism is to be "ruthless in that it will shrink neither from its own discoveries, nor from conflict with the powers that be."[40] That second part is the most important part to uphold. In the fights ahead, we must embody both mechanics and Luddites, able to wield wrenches and hammers according to the needs at hand. Writing in defense of the original Luddites and their ongoing relevance, Brian Merchant points out, "They were not opposed to progress, and certainly not to technology; most were skilled technicians themselves, who spent their days working on machines at home or in small shops."[41] What turned these mechanics into Luddites was knowing when it was time to stop tinkering at home and take to the streets, factories, and wherever else capital was imposing its future upon them. This is the same wisdom that must galvanize us today. Only then can we put the pieces together in ways that work for us, not against us.

Notes

Chapter One. Two Systems

1. Meghan O'Gieblyn (2016), As a God Might Be: Three Visions of Technological Progress, *Boston Review*, 9 February, accessed 10 January 2023: https://bostonreview.net/books-ideas/meghan-ogieblyn-god-might-be.

2. Allan Dafoe (2015), On Technological Determinism: A Typology, Scope Conditions, and a Mechanism, *Science, Technology, and Human Values* 40 (6): 1047–1076.

3. Kevin Kelly (2010), *What Technology Wants* (New York: Viking Press).

4. Langdon Winner (1978), *Autonomous Technology: Technics-Out-of-Control as a Theme in Political Thought* (Cambridge, MA: MIT Press).

5. Jathan Sadowski (2020c), *Too Smart: How Digital Capitalism Is Extracting Data, Controlling Our Lives, and Taking Over the World* (Cambridge, MA: MIT Press).

6. Winner (1978).

7. Keller Easterling (2014), *Extrastatecraft: The Power of Infrastructure Space* (New York: Verso).

8. Winner (1978, p. 323).

9. Milton Friedman (1970), A Friedman Doctrine: The Social Responsibility of Business Is to Increase Its Profits, *New York Times*, 13 September, accessed 21 December 2022: https://www.nytimes.com/1970/09/13/archives/a-friedman-doctrine-the-social-responsibility-of-business-is-to.html.

10. Karl Marx (1990), *Capital, Volume I*, trans. Ben Fowkes (New York: Penguin Classics), p. 253.

11. Marx (1990, p. 252).

12. Karl Marx (1992), *Capital, Volume II*, trans. David Fernbach (London: Penguin Classics), p. 185.

13. Søren Mau (2023), *Mute Compulsion: A Marxist Theory of the Economic Power of Capital* (London: Verso Books), chapter 1 (epub), quoting Karl Marx (1993b), *Grundrisse: Foundations of the Critique of Political Economy*, trans. Martin Nicolaus (Harmondsworth, UK: Penguin), p. 106.

14. William Cronon (1991), *Nature's Metropolis: Chicago and the Great West* (New York: W. W. Norton).

15. Marx (1990, p. 563).

16. Lucas Chancel, Thomas Piketty, Emmanuel Saez, and Gabriel Zucman (2022), *World Inequality Report 2022* (Paris: World Inequality Lab), accessed 16 December 2022: https://wir2022.wid.world. See also Phil A. Neel (2022), The Knife at Your Throat, *Brooklyn Rail*, October, accessed 16 December 2022: https://brooklynrail.org/2022/10/field-notes/The-Knife-At-Your-Throat.

17. Cynthia Cockburn (1981), The Material of Male Power, *Feminist Review* 9 (1): 41–58.

18. Jodi Dean (2017), Introduction, *The Communist Manifesto* (London: Pluto Press), p. 6; quoted in China Miéville (2022), *A Spectre, Haunting: On the Communist Manifesto* (Chicago: Haymarket Books).

19. Evgeny Morozov (2013), *To Save Everything, Click Here: The Folly of Technological Solutionism* (New York: PublicAffairs Books).

20. Sadowski (2020c, p. 52).

21. Ezra Klein (host), (2021), Ezra Klein Interviews Ted Chiang [Transcript], *New York Times*, 30 March, accessed 14 March 2023: https://www.nytimes.com/2021/03/30/podcasts/ezra-klein-podcast-ted-chiang-transcript.html.

22. Max Bank, Felix Duffy, Verena Leyendecker, and Margarida Silva (2021), *The Lobby Network: Big Tech's Web of Influence in the EU* (Brussels: Corporate Europe Observatory), accessed 12 January 2023: https://corporateeurope.org/en/2021/08/lobby-network-big-techs-web-influence-eu; Adam Satariano and Matina Stevis-Gridneff (2020), Big Tech Turns Its Lobbyists Loose on Europe, Alarming Regulators, *New York Times*, 14 December, accessed 12 January 2023: https://www.nytimes.com/2020/12/14/technology/big-tech-lobbying-europe.html; Cat Zakrzewski (2022), Tech Companies Spent Almost $70 Million Lobbying Washington in 2021 as

Congress Sought to Rein in Their Power, *Washington Post*, 21 January, accessed 12 January 2023: https://www.washingtonpost.com/technology/2022/01/21 /tech-lobbying-in-washington/.

23. Olivia Solon and Sabrina Siddiqui (2017), Forget Wall Street: Silicon Valley Is the New Political Power in Washington, *Guardian*, 3 September, accessed 12 January 2023: https://www.theguardian.com/technology/2017/sep/03 /silicon-valley-politics-lobbying-washington.

24. Jathan Sadowski and Roy Bendor (2019), Selling Smartness: Corporate Narratives and the Smart City as a Sociotechnical Imaginary, *Science, Technology & Human Values* 44 (3): 540–563; Jathan Sadowski (2020a), Cyberspace and Cityscapes: On the Emergence of Platform Urbanism, *Urban Geography* 41 (3): 448–452; Jathan Sadowski (2021b), Who Owns the Future City? Phases of Technological Urbanism and Shifts in Sovereignty, *Urban Studies* 58 (8): 1732–1744.

25. Jathan Sadowski (2023), Total Life Insurance: Logics of Anticipatory Control and Actuarial Governance in Insurance Technology, *Social Studies of Science*, https://doi.org/10.1177/03063127231186437.

26. Phoebe Wall Howard (2018), Data Could Be What Ford Sells Next as It Looks for New Revenue, *Detroit Free Press*, 13 November, accessed 19 February 2024: https://www.freep.com/story/money/cars/2018/11/13/ford-motor-credit-data-new-revenue/1967077002/.

27. Gary Marcus (2022), Deep Learning Is Hitting a Wall, *Nautilus*, 10 March, accessed 16 December 2022: https://nautil.us/deep-learning-is-hitting-a-wall-238440/.

28. Jathan Sadowski and Anthony Levenda (2020), The Anti-Politics of Smart Energy Regimes, *Political Geography* 81 (August): 102202.

29. Nick Chavez (2022), Technical Expertise and Communist Production, *Brooklyn Rail*, December/January, accessed 11 January 2023: https://brooklynrail .org/2023/12/field-notes/Technical-Expertise-and-Communist-Production; Martín Arboleda (2020), *Planetary Mine: Territories of Extraction under Late Capitalism* (London: Verso); Andreas Malm (2016), *Fossil Capital: The Rise of Steam Power and the Roots of Global Warming* (London: Verso); Cecilia Rikap (2021), *Capitalism, Power and Innovation: Intellectual Monopoly Capitalism Uncovered* (London: Routledge); Raj Patel and Jason W. Moore (2018), *A History of the World in Seven Cheap Things: A Guide to Capitalism, Nature, and the Future of the Planet* (Oakland: University of California Press).

30. Leo Marx (1987), Does Improved Technology Mean Progress? *Technology Review* 71 (January): 33–41, p. 34.

31. Marx (1987, p. 34).

32. Thao Phan, Jake Goldenfein, Declan Kuch, and Monique Mann (eds.) (2022), *Economies of Virtue: The Circulation of "Ethics" in AI* (Amsterdam: Institute of Network Cultures).

Chapter Two. Two Models

1. Stafford Beer (1985), *Diagnosing the System for Organizations* (Hoboken, NJ: Wiley), p. 99. For more on his career, I highly recommend starting with the history of Cybersyn, which aimed to synthesize Stafford Beer's cybernetic management with a socialist planned economy in Chile: Eden Medina (2014), *Cybernetic Revolutionaries: Technology and Politics in Allende's Chile* (Cambridge, MA: MIT Press); Evgeny Morozov (2023c), The Santiago Boys, accessed 11 September 2023: https://the-santiago-boys.com/.

2. Jathan Sadowski and Kaitlin Beegle (2023), Extractive and Expansive Networks of Web3, *Big Data & Society* 10 (1): 1–14.

3. John Carreyou (2018), *Bad Blood: Secrets and Lies in a Silicon Valley Startup* (New York: Knopf).

4. Hannah Alarazi (2021), Ex-Theranos CEO's Defense Emerges in Pre-Trial Battle, *Law360*, 4 May, accessed 7 February 2023: https://www.law360.com/articles/1381385/ex-theranos-ceo-s-defense-emerges-in-pre-trial-battle.

5. Matt Levine (2021), Startups Sometimes Stretch the Truth, *Bloomberg*, 27 February, accessed 7 February 2023: https://www.bloomberg.com/opinion/articles/2021-02-26/startups-sometimes-stretch-the-truth?sref=1kJVNqnU.

6. Mau (2023, chapter 1) (epub).

7. Lee Vinsel (2019), You're Doing It Wrong: Notes on Criticism and Technology Hype, *Medium*, 2 February, accessed 8 February 2023: https://sts-news.medium.com/youre-doing-it-wrong-notes-on-criticism-and-technology-hype-18b08b4307e5.

8. Cory Doctorow (2020), How to Destroy Surveillance Capitalism, *OneZero*, 26 August, accessed 8 February 2023: https://onezero.medium.com/how-to-destroy-surveillance-capitalism-8135e6744d59; Shoshana Zuboff (2019), *The Age of Surveillance Capitalism: The Fight for a Human Future at the New Frontier of Power* (New York: PublicAffairs).

9. Beer (1985, p. 99).

10. Jenna Burrell (2016), How the Machine "Thinks": Understanding Opacity in Machine Learning Algorithms, *Big Data & Society* 3 (1): 1–12; Frank Pasquale (2015), *The Black Box Society: The Secret Algorithms That Control Money and Information* (Cambridge, MA: Harvard University Press); Winner (1978).

11. Leo Marx (2010), Technology: The Emergence of a Hazardous Concept, *Technology and Culture* 51: 561–577.

12. Nick Chavez (2021), The Present and Future of Engineers, *Brooklyn Rail*, October, accessed 20 February 2023: https://brooklynrail.org/2021/10/field-notes/thinking-about-communism.

13. David F. Noble (1979), *America by Design: Science, Technology, and the Rise of Corporate Capitalism* (Oxford: Oxford University Press); David F. Noble (1984), *Forces of Production: A Social History of Industrial Automation* (New York: Knopf).

14. Marx (2010, p. 574).

15. I want to thank Thao Phan for raising the issue of gender as it relates to the masculine tropes of mechanics and for suggesting the possibility of recuperating the figure for more inclusive and critical purposes.

16. Cynthia Cockburn (1985), *The Machinery of Dominance: Women, Men, and Technical Know-How* (London: Pluto Press); Rayvon Fouché (2006), Say It Loud, I'm Black and I'm Proud: African Americans, American Artifactual Culture, and Black Vernacular Technological Creativity, *American Studies Quarterly* 58 (3): 639–661.

17. Cockburn (1981); Judy Wacjman (2004), *Technofeminism* (London: Polity Press); Wendy Faulkner (2000), Dualisms, Hierarchies and Gender in Engineering, *Social Studies of Science* 30 (5): 759–792; Charlton D. McIlwain (2020), *Black Software: The Internet and Racial Justice, from the AfroNet to Black Lives Matter* (Oxford: Oxford University Press); Lisa Nakamura (2014), Indigenous Circuits: Navajo Women and the Racialization of Early Electronic Manufacture, *American Quarterly* 66 (4): 919–941; Ruha Benjamin (2019), *Race after Technology: Abolitionist Tools for the New Jim Code* (London: Polity Press); Simone Browne (2015), *Dark Matters: On the Surveillance of Blackness* (Durham, NC: Duke University Press).

18. Jennifer S. Light (1999), When Computers Were Women, *Technology and Culture* 40 (3): 455–483; Kenneth Lipartito (1994), When Women Were

Switches: Technology, Work, and Gender in the Telephone Industry, 1890–1920, *American Historical Review* 99 (4): 1075–1111.

19. Mar Hicks (2018), *Programmed Inequality: How Britain Discarded Women Technologists and Lost Its Edge in Computing* (Cambridge, MA: MIT Press); Nathan L. Ensmenger (2012), *The Computer Boys Take Over Computers, Programmers, and the Politics of Technical Expertise* (Cambridge, MA: MIT Press).

20. Karen Throsby (2009), Revisiting "The Machinery of Dominance: Women, Men, and Technical Know-How," *Women's Studies Quarterly* 37 (1/2): 274–276.

21. Ian Manovel and Leigh Donoghue (2019), *Injecting Intelligence into Health Care* (Sydney: Accenture Consulting).

22. E. P. Thompson (1966), *The Making of the English Working Class* (New York: Vintage Books), p. 552.

23. For excellent work that details the real history of Luddism and its relevance for contemporary society, see these two books: Gavin Mueller (2021), *Breaking Things at Work: The Luddites Are Right about Why You Hate Your Job* (London: Verso); Brian Merchant (2023a), *Blood in the Machine: The Origins of the Rebellion against Big Tech* (New York: Little, Brown).

24. See the Wikipedia page for the full text of the short poem "And Did Those Feet in Ancient Times," plus helpful context for this popular phrase's meaning and usage. Accessed 2 March 2023: https://en.wikipedia.org/wiki/And_did_those_feet_in_ancient_time.

25. Friedrich Engels (2009), *Condition of the Working Class in England* (London: Penguin Classics).

26. Merchant (2023a).

27. Mueller (2021, p. 13).

28. David F. Noble (1995), *Progress without People: New Technology, Unemployment, and the Message of Resistance* (Toronto: Between the Lines), p. 7.

29. Adrian Randall (1998), The "Lessons" of Luddism, *Endeavour* 22 (4): 152–155.

30. Randall (1998, p. 153).

31. Randall (1998).

32. Phan et al. (2022).

33. Anna Lauren Hoffmann (2021), Terms of Inclusion: Data, Discourse, Violence, *New Media & Society* 23 (12): 3539–3556, p. 3548.

34. Karl Marx (1843), Letter from Marx to Arnold Ruge, accessed 9 February 2023: https://www.marxists.org/archive/marx/works/1843/letters/43_09-alt.htm.

Chapter Three. Innovation

1. Quoted in Leo Marx (1964), *The Machine in the Garden: Technology and the Pastoral Ideal in America* (Oxford: Oxford University Press), p. 195. See also David E. Nye (1996), *American Technological Sublime* (Cambridge, MA: MIT Press).

2. Marx (1964).

3. Marc Andreessen (2023a), The Techno-Optimist Manifesto, *a16z*, 16 October, accessed 23 November 2023: https://a16z.com/the-techno-optimist-manifesto/.

4. Langdon Winner (1986), *The Whale and the Reactor: A Search for Limits in an Age of High Technology* (Chicago: University of Chicago Press); Richard E. Sclove (1995), *Democracy and Technology* (New York: Guilford Press).

5. Robyn Klingler-Vidra (2014), Building a Venture Capital Market in Vietnam: Diffusion of a Neoliberal Market Strategy to a Socialist State, *Asian Studies Review* 38 (4): 582–600.

6. Tom Nicholas (2019), *VC: An American History* (Cambridge, MA: Harvard University Press).

7. Josh Lerner and Ramana Nanda (2020), Venture Capital's Role in Financing Innovation: What We Know and How Much We Still Need to Learn, *Journal of Economic Perspectives* 34 (3): 237–261.

8. Robyn Klingler-Vidra (2016), When Venture Capital Is Patient Capital: Seed Funding as a Source of Patient Capital for High-Growth Companies, *Socio-Economic Review* 14 (4): 691–708.

9. Tom Wolfe (1987), *The Bonfire of the Vanities* (New York: Farrar, Straus and Giroux).

10. Peter Lee (2022), Enhancing the Innovative Capacity of Venture Capital, *Yale Journal of Law and Technology* 24: 611–705.

11. Pascale Lehoux, Fiona A. Miller, Geneviève Daudelin, and David R. Urbach (2016), How Venture Capitalists Decide Which New Medical Technologies Come to Exist, *Science and Public Policy* 43 (3): 375–385.

12. Franziska Cooiman (2022), Imprinting the Economy: The Structural Power of Venture Capital, *Environment and Planning A: Economy and Space*, https://doi.org/10.1177/0308518X221136559.

13. Lee (2022); Nicholas (2019).

14. Lee (2022, pp. 629–630).

15. Franziska Cooiman (2023), Veni Vidi VC: The Backend of the Digital Economy and Its Political Making, *Review of International Political Economy* 30 (1): 229–251; Kean Birch (2023), Reflexive Expectations in Innovation Financing: An Analysis of Venture Capital as a Mode of Valuation, *Social Studies of Science* 53 (1): 29–48.

16. Peter Thiel and Blake Masters (2014), *Zero to One: Notes on Startups, or How to Build the Future* (New York: Crown Business).

17. Robyn Klingler-Vidra (2018), Building the Venture Capital State, *American Affairs* 2 (3): n.p.

18. Peter Lee (2018), Innovation and the Firm: A New Synthesis, *Stanford Law Review* 70 (5): 1431–1501.

19. Sadowski (2020a); Sadowski (2021b).

20. TrueBridge Capital Partners (2022), State of VC 2021: Breaking Every Record, *Forbes*, 14 June, accessed 15 March 2023: https://www.forbes.com/sites/truebridge/2022/06/14/state-of-vc-2021-breaking-every-record/?sh=654b75ad5fbe.

21. Mark Fisher (2010), *Capitalist Realism: Is There No Alternative?* (Winchester, UK: Zero Books), p. 2.

22. For further investigation and strong repudiation of this idea, see Mariana Mazzucato (2013), *The Entrepreneurial State: Debunking Public vs. Private Sector Myths* (New York: Anthem Press).

23. Eric Levitz (2020), America Has Central Planners. We Just Call Them "Venture Capitalists," *New York Magazine*, 3 December, accessed 10 March 2023: https://nymag.com/intelligencer/2020/12/wework-venture-capital-central-planning.html.

24. Edward Ongweso Jr. (2023), The Incredible Tantrum Venture Capitalists Threw over Silicon Valley Bank, *Slate*, 13 March, accessed 14 March 2023: https://slate.com/technology/2023/03/silicon-valley-bank-rescue-venture-capital-calacanis-sacks-ackman-tantrum.html; Matt Levine (2023), Startup Bank Had a Startup Bank Run, *Bloomberg*, 11 March, accessed 14 March 2023:

https://www.bloomberg.com/opinion/articles/2023-03-10/startup-bank-had
-a-startup-bank-run; Nathan Tankus (2023), Every Complex Banking Issue All
at Once: The Failure of Silicon Valley Bank in One Brief Summary and Five
Quick Implications, *Crises Notes*, 14 March, accessed 15 March 2023: https://
www.crisesnotes.com/every-complex-banking-issue-all-at-once-the-failure
-of-silicon-valley-bank-in-one-brief-summary-and-five-quick-implications/.

25. Christopher Anstey (2023), Larry Summers Warns Silicon Valley Bank
Collapse Has "Substantial Consequences" for America's Innovation System,
Fortune, 12 March, accessed 14 March 2023: https://fortune.com/2023/03/11
/larry-summers-warns-silicon-valley-bank-collapse-finance-consequences
-innovation-ventures/.

26. Ken Sweet, Christopher Rugaber, Chris Megerian, and Cathy Bussewitz (2023), US Government Moves to Stop Potential Banking Crisis, *AP News*,
13 March, accessed 14 March 2023: https://apnews.com/article/silicon-valley
-bank-bailout-yellen-deposits-failure-94f2185742981daf337c4691bbb9ec1e.

27. Paul Krugman (2023), How Bad Was the Silicon Valley Bank Bailout?
New York Times, 14 March, accessed 15 March 2023: https://www.nytimes
.com/2023/03/14/opinion/silicon-valley-bank-bailout.html.

28. This section draws from: Sadowski and Beegle (2023).

29. Erin Griffith and Cade Metz (2023b), "Let 1,000 Flowers Bloom": A.I.
Funding Frenzy Escalates, *New York Times*, 14 March, accessed 9 May 2023:
https://www.nytimes.com/2023/03/14/technology/ai-funding-boom.html.

30. Nilay Patel and Chris Dixon (2022), Chris Dixon Thinks Web3 Is the
Future of the Internet: Is It? *The Verge*, 12 April, accessed 17 April 2023: https://
www.theverge.com/23020727/decoder-chris-dixon-web3-cryptoa16z-vc
-silicon-valley-investing-podcast-interview.

31. Chris Dixon, Katie Haun, and Ali Yahya (2021), Crypto Fund III, *a16z*,
24 June, accessed 6 April 2022: https://a16z.com/2021/06/24/crypto-fund-iii/.

32. Jacob Kastrenakes (2022), Bored Ape Yacht Club Creator Raises $450
Million to Build an NFT Metaverse, *The Verge*, 22 March, accessed 6 April 2022:
https://www.theverge.com/2022/3/22/ 22991272/yuga-labs-seed-funding-a16z
-bored-ape-yacht-club-bayc-metaverse-other-side.

33. Rick Claypool (2022), Capitol Coin, *Public Citizen*, 8 March, accessed 6
April 2022: https://www.citizen.org/article/capitol-coin-cryptocurrency
-lobbying-revolving-door-report/.

34. Eric Lipton, Daisuke Wakabayashi, and Ephrat Livni (2021), Big Hires, Big Money and a D.C. Blitz: A Bold Plan to Dominate Crypto, *New York Times*, 29 October, accessed 6 April 2022: https://www.nytimes.com/2021/10/29/us/politics/andreessen-horowitz-lobbying-cryptocurrency.html.

35. Kiran Stacey (2022), Meet the "Crypto Caucus": The US Lawmakers Defending Digital Coins, *Financial Times*, 31 March, accessed 6 April 2022: https://www.ft.com/content/29f32905-1933-458e-aa29-7f1685109ea1.

36. Klingler-Vidra (2016).

37. Cooiman (2022, p. 1).

38. Pitchbook and NVCA (2022), *Venture Monitor: Q4 2022*, accessed 20 March 2023: https://files.pitchbook.com/website/files/pdf/Q4_2022_PitchBook-NVCA_Venture_Monitor.pdf.

39. Cooiman (2023).

40. Lerner and Nanda (2020).

41. David Harvey (2006), *Limits to Capital* (London: Verso), p. 95.

42. Rodrigo Fernandez, Ilke Adriaans, Tobias J. Klinge, and Reijer Hendrikse (2020), *Engineering Digital Monopolies: The Financialisation of Big Tech* (Amsterdam: SOMO).

43. Hilary J. Allen (2022), DeFi: Shadow Banking 2.0? *William & Mary Law Review*, https://doi.org/10.2139/ssrn.4038788.

44. Jathan Sadowski (2020b), The Internet of Landlords: Digital Platforms and New Mechanisms of Rentier Capitalism, *Antipode* 52 (2): 562–580.

45. Saule T. Omarova (2019), New Tech v. New Deal: Fintech as a Systemic Phenomenon, *Yale Journal on Regulation* 36 (2): 735–793.

46. Omarova (2019, p. 742).

47. Will Gornall and Ilya A. Strebulaev (2020), Squaring Venture Capital Valuations with Reality, *Journal of Financial Economics* 135: 120–143.

48. Birch (2023).

49. Shai Bernstein, Arthur Korteweg, and Kevin Laws (2017), Attracting Early Stage Investors: Evidence from a Randomized Field Experiment, *Journal of Finance* 72 (2): 509–538; Lee (2022).

50. Lee (2022); Cooiman (2022).

51. Pitchbook and NVCA (2022, p. 21).

52. Lee (2022).

53. Lee (2022).

54. Steven Bertoni (2017), WeWork's $20 Billion Office Party: The Crazy Bet That Could Change How the World Does Business, *Forbes*, 2 October, accessed 15 March 2023: https://www.forbes.com/sites/stevenbertoni/2017/10/02/the-way-we-work/?sh=1f1f24fe1b18.

55. Harvey (2006, p. 267).

56. David Harvey (2017), *Marx, Capital and the Madness of Economic Reason* (London: Profile Books).

57. Karl Marx (1993a), *Capital, Volume III*, trans. David Fernbach (London: Penguin), p. 603.

58. Marx (1993a, p. 609).

59. Mads Borup, Nik Brown, Kornelia Konrad, and Harro van Lente (2006), The Sociology of Expectations in Science and Technology, *Technology Analysis & Strategic Management* 18 (3/4): 285–298; Harro van Lente, Charlotte Spitters, and Alexander Peine (2013), Comparing Technological Hype Cycles: Towards a Theory, *Technological Forecasting & Social Change* 80 (8): 1615–1628.

60. Sadowski and Bendor (2019).

Chapter Four. Data

1. There is a hefty critical literature focused on picking apart the metaphors of data, with a particular focus on "data mining" and "new oil": Lisa Gitelman (ed.) (2013), *"Raw Data" Is an Oxymoron* (Cambridge, MA: MIT Press); Cornelius Puschmann and Jean Burgess (2014), Metaphors of Big Data, *International Journal of Communication* 8: 1609–1709; Luke Stark and Anna Lauren Hoffmann (2019), Data Is the New What? Popular Metaphors and Professional Ethics in Emerging Data Culture, *Journal of Cultural Analytics* 4 (1): 1–22; Sy Taffel (2023), Data and Oil: Metaphor, Materiality and Metabolic Rifts, *New Media & Society* 25 (5): 980–998.

2. *Economist* (2017), The World's Most Valuable Resource Is No Longer Oil, but Data, 6 May, accessed 11 April 2023: https://www.economist.com/leaders/2017/05/06/the-worlds-most-valuable-resource-is-no-longer-oil-but-data.

3. *Economist* (2017, n.p.).

4. Howard (2018).

5. Alistair Fraser (2022), "You Can't Eat Data"? Moving beyond the Misconfigured Innovations of Smart Farming, *Journal of Rural Studies* 91 (April): 200–207.

6. Taffel (2021, p. 4).

7. Siemens (2014), Siemens Smart Data, YouTube, 4 September, accessed 12 April 2023: https://www.youtube.com/watch?v=ZxoO-DvHQRw.

8. IBM (2014), A World Made with Data. Made with IBM, YouTube, 27 May, accessed 12 April 2023: https://www.youtube.com/watch?v=QCgzrOUd_Dc.

9. Sadowski (2020c).

10. Jathan Sadowski (2019), When Data Is Capital: Datafication, Accumulation, and Extraction, *Big Data & Society* 6 (1): 1–12.

11. Marx (1990, p. 416).

12. Joseph Turow (2017), *The Aisles Have Eyes: How Retailers Track Your Shopping, Strip Your Privacy, and Define Your Power* (New Haven, CT: Yale University Press).

13. Jon Keegan (2023), Forget Milk and Eggs: Supermarkets Are Having a Fire Sale on Data about You, *The Markup*, 16 February, accessed 12 April 2023: https://themarkup.org/privacy/2023/02/16/forget-milk-and-eggs-supermarkets -are-having-a-fire-sale-on-data-about-you.

14. Keegan (2023).

15. Marion Fourcade and Kieran Healy (2017), Seeing Like a Market, *Socio-Economic Review* 15 (1): 9–29.

16. Amba Kak and Sarah Myers West (2023), *AI Now 2023 Landscape: Confronting Tech Power* (New York: AI Now Institute).

17. Marx (1990, p. 253).

18. MIT Technology Review Custom and Oracle (2016), *The Rise of Data Capital*, accessed 12 April 2023: http://files.technologyreview.com/whitepapers /MIT_Oracle+Report-The_Rise_of_Data_Capital.pdf.

19. Marx (1990, p. 254).

20. Stanford Graduate School of Business (2017), Andrew Ng: Artificial Intelligence Is the New Electricity, YouTube, 2 February, accessed 12 April 2023: https://www.youtube.com/watch?v=21EiKfQYZXc.

21. Fourcade and Healy (2017, p. 13).

22. Kak and West (2023).

23. Pratyusha Ria Kalluri, William Agnew, Myra Cheng, Kentrell Owens, Luca Soldaini, and Abeba Birhane (2023), The Surveillance AI Pipeline, *arXiv*, 26 September, accessed 27 November 2023: https://arxiv.org/abs/2309.15084.

24. Kalluri et al. (2023, pp. 3–4).

25. Kalluri et al. (2023, p. 1).

26. Tekla S. Perry (2023), 10 Graphs That Sum Up the State of AI in 2023: The AI Index Tracks Breakthroughs, GPT Training Costs, Misuse, Funding, and More, *IEEE Spectrum*, 8 April, accessed 13 April 2023: https://spectrum.ieee.org/state-of-ai-2023.

27. Perry (2023).

28. Meredith Whittaker (2021), The Steep Cost of Capture, *ACM Interactions* 28 (6): 50–55.

29. Kalluri et al. (2023).

30. Donna Haraway (1988), Situated Knowledges: The Science Question in Feminism and the Privilege of Partial Perspective, *Feminist Studies* 14 (3): 581.

31. Jathan Sadowski and Evan Selinger (2014), Creating a Taxonomic Tool for Technocracy and Applying It to Silicon Valley, *Technology in Society* 38: 161–168.

32. Kalluri et al. (2023, p. 10).

33. Dan McQuillan (2018), Data Science as Machinic Neoplatonism, *Philosophy and Technology* 31: 261.

34. Salomé Viljoen (2021), A Relational Theory of Data Governance, *Yale Law Journal* 131 (2): 573–654.

35. Jenna Burrell (2016), How the Machine "Thinks": Understanding Opacity in Machine Learning Algorithms, *Big Data & Society* 3 (1): 1–12.

36. OpenAI (2023), *GPT-4 Technical Report*, accessed 24 April 2023: https://cdn.openai.com/papers/gpt-4.pdf.

37. Frank Pasquale (2015), *The Black Box Society: The Secret Algorithms That Control Money and Information* (Cambridge, MA: Harvard University Press).

38. Jason (2023), If You're in Crypto Pivot to AI, Twitter post, 9 June, accessed 24 November 2023: https://twitter.com/Jason/status/1666874821077250048?lang=en.

39. Kak and West (2023).

40. Kak and West (2023, p. 6).

41. Dieuwertje Luitse and Wiebke Denkena (2021), The Great Transformer: Examining the Role of Large Language Models in the Political Economy of AI, *Big Data & Society* 8 (2): 1–14; Whittaker (2021).

42. Henry Kissinger, Eric Schmidt, and Daniel Huttenlocher (2021), *The Age of AI: And Our Human Future* (New York: Little, Brown).

43. Kate Kaye (2022), Inside Eric Schmidt's Push to Profit from an AI Cold War with China, *Protocol*, 31 October, accessed 1 May 2023: https://www.protocol.com/enterprise/eric-schmidt-ai-china.

44. Evgeny Morozov (2023a), AI: The Key Battleground for Cold War 2.0? *Le Monde Diplomatique*, May, accessed 1 May 2023: https://mondediplo.com/2023/05/02china.

45. Alex Karp (2023), Our Oppenheimer Moment: The Creation of A.I. Weapons, *New York Times*, 25 July, accessed 3 August 2023: https://www.nytimes.com/2023/07/25/opinion/karp-palantir-artificial-intelligence.html.

46. Palmer Luckey (2018), Disrupting Defense: How Tech Can, and Should, Support National Security, Web Summit, 16 November, accessed 21 August 2023: https://www.youtube.com/watch?v=0G4FR1pepu4.

47. Patel and Moore (2018).

48. Emily Denton, Alex Hanna, Razvan Amironesei, Andrew Smart, and Hilary Nicole (2021), On the Genealogy of Machine Learning Datasets: A Critical History of ImageNet, *Big Data & Society* 8 (2): 1–14.

49. Kate Crawford and Trevor Paglen (2021), Excavating AI: The Politics of Images in Machine Learning Training Sets, *AI & Society* 36: 1105–1116.

50. Jenna Burrell and Marion Fourcade (2021), The Society of Algorithms, *Annual Review of Sociology* 47 (1): 213–237; Meredith Broussard (2018), *Artificial Unintelligence: How Computers Misunderstand the World* (Cambridge, MA: MIT Press); Cathy O'Neill (2016), *Weapons of Math Destruction* (New York: Crown).

51. Nithya Sambasivan, Shivani Kapania, Hannah Highfill, Diana Akrong, Praveen Paritosh, and Lora Aroyo (2021), "Everyone Wants to Do the Model Work, Not the Data Work": Data Cascades in High-Stakes AI, *CHI '21: Proceedings of the 2021 CHI Conference on Human Factors in Computing Systems*, Article no. 39.

52. Sarah Myers West (2019), Data Capitalism: Redefining the Logics of Surveillance and Privacy, *Business & Society* 58 (1): 20–41; Matthew Crain (2021), *Profit over Privacy: How Surveillance Advertising Conquered the Internet* (Minneapolis: University of Minnesota Press).

53. Kevin Schaul, Szu Yu Chen, and Nitasha Tiku (2023), Inside the Secret List of Websites That Make AI Like ChatGPT Sound Smart, *Washington Post*, 19 April, accessed 24 April 2023: https://www.washingtonpost.com/technology/interactive/2023/ai-chatbot-learning/.

54. Ina Fried (2023), 1 Big Thing: How We All Became AI's Brain Donors, *Axios*, 24 April, accessed 26 April 2023: https://www.axios.com/newsletters/axios-login-4fc52afb-3c90-4bea-ad3735b90c77ed9f.html.

55. Paresh Dave (2023), Stack Overflow Will Charge AI Giants for Training Data, *Wired*, 20 April, accessed 24 April 2023: https://www.wired.com/story/stack-overflow-will-charge-ai-giants-for-training-data/; Mike Isaac (2023), Reddit Wants to Get Paid for Helping to Teach Big A.I. Systems, *New York Times*, 18 April, accessed 24 April 2023: https://www.nytimes.com/2023/04/18/technology/reddit-ai-openai-google.html.

56. Will Knight (2023), OpenAI's CEO Says the Age of Giant AI Models Is Already Over, *Wired*, 17 April, accessed 24 April 2023: https://www.wired.com/story/openai-ceo-sam-altman-the-age-of-giant-ai-models-is-already-over/.

57. Sam Altman (2022), We Will Have to Monetize It Somehow at Some Point; the Compute Costs Are Eye-Watering, Twitter post, 5 December, accessed 24 April 2023: https://twitter.com/sama/status/1599669571795185665?lang=en.

58. OpenAI Charter, accessed 24 April 2023: https://openai.com/charter.

59. Sadowski (2019).

60. Rebecca Giblin and Cory Doctorow (2022), *Chokepoint Capitalism: How Big Tech and Big Content Captured Creative Labor Markets and How We'll Win Them Back* (Boston: Beacon Press).

61. Schaul et al. (2023).

62. Jathan Sadowski, Salomé Viljoen, and Meredith Whittaker (2021), Everyone Should Decide How Their Digital Data Are Used—Not Just Tech Companies, *Nature* 595: 169–171.

63. Marx (1990, p. 926).

64. Benjamin N. Jacobsen (2023), Machine Learning and the Politics of Synthetic Data, *Big Data & Society* 10 (1): 2.

65. Jacobsen (2023, p. 2).

66. Madhumita Murgia (2023), Why Computer-Made Data Is Being Used to Train AI Models, *Financial Times*, 19 July, accessed 21 July 2023: https://www.ft.com/content/053ee253-820e-453a-a1d5-0f24985258de.

67. Sina Alemohammad, Josue Casco-Rodriguez, Lorenzo Luzi, Ahmed Imtiaz Humayun, Hossein Babaei, Daniel LeJeune, Ali Siahkoohi, and Richard G. Baraniuk (2023), Self-Consuming Generative Models Go MAD, *arXiv*, 4 July, accessed 21 July 2023: https://arxiv.org/abs/2307.01850.

68. Alemohammad et al. (2023, p. 1).

Chapter Five. Labor

1. Tom Standage (2002), *The Turk: The Life and Times of the Famous Eighteenth-Century Chess-Playing Machine* (New York: Walker).

2. Gaby Wood (2002), Living Dolls: A Magical History of the Quest for Mechanical Life by Gaby Wood, *Guardian*, 16 February, accessed 16 May 2023: https://www.theguardian.com/books/2002/feb/16/extract.gabywood.

3. Paul Mozur (2018), Inside China's Dystopian Dreams: A.I., Shame and Lots of Cameras, *New York Times*, 8 July, accessed 16 May 2023: https://www.nytimes.com/2018/07/08/business/china-surveillance-technology.html.

4. Mary L. Gray and Siddharth Suri (2019), *Ghost Work: How to Stop Silicon Valley from Building a New Global Underclass* (Boston: Houghton Mifflin Harcourt); Sarah T. Roberts (2019), *Behind the Screen: Content Moderation in the Shadows of Social Media* (New Haven, CT: Yale University Press).

5. This chapter is a significantly expanded and updated version of an essay I wrote for *Real Life Magazine* in August 2018, where I first coined the term *Potemkin AI*. In a nice case of synchronicity, my friend and collaborator Astra Taylor independently wrote an essay for *Logic Magazine* that came out the same week of August 2018 where she coined the term *fauxtomation*, which analyzed this same issue from a complementary perspective. Not long after, social scientists Mary Gray and Siddharth Suri added more depth to the critical analysis of the "new global underclass" that supports Silicon Valley with their 2019 book, *Ghost Work*. This work all builds on earlier investigations by scholars like Lilly Irani into the hidden workforces and "data janitors" behind digital technologies (2015, The Cultural Work of Microwork, *New Media & Society* 17 [5]: 720–739). Together these concepts and their research all contribute to the same goals of materialist analysis that motivate this book.

6. Aaron Benanav (2020), *Automation and the Future of Work* (London: Verso).

7. Malcolm Harris (2023), *Palo Alto: A History of California, Capitalism, and the World* (New York: Little, Brown).

8. Veena Dubal (2023), On Algorithmic Wage Discrimination, UC San Francisco Research Paper, accessed 12 May 2023: http://dx.doi.org/10.2139/ssrn.4331080; Karen Gregory (2021), "My Life Is More Valuable Than This": Understanding Risk among On-Demand Food Couriers in Edinburgh, *Work,*

Employment and Society 35 (2): 316–331; Karen Gregory and Jathan Sadowski (2021), Biopolitical Platforms: The Perverse Virtues of Digital Labour, *Journal of Cultural Economy* 14 (6): 662–674; Niels van Doorn (2017), Platform Labor: On the Gendered and Racialized Exploitation of Low-Income Service Work in the "On-Demand" Economy, *Information, Communication & Society* 20: 898–914; Niels van Doorn and Adam Badger (2020), Platform Capitalism's Hidden Abode: Producing Data Assets in the Gig Economy, *Antipode* 52: 1475–1495.

9. Olivia Solon (2018), The Rise of "Pseudo-AI": How Tech Firms Quietly Use Humans to Do Bots' Work, *Guardian*, 6 July, accessed 16 May 2023: https://www.theguardian.com/technology/2018/jul/06/artificial-intelligence-ai-humans-bots-tech-companies; Astra Taylor (2018), The Automation Charade, *Logic*, 1 August, accessed 16 May 2023: https://logicmag.io/failure/the-automation-charade/; Moritz Altenried (2020), The Platform as Factory: Crowdwork and the Hidden Labour behind Artificial Intelligence, *Capital & Class* 44 (2): 145–158.

10. Douglas MacMillan (2018), Tech's "Dirty Secret": The App Developers Sifting through Your Gmail, *Wall Street Journal*, 2 July, accessed 16 May 2023: https://www.wsj.com/articles/techs-dirty-secret-the-app-developers-sifting-through-your-gmail-1530544442.

11. Casey Newton (2018), Facebook Is Shutting Down M, Its Personal Assistant Service That Combined Humans and AI, *The Verge*, 8 January, accessed 16 May 2023: https://www.theverge.com/2018/1/8/16856654/facebook-m-shutdown-bots-ai.

12. MacMillan (2018).

13. Aliya Ram (2019), Europe's AI Start-Ups Often Do Not Use AI, Study Finds, *Financial Times*, 5 March, accessed 9 May 2023: https://www.ft.com/content/21b19010-3e9f-11e9-b896-fe36ec32aece.

14. Ram (2019).

15. Cade Metz (2023), Generative A.I. Start-Up Cohere Valued at about $2 Billion in Funding Round, *New York Times*, 2 May, accessed 9 May 2023: https://www.nytimes.com/2023/05/02/technology/generative-ai-start-up-cohere-funding.html; Erin Griffith and Cade Metz (2023a), Anthropic, an A.I. Start-Up, Is Said to Be Close to Adding $300 Million, *New York Times*, 27 January, accessed 9 May 2023: https://www.nytimes.com/2023/01/27/technology/anthropic-ai-funding.html.

16. Erin Griffith and Cade Metz (2023b), "Let 1,000 Flowers Bloom": A.I. Funding Frenzy Escalates, *New York Times*, 14 March, accessed 9 May 2023: https://www.nytimes.com/2023/03/14/technology/ai-funding-boom.html.

17. Ingrid Lunden (2023), France's Mistral AI Blows in with a $113M Seed Round at a $260M Valuation to Take On OpenAI, *TechCrunch*, 14 June, accessed 15 June 2023: https://techcrunch.com/2023/06/13/frances-mistral-ai-blows-in-with-a-113m-seed-round-at-a-260m-valuation-to-take-on-openai.

18. Billy Perrigo (2023), Exclusive: OpenAI Used Kenyan Workers on Less Than $2 Per Hour to Make ChatGPT Less Toxic, *Time*, 18 January, accessed 9 May 2023: https://time.com/6247678/openai-chatgpt-kenya-workers/.

19. Reed Albergotti and Louise Matsakis (2023), OpenAI Has Hired an Army of Contractors to Make Basic Coding Obsolete, *Semafor*, 28 January, accessed 9 May 2023: https://www.semafor.com/article/01/27/2023/openai -has-hired-an-army-of-contractors-to-make-basic-coding-obsolete.

20. Astute Analytica (2023), *Global Data Annotation Tools Market, by Data Type, by Technology, by Device Type, by End-Users, Estimation and Forecast, 2017–2030*, accessed 9 May 2023: https://www.researchandmarkets.com/reports /5638906/global-data-annotation-tools-market-by-data?utm_campaign= 1741649+-+The+Worldwide+Data+Annotation+Tools+Industry+is+Expected +to+Reach+%2413.2+Billion+by+2030.

21. Neil Pollock and Robin Williams (2010), The Business of Expectations: How Promissory Organizations Shape Technology and Innovation, *Social Studies of Science* 40 (4): 525–548.

22. Mohammad Amir Anwar and Mark Graham (2020), Digital Labour at Economic Margins: African Workers and the Global Information Economy, *Review of African Political Economy* 47 (163): 95–105.

23. Irani (2015).

24. Michael Richardson, Jake Goldfein, and Thao Phan (2021), Privatising the Sky: Drone Delivery Promises Comfort and Speed, but at a Cost to Workers and Communities, *The Conversation*, 4 October, accessed 10 May 2021: https:// theconversation.com/privatising-the-sky-drone-delivery-promises-comfort-and-speed-but-at-a-cost-to-workers-and-communities-166960.

25. Mark Graham and Mohammad Amir Anwar (2019), The Global Gig Economy: Towards a Planetary Labour Market?, *First Mind* 24 (4), https:// doi.org/10.5210/fm.v24i4.9913; Nick Couldry and Ulises A. Mejias (2019),

Data Colonialism: Rethinking Big Data's Relation to the Contemporary Subject, *Television & New Media* 20 (4): 336–349; Jim Thatcher, David O'Sullivan, and Dillon Mahmoudi (2016), Data Colonialism through Accumulation by Dispossession: New Metaphors for Daily Data, *Environment and Planning D* 34 (6): 990–1006; Sadowski (2019).

26. Daniel Greene and Daniel Joseph (2015), The Digital Spatial Fix, *TripleC* 13 (2): 223–247; Rosa Luxemburg (1951), *The Accumulation of Capital* (New York: Monthly Review Press).

27. Michel Wahome and Mark Graham (2020), Spatially Shaped Imaginaries of the Digital Economy, *Information, Communication & Society* 23 (8): 1123–1138.

28. Karen Gregory and Miguel Paredes Maldonado (2020), Delivering Edinburgh: Uncovering the Digital Geography of Platform Labour in the City, *Information, Communication & Society* 23 (8): 1187–1202.

29. Burrell (2016).

30. Zachary C. Lipton and Jacob Steinhardt (2019), Troubling Trends in Machine Learning Scholarship: Some ML Papers Suffer from Flaws That Could Mislead the Public and Stymie Future Research, *ACM Queue* 17 (1): 45–77.

31. Anya E. R. Prince and Daniel Schwarcz (2020), Proxy Discrimination in the Age of Artificial Intelligence and Big Data, *Iowa Law Review* 105: 1257–1318.

32. Pasquale (2015).

33. Julia Angwin, Jeff Larson, Surya Mattu, and Lauren Kirchner (2016), Machine Bias, *ProPublica*, 23 May, accessed 16 May 2023: https://www.propublica.org/article/machine-bias-risk-assessments-in-criminal-sentencing.

34. Byung-Chul Han (2017), *Psychopolitics: Neoliberalism and New Technologies of Power*, trans. Erik Butler (London: Verso), p. 14.

35. Jathan Sadowski (2022b), Lords of the Platform: Rentier Capitalism and the Platform Economy, in *Platform Labour and Global Logistics: A Research Companion*, ed. Immanuel Ness (London: Routledge).

36. Christopher Intagliata (2011), The Origin of the Word "Robot," *Science Friday*, 22 April, accessed 16 May 2023: https://www.sciencefriday.com/segments/the-origin-of-the-word-robot/.

37. Kotaro Hara, Abigail Adams, Kristy Milland, Saiph Savage, Chris Callison-Burch, and Jeffrey P. Bigham (2018), A Data-Driven Analysis of Workers' Earnings on Amazon Mechanical Turk, *Proceedings of the 2018 CHI Conference on Human Factors in Computing Systems (CHI '18)*, Paper 449, pp. 1–14.

38. Leslie Hook (2016), The Humans behind Mechanical Turk's Artificial Intelligence, *Financial Times*, 26 October, accessed 16 May 2023: https://www.ft.com/content/17518034-6f77-11e6-9ac1-1055824ca907.

39. Ariel Bogle (2022), Behind "Miracle" AI Is an Army of "Ghost Workers"—and They're Speaking Out about Appen, *ABC News*, 14 October, accessed 10 May 2023: https://www.abc.net.au/news/science/2022-10-14/artificial-intelligence-ai-appen-data-labelling-ghost-workers/101531084.

40. Paola Tubaro, Antonio A. Casilli, and Marion Coville (2020), The Trainer, the Verifier, the Imitator: Three Ways in Which Human Platform Workers Support Artificial Intelligence, *Big Data & Society* 7 (1): 1–12.

41. Irani (2015, p. 730).

42. Graham and Anwar (2019, n.p.).

43. Irani (2015, p. 723).

44. David Harvey (2014), *Seventeen Contradictions and the End of Capitalism* (London: Profile Books).

45. Carl Benedikt Frey and Michael A. Osborne (2013), The Future of Employment: How Susceptible Are Jobs to Computerisation?, accessed 12 May 2023: https://www.oxfordmartin.ox.ac.uk/downloads/academic/The_Future_of_Employment.pdf.

46. Tyna Eloundou, Sam Manning, Pamela Mishkin, and Daniel Rock (2023), GPTs Are GPTs: An Early Look at the Labor Market Impact Potential of Large Language Models, *arXiv*, 23 March, accessed 12 May 2023: https://arxiv.org/abs/2303.10130.

47. Aaron Benanav (2023), The Revolution Will Not Be Brought to You by ChatGPT, *New Statesman*, 11 April, accessed 12 May 2023: https://www.newstatesman.com/ideas/2023/04/revolution-brought-chatgpt-artificial-intelligence.

48. Benanav (2020).

49. Martin Krzywdzinski (2021), Automation, Digitalization, and Changes in Occupational Structures in the Automobile Industry in Germany, Japan, and the United States: A Brief History from the Early 1990s until 2018, *Industrial and Corporate Change* 30 (3): 499–535.

50. Krzywdzinski (2021, p. 508).

51. Marx (1990, p. 548).

52. Marx (1990, p. 548).

53. Alessandro Delfanti and Bronwyn Frey (2020), Humanly Extended Automation or the Future of Work Seen through Amazon Patents, *Science, Technology & Human Values* 46 (3): 655.

54. Gary Becker (1993), *Human Capital: A Theoretical and Empirical Analysis, with Special Reference to Education* (3rd ed.) (Chicago: University of Chicago Press), p. 16.

55. Laura Preston's personal website, accessed 30 November 2023: https://www.laurahpreston.com/.

56. Laura Preston (2023), Human_Fallback, *n+1 magazine*, accessed 15 May 2023: https://www.nplusonemag.com/issue-44/essays/human_fallback/.

Chapter Six. Landlords

1. Giblin and Doctrow (2022).

2. Adam Smith (1999), *The Wealth of Nations, Books I–III* (London: Penguin Classics); David Ricardo (2004), *The Principles of Political Economy and Taxation* (New York: Dover); Marx (1993a); John Maynard Keynes (1936), *The General Theory of Employment, Interest and Money* (New York: Harcourt, Brace); Harvey (2006); Anne Haila (1988), Land as a Financial Asset: The Theory of Urban Rent as a Mirror of Economic Transformation, *Antipode* 20 (2): 79–101; Brett Christophers (2020), *Rentier Capitalism: Who Owns the Economy, and Who Pays for It?* (London: Verso).

3. Brett Christophers (2010), On Voodoo Economics: Theorising Relations of Property, Value, and Contemporary Capitalism, *Transactions of the Institute of British Geographers* 35 (1): 94–108.

4. Michael Neocosmos (1986), Marx's Third Class: Capitalist Landed Property and Capitalist Development, *Journal of Peasant Studies* 13 (3): 5–44.

5. Marx (1993a, p. 1023).

6. Mau (2023, introduction) (epub).

7. Heather Somerville (2021), Silicon Valley's Deal Machine Is Cranking: "I've Never Seen It This Frenzied," *Wall Street Journal*, 21 April, accessed 27 April 2021: https://www.wsj.com/articles/startups-crack-records-as-more-money-flows-to-silicon-valley-11619004801.

8. United Nations Conference on Trade and Development (2019), *Digital Economy Report: Value Creation and Capture; Implications for Developing Countries* (Geneva: United Nations).

9. Paul E. Steiger (2014), What a Difference 25 Years Makes, *CNBC*, 2 May, accessed 10 July: https://www.cnbc.com/2014/04/29/what-a-difference-25-years-makes.html.

10. Lyle Daly (2023), The Largest Companies by Market Cap in 2023, *The Motley Fool*, 7 July, accessed 10 July 2023: https://www.fool.com/research/largest-companies-by-market-cap/.

11. Kean Birch (2020b), Technoscience Rent: Toward a Theory of Rentiership for Technoscientific Capitalism, *Science, Technology, and Human Values* 45 (1): 3–33; David Harvey (2010), *The Enigma of Capital and the Crises of Capitalism* (London: Profile).

12. Nick Srnicek (2017), *Platform Capitalism* (Cambridge: Polity); Paul Langley and Andrew Leyshon (2017), Platform Capitalism: The Intermediation and Capitalisation of Digital Economic Circulation, *Finance and Society* 3 (1): 11–31; Jean-Christophe Plantin, Carl Lagoze, Paul N. Edwards, and Christian Sandvig (2018), Infrastructure Studies Meet Platform Studies in the Age of Google and Facebook, *New Media and Society* 20 (1): 293–310.

13. Kean Birch (2020a), Automated Neoliberalism? The Digital Organisation of Markets in Technoscientific Capitalism, *New Formations: A Journal of Culture/Theory/Politics* 100: 10–27.

14. Kean Birch (2015), *We Have Never Been Neoliberal* (Alresford, UK: Zero Books), p. 112.

15. Callum Ward and Manuel B. Aalbers (2016), "The Shitty Rent Business": What's the Point of Land Rent Theory? *Urban Studies* 53 (9): 1760–1783.

16. Alex Ivanovs (2023), Zoom's Updated Terms of Service Permit Training AI on User Content without Opt-Out, *Stack Diary*, 7 August, accessed 8 August 2023: https://stackdiary.com/zoom-terms-now-allow-training-ai-on-user-content-with-no-opt-out/.

17. Samantha Cole (2023), Zoom Changes TOS to Say It Won't Train AI on Your Calls "without Your Consent" after Backlash, *Vice Motherboard*, 8 August, accessed 17 August 2023: https://www.vice.com/en/article/wxjgvy/zoom-changes-tos-to-say-it-wont-train-ai-on-your-calls-without-your-consent-after-backlash.

18. Brian Merchant (2023b), These Apps and Websites Use Your Data to Train AI: You're Probably Using One Right Now, *Los Angeles Times*, 16 August, accessed 17 August 2023: https://www.latimes.com/business/technology/story/2023-08-16/column-its-not-just-zoom-how-websites-and-apps-harvest-your-data-to-build-ai.

19. Kean Birch (2016), Market vs. Contract? The Implications of Contractual Theories of Corporate Governance to the Analysis of Neoliberalism, *Ephemera: Theory & Politics in Organizations* 16 (1): 107-133; Eyal Zamir (2014), Contract Law and Theory: Three Views of the Cathedral, *University of Chicago Law Review* 81: 2077-2123.

20. Yolande Strengers, Jathan Sadowski, Zhuying Li, Anna Shimshak, and Florian "Floyd" Mueller (2021), What Can HCI Learn from Sexual Consent? A Feminist Process of Embodied Consent for Interactions with Emerging Technologies, *CHI '21: Proceedings of the 2021 CHI Conference on Human Factors in Computing Systems*, Article no. 405, pp. 1-13.

21. Brett Christophers (2019), The Problem of Rent, *Critical Historical Studies* 6 (2): 303-323.

22. Guy Standing (2016), *The Corruption of Capitalism: Why Rentiers Thrive and Work Does Not Pay* (London: Biteback).

23. Mariana Mazzucato (2018), *The Value of Everything: Making and Taking in the Global Economy* (London: Allen Lane).

24. Evgeny Morozov (2022), Critique of Techno-Feudal Reason, *New Left Review* 133/134 (1): 89-126.

25. This chapter is a significantly expanded and updated version of my article: Sadowski (2020b).

26. Sadowski (2020c).

27. Ward and Aalbers (2016, p. 1762).

28. Pete Bigelow (2015), General Motors Says It Owns Your Car's Software, *Autoblog*, 20 May, accessed 20 July 2023: http://www.autoblog.com/2015/05/20/general-motors-says-owns-your-car-software/.

29. Luis F. Alvarez Leon (2019), Counter-Mapping the Spaces of Autonomous Driving, *Cartographic Perspectives* 92 (1): 10-23.

30. Jason Koebler (2018), Tractor-Hacking Farmers Are Leading a Revolt against Big Tech's Repair Monopolies, *Vice Motherboard*, 15 February, accessed 20 July 2023: https://www.vice.com/en/article/kzp7ny/tractor-hacking-right-to-repair.

31. Howard (2018).

32. Matthew Gault and Jason Koebler (2021), Biden's Right to Repair Order Covers Electronics, Not Just Tractors, *Vice Motherboard*, 9 July, accessed 12 July 2023: https://www.vice.com/en/article/y3d5yb/bidens-right-to-repair-executive-order-covers-electronics-not-just-tractors; Jason Koebler (2023), Biden Administration Changes Mind, Says Car Companies Shouldn't Ignore Overwhelmingly Popular Car Repair Law Anymore, *404 Media*, 22 August, accessed 23 August 2023: https://www.404media.co/biden-administration-changes-mind-says-car-companies-shouldnt-ignore-overwhelmingly-popular-car-repair-law-anymore/.

33. Jason Koebler (2020), Why Repair Techs Are Hacking Ventilators with DIY Dongles from Poland, *Vice Motherboard*, 9 July, accessed 25 July 2023: https://www.vice.com/en/article/3azv9b/why-repair-techs-are-hacking-ventilators-with-diy-dongles-from-poland.

34. Cory Doctorow (2023), *The Internet Con: How to Seize the Means of Computation* (London: Verso), p. 63.

35. Megan Nethercote (2023), Platform Landlords: Renters, Personal Data and New Digital Footholds of Urban Control, *Digital Geography and Society* 5 (December): 100060.

36. Joe Shaw (2018), Platform Real Estate: Theory and Practice of New Urban Real Estate Markets, *Urban Geography* 41 (8): 1037–1064.

37. Desiree Fields (2022), Automated Landlord: Digital Technologies and Post-Crisis Financial Accumulation, *Environment and Planning A: Economy and Space* 54 (1): 160–181.

38. Daniel Greene (2022), Landlords of the Internet: Big Data and Big Real Estate, *Social Studies of Science* 52 (6): 904–927.

39. Shaw (2018, pp. 1039–1040).

40. Dallas Rogers (2017), *The Geopolitics of Real Estate: Reconfiguring Property, Capital, and Rights* (London: Rowman & Littlefield).

41. Giulia Dal Maso, Shanthi Robertson, and Dallas Rogers (2019), Cultural Platform Capitalism: Extracting Value from Cultural Asymmetries in RealTech, *Social and Cultural Geography* 22 (4): 565–580.

42. Dallas Rogers (2016), Uploading Real Estate, in *Housing and Home Unbound: Intersections in Economics, Environment, and Politics in Australia*, ed. N. Cook, A. Davison, and L. Crabtree (Melbourne: Routledge), pp. 23–38.

43. Kevin Fox Gotham (2009), Creating Liquidity Out of Spatial Fixity: The Secondary Circuit of Capital and the Subprime Mortgage Crisis, *International Journal of Urban and Regional Research* 33 (2): 355–371; Kathe Newman (2009), Post-Industrial Widgets: Capital Flows and the Production of the Urban, *International Journal of Urban and Regional Research* 33 (2): 314–331.

44. Fields (2022).

45. Erin McElroy and Manon Vergerio (2022), Automating Gentrification: Landlord Technologies and Housing Justice Organizing in New York City Homes, *Environment and Planning D: Society and Space* 40 (4): 607–626.

46. Heather Vogell (2022), Rent Going Up? One Company's Algorithm Could Be Why, *ProPublica*, 15 October, accessed 20 July 2023: https://www.propublica.org/article/yieldstar-rent-increase-realpage-rent.

47. Vogell (2022).

48. Vogell (2022).

49. Joe Beswick, Georgia Alexandri, Michael Byrne, Sònia Vives-Miró, Desiree Fields, Stuart Hodkinson, and Michael Janoschka (2016), Speculating on London's Housing Future: The Rise of Global Corporate Landlords in "Post-Crisis" Urban Landscapes, *City* 20 (2): 321–341.

50. Desiree Fields (2018), Constructing a New Asset Class: Property-Led Financial Accumulation after the Crisis, *Economic Geography* 94 (2): 118–140.

51. Fields (2018, p. 120).

52. Nethercote (2023).

53. Fields (2022, p. 176).

54. Greene (2022, p. 904).

55. Drew FitzGerald (2014), Equinix Inc., the Internet's Biggest Landlord, *Wall Street Journal*, 29 October, accessed 24 July 2023: https://www.wsj.com/articles/equinix-inc-the-internets-biggest-landlord-1414451918.

56. Greene (2022, p. 919).

57. Greene (2022, p. 915).

58. Greene (2022, p. 920).

Chapter Seven. Risk

1. Greta R. Krippner (2005), The Financialization of the American Economy, *Socio-Economic Review* 3: 173–208; Mike Konczal and Nell Abernathy

(2015), *Defining Financialization* (New York: Roosevelt Institute); Paul Langley (2021), Assets and Assetization in Financialized Capitalism, *Review of International Political Economy* 28 (2): 382–393.

2. Wendy Brown (2015), *Undoing the Demos: Neoliberalism's Stealth Revolution* (Cambridge, MA: MIT Press); David Harvey (2008), *A Brief History of Neoliberalism* (Oxford: Oxford University Press); Maurizio Lazzarato (2009), Neoliberalism in Action: Inequality, Insecurity and the Reconstitution of the Social, *Theory, Culture & Society* 26 (6): 109–133; Jamie Peck and Adam Tickell (2002), Neoliberalizing Space, *Antipode* 34 (3): 380–404.

3. Christina Scharff (2016), The Psychic Life of Neoliberalism: Mapping the Contours of Entrepreneurial Subjectivity, *Theory, Culture & Society* 33 (6): 107–122; Gregory and Sadowski (2021); Malcolm Harris (2017), *Kids These Days: Human Capital and the Making of Millennials* (New York: Little, Brown).

4. I have done extensive work on the political economy of FIRE and technology. For more, see the following articles: Sophia Maalsen and Jathan Sadowski (2019), The Smart Home on FIRE: Amplifying and Accelerating Domestic Discipline, *Surveillance & Society* 16 (1/2): 118–124; Jathan Sadowski, Yolande Strengers, and Jenny Kennedy (2024), More Work for Big Mother: Revaluing Care and Control in Smart Homes, *Environment and Planning A: Economy and Space* 56 (1): 330–345; Jathan Sadowski (2022a), FIRE Watchers: The Centrality of Surveillance (Studies) for Finance, Insurance, Real Estate, *Surveillance & Society* 20 (4): 450–454; Sadowski and Beegle (2023); Jathan Sadowski (2023), Total Life Insurance: Logics of Anticipatory Control and Actuarial Governance in Insurance Technology, *Social Studies of Science*, https://doi.org/10.1177/03063127231186437.

5. Marion Fourcade and Kieran Healy (2013), Classification Situations: Life-Chances in the Neoliberal Era, *Accounting, Organizations and Society* 38 (8): 559–572.

6. Rob Aitken (2017), "All Data Is Credit Data": Constituting the Unbanked, *Competition & Change* 21 (4): 274–300.

7. Prince and Schwarcz (2020).

8. Angwin et al. (2016).

9. Michel Foucault (1980), *Power/Knowledge: Selected Interviews and Other Writings, 1972–1977* (New York: Vintage).

10. Geoffrey Bowker and Susan Leigh Star (2000), *Sorting Things Out: Classification and Its Consequences* (Cambridge, MA: MIT Press).

11. Brown (2015, p. 123).

12. Brown (2015, p. 124).

13. Daniela Gabor (2021), The Wall Street Consensus, *Development and Change* 52: 429–459; Daniela Gabor (2022), The Wall Street Consensus at COP27, *Phenomenal World*, 19 November, accessed 3 August 2023: https://www.phenomenalworld.org/analysis/the-wall-street-consensus-at-cop27/.

14. Gabor (2021, p. 430).

15. Gabor (2021, p. 429).

16. Vanessa Houlder and Nathalie Thomas (2023), Lex In Depth: How Investors Are Underpricing Climate Risks, *Financial Times*, 17 August, accessed 18 August 2023: https://www.ft.com/content/899472a8-e5e2-4fde-bc91-7e548ba35294.

17. Margot E. Kaminski (2023), Regulating the Risks of AI, *Boston University Law Review* 103: 1347–1411.

18. Kaminski (2023, p. 1352).

19. Kaminski (2023, p. 1352).

20. *xkcd* (2017), Machine Learning, 17 May, accessed 7 August 2023: https://xkcd.com/1838/. The "Pile" is also the name for one of the largest and widest used datasets of English text for training large language models. It is made up of nearly two dozen other large datasets—including Wikipedia, arXiv, GitHub, and YouTube subtitles—all *compiled* together. Note that the *xkcd* comic came out years before the Pile was created, so "stir the pile" is just a nice coincidence, not a direct reference.

21. Louise Amoore (2020), *Cloud Ethics: Algorithms and the Attributes of Ourselves and Others* (Durham, NC: Duke University Press), pp. 14, 81.

22. Donald Rumsfeld (2002), DoD News Briefing: Secretary Rumsfeld and Gen. Myers, US Department of Defense, 12 February, accessed 7 August 2023: https://archive.md/20180320091111/http://archive.defense.gov/Transcripts/Transcript.aspx?TranscriptID=2636#selection-401.0-406.0.

23. Sarah Brayne (2017), Big Data Surveillance: The Case of Policing, *American Sociological Review* 82 (5): 977–1008; Philippa Metcalfe and Lina Dencik (2019), The Politics of Big Borders: Data (In)Justice and the Governance Of Refugees, *First Monday* 24 (4): n.p.; Sadowski (2020c).

24. Justin Jouvenal (2016), The New Way Police Are Surveilling You: Calculating Your Threat "Score," *Washington Post*, 10 January, accessed 8 August 2023: https://www.washingtonpost.com/local/public-safety/the-new-way

-police-are-surveilling-you-calculating-your-threat-score/2016/01/10
/e42bccac-8e15-11e5-baf4-bdf37355daoc_story.html.

25. Aitken (2017).

26. Zest AI (n.d.), AI-Driven Credit Underwriting Software, accessed 8 August 2023: https://www.zest.ai/.

27. Duncan Minty (2022), Why the Clearview Ruling Matters to Insurers, *Ethics and Insurance*, 25 May, accessed 8 August 2023: https://www.ethicsand insurance.info/why-the-clearview-ruling-matters-to-insurers/.

28. Barbara Kiviat (2019), The Moral Limits of Predictive Practices: The Case of Credit-Based Insurance Scores, *American Sociological Review* 84 (6): 1134–1158.

29. Dan Bouk (2015), *How Our Days Became Numbered: Risk and the Rise of the Statistical Individual* (Chicago: University of Chicago Press); Caley Horan (2021), *Insurance Era: Risk, Governance, and the Privatization of Security in Postwar America* (Chicago: University of Chicago Press).

30. Eva Constantaras, Gabriel Geiger, Justin-Casimir Braun, Dhruv Mehrotra, and Htet Aung (2023), Inside the Suspicion Machine, *Wired*, 6 March, accessed 8 August 2023: https://www.wired.com/story/welfare-state-algorithms/.

31. Constantaras et al. (2023, n.p.).

32. Manon Romain, Adrien Senecat, Soizic Pénicaud, Gabriel Geiger, and Justin-Casimir Braun (2023), How We Investigated France's Mass Profiling Machine, *Lighthouse Reports*, 4 December, accessed 31 December 2023: https:// www.lighthousereports.com/methodology/how-we-investigated-frances -mass-profiling-machine/.

33. Virginia Eubanks (2018), *Automating Inequality: How High-Tech Tools Profile, Police, and Punish the Poor* (New York: St. Martin's Press).

34. Julia Dressel and Hany Farid (2018), The Accuracy, Fairness, and Limits of Predicting Recidivism, *Science Advances* 4 (1): 1.

35. Sun-ha Hong (2023), Prediction as Extraction of Discretion, *Big Data & Society* 10 (1): 1–11.

36. Langdon Winner (1980), Do Artifacts Have Politics?, *Daedalus* 109 (1): 121–136, pp. 125–126.

37. Jonathan Simon (1988), The Ideological Effects of Actuarial Practices, *Law & Society Review* 22 (4): 771–800.

38. Bouk (2015); Horan (2021).

39. Bouk (2015, p. 56, original emphasis).

40. Bouk (2015, pp. 78–79).

41. Bouk (2015, p. 84).

42. Regina Austin (1983), The Insurance Classification Controversy, *University of Pennsylvania Law Review* 131 (3): 517–583.

43. EIOPA (2019), *Big Data Analytics in Motor and Health Insurance: Thematic Review*, p. 38, accessed 10 August 2023: https://register.eiopa.europa.eu /Publications/EIOPA_BigDataAnalytics_ThematicReview_April2019.pdf.

44. EIOPA (2019, p. 38).

45. Laurence Barry and Arthur Charpentier (2020), Personalization as a Promise: Can Big Data Change the Practice of Insurance? *Big Data & Society* 7 (1): 1–12; Liz McFall, Gert Meyers, and Ine Van Hoyweghen (2020), The Personalisation of Insurance: Data, Behaviour and Innovation, *Big Data & Society* 7 (2): 1–11; Sadowski (2023).

46. Greta R. Krippner (2023), Unmasked: A History of the Individualization of Risk, *Sociological Theory* 41 (2): 83–104.

47. Peter Littlejohns (2020), Aviva's Colm Holmes on Claims Inflation, Stupid Drivers and Commercial Insurance, *NS Insurance*, 7 February, accessed 16 August 2023: https://www.nsinsur-ance.com/analysis/aviva-colm-holmes-claims-inflation/.

48. Greta R. Krippner and Daniel Hirschman (2022), The Person of the Category: The Pricing of Risk and the Politics of Classification in Insurance and Credit, *Theory and Society* 51: 685–727.

49. Bouk (2015, p. 56).

50. Sadowski (2023).

51. Rick Swedloff (2020), The New Regulatory Imperative for Insurance, *Boston College Law Review* 61 (6): 2031–2084.

52. Zofia Bednarz and Kayleen Manwaring (2022), Hidden Depths: The Effects of Extrinsic Data Collection on Consumer Insurance Contracts, *Computer Law & Security Review* 45: 1–23.

53. Angela Zeier Röschmann, Matthias Erny, and Joël Wagner (2022), On the (Future) Role of On-Demand Insurance: Market Landscape, Business Model and Customer Perception, *The Geneva Papers on Risk and Insurance— Issues and Practice* 47: 603–642.

54. Duncan Minty (2021), Is Settlement Walking Now Part of UK Insurance, *Ethics and Insurance*, 18 March, accessed 16 August 2023: https:// www.ethicsandinsurance.info/settlement-walking/.

55. Patrick Rucker, Maya Miller, and David Armstrong (2023), How Cigna Saves Millions by Having Its Doctors Reject Claims without Reading Them, *ProPublica*, 25 March, accessed 16 August 2023: https://www.propublica.org/article/cigna-pxdx-medical-health-insurance-rejection-claims.

56. Burrell (2016); Prince and Schwarcz (2020).

57. Bouk (2015, p. xx).

58. Krippner (2023, p. 84).

59. François Ewald (2020), *The Birth of Solidarity: The History of the French Welfare State*, ed. Melinda Cooper (Durham, NC: Duke University Press).

60. Krippner (2023, p. 88).

61. Krippner (2023, p. 89).

62. For more in-depth work on behavioral insurance, see Jathan Sadowski, Kelly Lewis, and Zofia Bednarz (2024), Risk, Value, Vitality: The Moral Economy of a Global Behavioral Insurance Platform, *Economy and Society*, https://doi.org/10.1080/03085147.2024.2328992; Hugo Jeanningros and Liz McFall (2020), The Value of Sharing: Branding and Behaviour in a Life and Health Insurance Company, *Big Data & Society* 7 (2): 1–15; Gert Meyers and Ine Van Hoyweghen (2018), Enacting Actuarial Fairness in Insurance: From Fair Discrimination to Behaviour-Based Fairness, *Science as Culture* 27 (4): 413–438; Gert Meyers and Ine Van Hoyweghen (2020), "Happy Failures": Experimentation with Behaviour-Based Personalisation in Car Insurance, *Big Data & Society* 7 (1): 1–14; Maiju Tanninen, Turo-Kimmo Lehtonen, and Minna Ruckenstein (2021), Tracking Lives, Forging Markets, *Journal of Cultural Economy* 14 (4): 449–463.

63. Sadowski et al. (2024).

64. Jeremy Houghton Shuwen Wong (2020), Case Study—AIA Vitality, *Shared Value Project*, accessed 5 July 2023: https://sharedvalue.org.au/wp-content/uploads/2020/08/AIA-Vitality_Case-Study.pdf.

65. Richard Ericson, Aaron Doyle, and Dean Barry (2003), *Insurance as Governance* (Toronto: University of Toronto Press).

Chapter Eight. Futures

1. See, for example: Jenny Andersson (2018), *The Future of the World: Futurology, Futurists, and the Struggle for the Post Cold War Imagination* (Oxford: Oxford University Press); Jenny Andersson (2020), Ghost in a Shell: The Scenario Tool and the World Making of Royal Dutch Shell, *Business History Review*

94: 729–751; Jennifer M. Gidley (2017), *The Future: A Very Short Introduction* (Oxford: Oxford University Press); Sun-ha Hong (2022), Predictions without Futures, *History and Theory* 61 (3): 371–390; Heonju Son (2015), The History of Western Future Studies: An Exploration of the Intellectual Traditions and Three-Phase Periodization, *Futures* 66: 120–133.

2. Andersson (2018).

3. Andersson (2020).

4. Andersson (2020, p. 730).

5. Andersson (2020, pp. 730–731).

6. David Graeber (2012), Of Flying Cars and the Declining Rate of Profit, *The Baffler*, March, accessed 4 September 2023: https://thebaffler.com/salvos /of-flying-cars-and-the-declining-rate-of-profit; Devon Powers (2019), *On Trend: The Business of Forecasting the Future* (Champaign-Urbana: University of Illinois Press); Fred Turner (2006), *From Counterculture to Cyberculture Stewart Brand, the Whole Earth Network, and the Rise of Digital Utopianism* (Chicago: University of Chicago Press).

7. Andersson (2018, p. 10).

8. Yiwen Lu (2023), Generative A.I. Can Add $4.4 Trillion in Value to Global Economy, Study Says, *New York Times*, 14 June, accessed 29 August 2023: https://www.nytimes.com/2023/06/14/technology/generative-ai-global -economy.html.

9. McKinsey & Company (2022), Value Creation in the Metaverse, accessed 29 August 2023: https://www.mckinsey.com/capabilities/growth-marketing -and-sales/our-insights/value-creation-in-the-metaverse.

10. Pollock and Williams (2010).

11. Borup et al. (2006); Adam Hedgecoe (2010), Bioethics and the Reinforcement of Socio-Technical Expectations, *Social Studies of Science* 40 (2): 163–186; David Kirby (2010), The Future Is Now: Diegetic Prototypes and the Role of Popular Films in Generating Real-World Technological Development, *Social Studies of Science* 40 (1): 41–70; Harro van Lente (2012), Navigating Foresight in a Sea of Expectations: Lessons from the Sociology of Expectations, *Technology Analysis and Strategic Management* 24 (8): 769–782; Pollock and Williams (2010); Cynthia Selin (2007), Expectations and the Emergence of Nanotechnology, *Science, Technology & Human Values* 32 (2): 196–220; Cynthia Selin (2008), The Sociology of the Future: Tracing Stories of Technology and Time, *Sociology Compass* 2 (6): 1878–1895.

12. Borup et al. (2006, pp. 285–286).

13. Pollock and Williams (2010, p. 548).

14. Mau (2023, chapter 1) (epub).

15. van Lente (2012, p. 773).

16. Michel Foucault (2001), The Subject and Power, in *Power*, ed. James D. Faubion (New York: The New Press), p. 341.

17. Fisher (2010).

18. Borup et al. (2006); van Lente, Spitters, and Peine (2013); Martin Steinert and Larry Leifer (2010), Scrutinizing Gartner's Hype Cycle Approach, *Proceedings of PICMET 2010 Technology Management for Global Economic Growth*, Phuket, Thailand, pp. 1–13, https://ieeexplore.ieee.org/document/5603442.

19. Powers (2019, p. 3).

20. Sadowski and Bendor (2019).

21. Joel Dinerstein (2006), Technology and Its Discontents: On the Verge of the Posthuman, *American Quarterly* 58 (3): 569, 573.

22. Hong (2022, p. 372).

23. This section is derived from Jathan Sadowski (2021a), Future Schlock, *Real Life Magazine*, 25 January, accessed 5 September 2023: https://reallifemag.com/future-schlock/.

24. Morozov (2013).

25. Steven Levy (2023), What OpenAI Really Wants, *Wired*, 5 September 2023, accessed 8 September 2023: https://www.wired.com/story/what-openai-really-wants/.

26. *Forbes* (2023), Elon Musk, accessed 6 September 2023: https://www.forbes.com/profile/elon-musk/?list=billionaires&sh=215a10767999.

27. Erik Olin Wright (2010), *Envisioning Real Utopias* (London: Verso Books).

28. Erik Olin Wright (2013), Transforming Capitalism through Real Utopias, *American Sociological Review* 78: 1–25.

29. Evgeny Morozov (2023b), The Lessons of Chile's Struggle against Big Tech, *New Statesman*, 9 September, accessed 11 September 2023: https://www.newstatesman.com/the-weekend-essay/2023/09/salvador-allende-fight-big-tech.

30. David Graeber and David Wengrow (2022), *The Dawn of Everything: A New History of Humanity* (London: Penguin Press).

31. Graeber and Wengrow (2022).

32. Marc Andreessen (2020), It's Time to Build, *a16z*, 18 April, accessed 7 September 2023: https://a16z.com/its-time-to-build/.

33. Marc Andreessen (2023b), Why AI Will Save the World, *a16z*, 6 June, accessed 7 September 2023: https://a16z.com/ai-will-save-the-world/.

34. Andreessen (2023a).

35. David Graeber (2013), A Practical Utopian's Guide to the Coming Collapse, *The Baffler*, April, accessed 7 September 2023: https://thebaffler.com/salvos/a-practical-utopians-guide-to-the-coming-collapse.

36. David Ciepley (2013), Beyond Public and Private: Toward a Political Theory of the Corporation, *American Political Science Review* 107 (1): 139–158.

37. Quinn Slobodian (2023), *Crack-Up Capitalism: Market Radicals and the Dream of a World without Democracy* (New York: Metropolitan Books).

38. Anne Case and Angus Deaton (2020), *Deaths of Despair and the Future of Capitalism* (Princeton, NJ: Princeton University Press).

39. Walter Benjamin (2003), *Selected Writings, Volume 4, 1938–1940*, ed. H. Eiland and M. W. Jennings (Cambridge, MA: Harvard University Press), p. 402.

40. Marx (1843).

41. Merchant (2023c).

Bibliography

Aitken, Rob (2017). "All Data Is Credit Data": Constituting the Unbanked. *Competition & Change* 21 (4): 274–300.

Alarazi, Hannah (2021). Ex-Theranos CEO's Defense Emerges in Pre-Trial Battle. *Law360*, 4 May. Accessed 7 February 2023: https://www.law360.com/articles/1381385/ex-theranos-ceo-s-defense-emerges-in-pre-trial-battle

Albergotti, Reed, and Louise Matsakis (2023). OpenAI Has Hired an Army of Contractors to Make Basic Coding Obsolete. *Semafor*, 28 January. Accessed 9 May 2023: https://www.semafor.com/article/01/27/2023/openai-has-hired-an-army-of-contractors-to-make-basic-coding-obsolete

Alemohammad, Sina, Josue Casco-Rodriguez, Lorenzo Luzi, Ahmed Imtiaz Humayun, Hossein Babaei, Daniel LeJeune, Ali Siahkoohi, and Richard G. Baraniuk (2023). Self-Consuming Generative Models Go MAD. *arXiv*, 4 July. Accessed 21 July 2023: https://arxiv.org/abs/2307.01850

Allen, Hilary J. (2022). DeFi: Shadow Banking 2.0? *William & Mary Law Review*. https://doi.org/10.2139/ssrn.4038788

Altenried, Moritz (2020). The Platform as Factory: Crowdwork and the Hidden Labour behind Artificial Intelligence. *Capital & Class* 44 (2): 145–158.

Altman, Sam (2022). We Will Have to Monetize It Somehow at Some Point; the Compute Costs Are Eye-Watering. Twitter post, 5 December. Accessed 24 April 2023: https://twitter.com/sama/status/1599669571795185665

Alvarez Leon, Luis F. (2019). Counter-Mapping the Spaces of Autonomous Driving. *Cartographic Perspectives* 92 (1): 10–23.

Amoore, Louise (2020). *Cloud Ethics: Algorithms and the Attributes of Ourselves and Others*. Durham, NC: Duke University Press.

Andersson, Jenny (2018). *The Future of the World: Futurology, Futurists, and the Struggle for the Post–Cold War Imagination*. Oxford: Oxford University Press.

Andersson, Jenny (2020). Ghost in a Shell: The Scenario Tool and the World Making of Royal Dutch Shell. *Business History Review* 94: 729–751.

Andreessen, Marc (2020). It's Time to Build. *a16z*, 18 April. Accessed 7 September 2023: https://a16z.com/its-time-to-build/

Andreessen, Marc (2023a). The Techno-Optimist Manifesto. *a16z*, October 16. Accessed 23 November 2023: https://a16z.com/the-techno-optimist -manifesto/

Andreessen, Marc (2023b). Why AI Will Save the World. *a16z*, 6 June. Accessed 7 September 2023: https://a16z.com/ai-will-save-the-world/

Angwin, Julia, Jeff Larson, Surya Mattu, and Lauren Kirchner (2016). Machine Bias. *ProPublica*, 23 May. Accessed 16 May 2023: https://www .propublica.org/article/machine-bias-risk-assessments-in-criminal -sentencing

Anstey, Christopher (2023). Larry Summers Warns Silicon Valley Bank Collapse Has "Substantial Consequences" for America's Innovation System. *Fortune*, 12 March. Accessed 14 March 2023: https://fortune.com /2023/03/11/larry-summers-warns-silicon-valley-bank-collapse-finance -consequences-innovation-ventures/

Anwar, Mohammad Amir, and Mark Graham (2020). Digital Labour at Economic Margins: African Workers and the Global Information Economy. *Review of African Political Economy* 47 (163): 95–105.

Arboleda, Martín (2020). *Planetary Mine: Territories of Extraction under Late Capitalism*. London: Verso.

Astute Analytica (2023). *Global Data Annotation Tools Market, by Data Type, by Technology, by Device Type, by End-Users, Estimation and Forecast, 2017–2030*. Accessed 9 May 2023: https://www.researchandmarkets.com /reports/5638906/global-data-annotation-tools-market-by-data?utm_ campaign=1741649+-+The+Worldwide+Data+Annotation+Tools+Industr y+is+Expected+to+Reach+%2413.2+Billion+by+2030

Austin, Regina (1983). The Insurance Classification Controversy. *University of Pennsylvania Law Review* 131 (3): 517–583.

Bank, Max, Felix Duffy, Verena Leyendecker, and Margarida Silva (2021). *The Lobby Network: Big Tech's Web of Influence in the EU*. Brussels: Corporate Europe Observatory. Accessed 12 January 2023: https://corporateeurope.org/en/2021/08/lobby-network-big-techs-web-influence-eu

Barry, Laurence, and Arthur Charpentier (2020). Personalization as a Promise: Can Big Data Change the Practice of Insurance? *Big Data & Society* 7 (1): 1–12.

Becker, Gary (1993). *Human Capital: A Theoretical and Empirical Analysis, with Special Reference to Education* (3rd ed.). Chicago: University of Chicago Press.

Bednarz, Zofia, and Kayleen Manwaring (2022). Hidden Depths: The Effects of Extrinsic Data Collection on Consumer Insurance Contracts. *Computer Law & Security Review* 45: 1–23.

Beer, Stafford (1985). *Diagnosing the System for Organizations*. Hoboken, NJ: Wiley.

Benanav, Aaron (2020). *Automation and the Future of Work*. London: Verso.

Benanav, Aaron (2023). The Revolution Will Not Be Brought to You by ChatGPT. *New Statesman*, 11 April. Accessed 12 May 2023: https://www.newstatesman.com/ideas/2023/04/revolution-brought-chatgpt-artificial-intelligence

Benjamin, Ruha (2019). *Race after Technology: Abolitionist Tools for the New Jim Code*. London: Polity Press.

Benjamin, Walter (2003). *Selected Writings, Volume 4, 1938–1940*, edited by H. Eiland and M. W. Jennings. Cambridge, MA: Harvard University Press.

Bernstein, Shai, Arthur Korteweg, and Kevin Laws (2017). Attracting Early Stage Investors: Evidence from a Randomized Field Experiment. *Journal of Finance* 72 (2): 509–538.

Bertoni, Steven (2017). WeWork's $20 Billion Office Party: The Crazy Bet That Could Change How the World Does Business. *Forbes*, 2 October. Accessed 15 March 2023: https://www.forbes.com/sites/stevenbertoni/2017/10/02/the-way-we-work/?sh=1f1f24fe1b18

Beswick, Joe, Georgia Alexandri, Michael Byrne, Sònia Vives-Miró, Desiree Fields, Stuart Hodkinson, and Michael Janoschka (2016). Speculating on

London's Housing Future: The Rise of Global Corporate Landlords in "Post-Crisis" Urban Landscapes. *City* 20 (2): 321–341.

Bigelow, Pete (2015). General Motors Says It Owns Your Car's Software. *Autoblog*, 20 May. Accessed 20 July 2023: http://www.autoblog.com/2015/05/20/general-motors-says-owns-your-car-software/

Birch, Kean (2015). *We Have Never Been Neoliberal*. Alresford, UK: Zero Books.

Birch, Kean (2016). Market vs. Contract? The Implications of Contractual Theories of Corporate Governance to the Analysis of Neoliberalism. *Ephemera: Theory & Politics in Organizations* 16 (1): 107–133.

Birch, Kean (2020a). Automated Neoliberalism? The Digital Organisation of Markets in Technoscientific Capitalism. *New Formations: A Journal of Culture/Theory/Politics* 100: 10–27.

Birch, Kean (2020b). Technoscience Rent: Toward a Theory of Rentiership for Technoscientific Capitalism. *Science, Technology, and Human Values* 45 (1): 3–33.

Birch, Kean (2023). Reflexive Expectations in Innovation Financing: An Analysis of Venture Capital as a Mode of Valuation. *Social Studies of Science* 53 (1): 29–48.

Bogle, Ariel (2022). Behind "Miracle" AI Is an Army of "Ghost Workers"—and They're Speaking Out about Appen. *ABC News*, 14 October. Accessed 10 May 2023: https://www.abc.net.au/news/science/2022-10-14/artificial-intelligence-ai-appen-data-labelling-ghost-workers/101531084

Borup, Mads, Nik Brown, Kornelia Konrad, and Harro van Lente (2006). The Sociology of Expectations in Science and Technology. *Technology Analysis & Strategic Management* 18 (3/4): 285–298.

Bouk, Dan (2015). *How Our Days Became Numbered: Risk and the Rise of the Statistical Individual*. Chicago: University of Chicago Press.

Bowker, Geoffrey, and Susan Leigh Star (2000). *Sorting Things Out: Classification and Its Consequences*. Cambridge, MA: MIT Press.

Brayne, Sarah (2017). Big Data Surveillance: The Case of Policing. *American Sociological Review* 82 (5): 977–1008.

Broussard, Meredith (2018). *Artificial Unintelligence: How Computers Misunderstand the World*. Cambridge, MA: MIT Press.

Brown, Wendy (2015). *Undoing the Demos: Neoliberalism's Stealth Revolution*. Cambridge, MA: MIT Press.

Browne, Simone (2015). *Dark Matters: On the Surveillance of Blackness*. Durham, NC: Duke University Press.

Burrell, Jenna (2016). How the Machine "Thinks": Understanding Opacity in Machine Learning Algorithms. *Big Data & Society* 3 (1): 1–12.

Burrell, Jenna, and Marion Fourcade (2021). The Society of Algorithms. *Annual Review of Sociology* 47 (1): 213–237.

Carreyou, John (2018). *Bad Blood: Secrets and Lies in a Silicon Valley Startup*. New York: Knopf.

Case, Anne, and Angus Deaton (2020). *Deaths of Despair and the Future of Capitalism*. Princeton, NJ: Princeton University Press.

Chancel, Lucas, Thomas Piketty, Emmanuel Saez, and Gabriel Zucman (2022). *World Inequality Report 2022*. Paris: World Inequality Lab. Accessed 16 December 2022: https://wir2022.wid.world

Chavez, Nick (2021). The Present and Future of Engineers. *Brooklyn Rail*, October. Accessed 20 February 2023: https://brooklynrail.org/2021/10/field-notes/thinking-about-communism

Chavez, Nick (2022). Technical Expertise and Communist Production. *Brooklyn Rail*, December/January. Accessed 11 January 2023: https://brooklynrail.org/2023/12/field-notes/Technical-Expertise-and-Communist-Production

Christophers, Brett (2010). On Voodoo Economics: Theorising Relations of Property, Value, and Contemporary Capitalism. *Transactions of the Institute of British Geographers* 35 (1): 94–108.

Christophers, Brett (2019). The Problem of Rent. *Critical Historical Studies* 6 (2): 303–323.

Christophers, Brett (2020). *Rentier Capitalism: Who Owns the Economy, and Who Pays for It?* London: Verso.

Ciepley, David (2013). Beyond Public and Private: Toward a Political Theory of the Corporation. *American Political Science Review* 107 (1): 139–158.

Claypool, Rick (2022). Capitol Coin. *Public Citizen*, 8 March. Accessed 6 April 2022: https://www.citizen.org/article/capitol-coin-cryptocurrency-lobbying-revolving-door-report/

Cockburn, Cynthia (1981). The Material of Male Power. *Feminist Review* 9 (1): 41–58.

Cockburn, Cynthia (1985). *The Machinery of Dominance: Women, Men, and Technical Know-How*. London: Pluto Press.

Cole, Samantha (2023). Zoom Changes TOS to Say It Won't Train AI on Your Calls "without Your Consent" after Backlash. *Vice Motherboard*, 8 August. Accessed 17 August 2023: https://www.vice.com/en/article/wxjgvy /zoom-changes-tos-to-say-it-wont-train-ai-on-your-calls-without-your -consent-after-backlash

Constantaras, Eva, Gabriel Geiger, Justin-Casimir Braun, Dhruv Mehrotra, and Htet Aung (2023). Inside the Suspicion Machine. *Wired*, 6 March. Accessed 8 August 2023: https://www.wired.com/story/welfare-state-algorithms/

Cooiman, Franziska (2022). Imprinting the Economy: The Structural Power of Venture Capital. *Environment and Planning A: Economy and Space.* https://doi.org/10.1177/0308518X221136559

Cooiman, Franziska (2023). Veni Vidi VC: The Backend of the Digital Economy and Its Political Making. *Review of International Political Economy* 30 (1): 229–251.

Couldry, Nick, and Ulises A. Mejias (2019). Data Colonialism: Rethinking Big Data's Relation to the Contemporary Subject. *Television & New Media* 20 (4): 336–349.

Crain, Matthew (2021). *Profit over Privacy: How Surveillance Advertising Conquered the Internet.* Minneapolis: University of Minnesota Press.

Crawford, Kate, and Trevor Paglen (2021). Excavating AI: The Politics of Images in Machine Learning Training Sets. *AI & Society* 36: 1105–1116.

Cronon, William (1991). *Nature's Metropolis: Chicago and the Great West.* New York: W. W. Norton.

Dafoe, Allan (2015). On Technological Determinism: A Typology, Scope Conditions, and a Mechanism. *Science, Technology, and Human Values* 40 (6): 1047–1076.

Dal Maso, Giulia, Shanthi Robertson, and Dallas Rogers (2019). Cultural Platform Capitalism: Extracting Value from Cultural Asymmetries in RealTech. *Social and Cultural Geography* 22 (4): 565–580.

Daly, Lyle (2023). The Largest Companies by Market Cap in 2023. *The Motley Fool*, 7 July. Accessed 10 July 2023: https://www.fool.com/research /largest-companies-by-market-cap/

Dave, Paresh (2023). Stack Overflow Will Charge AI Giants for Training Data. *Wired*, 20 April. Accessed 24 April 2023: https://www.wired.com/story /stack-overflow-will-charge-ai-giants-for-training-data/

Dean, Jodi (2017). Introduction. *The Communist Manifesto*. London: Pluto Press.

Delfanti, Alessandro, and Bronwyn Frey (2020). Humanly Extended Automation or the Future of Work Seen through Amazon Patents. *Science, Technology & Human Values* 46 (3): 655–682.

Denton, Emily, Alex Hanna, Razvan Amironesei, Andrew Smart, and Hilary Nicole (2021). On the Genealogy of Machine Learning Datasets: A Critical History of ImageNet. *Big Data & Society* 8 (2): 1–14.

Dinerstein, Joel (2006). Technology and Its Discontents: On the Verge of the Posthuman. *American Quarterly* 58 (3): 569–595.

Dixon, Chris, Katie Haun, and Ali Yahya (2021). Crypto Fund III. *a16z*, 24 June. Accessed 6 April 2022: https://a16z.com/2021/06/24/crypto -fund-iii/

Doctorow, Cory (2020). How to Destroy Surveillance Capitalism. *OneZero*, 26 August. Accessed 8 February 2023: https://onezero.medium.com/how-to-destroy-surveillance-capitalism-8135e6744d59

Doctorow, Cory (2023). *The Internet Con: How to Seize the Means of Computation*. London: Verso.

Dressel, Julia, and Hany Farid (2018). The Accuracy, Fairness, and Limits of Predicting Recidivism. *Science Advances* 4 (1): 1–5.

Dubal, Veena (2023). On Algorithmic Wage Discrimination. University of California, San Francisco Research Paper. Accessed 12 May 2023: http:// dx.doi.org/10.2139/ssrn.4331080

Easterling, Keller (2014). *Extrastatecraft: The Power of Infrastructure Space*. New York: Verso.

Economist (2017). The World's Most Valuable Resource Is No Longer Oil, but Data. 6 May. Accessed 11 April 2023: https://www.economist.com/leaders /2017/05/06/the-worlds-most-valuable-resource-is-no-longer-oil-but -data

EIOPA (2019). *Big Data Analytics in Motor and Health Insurance: Thematic Review*. Accessed 10 August 2023: https://register.eiopa.europa.eu /Publications/EIOPA_BigDataAnalytics_ThematicReview_April2019.pdf

Eloundou, Tyna, Sam Manning, Pamela Mishkin, and Daniel Rock (2023). GPTs Are GPTs: An Early Look at the Labor Market Impact Potential of Large Language Models. *arXiv*, 23 March. Accessed 12 May 2023: https:// arxiv.org/abs/2303.10130

Engels, Friedrich (2009). *Condition of the Working Class in England*. London: Penguin Classics.

Ensmenger, Nathan L. (2012). *The Computer Boys Take Over Computers, Programmers, and the Politics of Technical Expertise*. Cambridge, MA: MIT Press.

Ericson, Richard, Aaron Doyle, and Dean Barry (2003). *Insurance as Governance*. Toronto: University of Toronto Press.

Eubanks, Virginia (2018). *Automating Inequality: How High-Tech Tools Profile, Police, and Punish the Poor*. New York: St. Martin's Press.

Ewald, François (2020). *The Birth of Solidarity: The History of the French Welfare State*, edited by Melinda Cooper. Durham, NC: Duke University Press.

Faulkner, Wendy (2000). Dualisms, Hierarchies and Gender in Engineering. *Social Studies of Science* 30 (5): 759–792.

Fernandez, Rodrigo, Ilke Adriaans, Tobias J. Klinge, and Reijer Hendrikse (2020). *Engineering Digital Monopolies: The Financialisation of Big Tech*. Amsterdam: SOMO.

Fields, Desiree (2018). Constructing a New Asset Class: Property-Led Financial Accumulation after the Crisis. *Economic Geography* 94 (2): 118–140.

Fields, Desiree (2022). Automated Landlord: Digital Technologies and Post-Crisis Financial Accumulation. *Environment and Planning A: Economy and Space* 54 (1): 160–181.

Fisher, Mark (2010). *Capitalist Realism: Is There No Alternative?* Winchester, UK: Zero Books.

FitzGerald, Drew (2014). Equinix Inc., the Internet's Biggest Landlord. *Wall Street Journal*, 29 October. Accessed 24 July 2023: https://www.wsj.com/articles/equinix-inc-the-internets-biggest-landlord-1414451918

Forbes (2023). Elon Musk. Accessed 6 September 2023: https://www.forbes.com/profile/elon-musk/?list=billionaires&sh=215a10767999

Foucault, Michel (1980). *Power/Knowledge: Selected Interviews and Other Writings, 1972–1977*. New York: Vintage.

Foucault, Michel (2001). The Subject and Power. In *Power*, edited by James D. Faubion. New York: The New Press.

Fouché, Rayvon (2006). Say It Loud, I'm Black and I'm Proud: African Americans, American Artifactual Culture, and Black Vernacular Technological Creativity. *American Studies Quarterly* 58 (3): 639–661.

Fourcade, Marion, and Kieran Healy (2013). Classification Situations: Life-Chances in the Neoliberal Era. *Accounting, Organizations and Society* 38 (8): 559–572.

Fourcade, Marion, and Kieran Healy (2017). Seeing Like a Market. *Socio-Economic Review* 15 (1): 9–29.

Fraser, Alistair (2022). "You Can't Eat Data"? Moving beyond the Misconfigured Innovations of Smart Farming. *Journal of Rural Studies* 91 (April): 200–207.

Frey, Carl Benedikt, and Michael A. Osborne (2013). The Future of Employment: How Susceptible Are Jobs to Computerisation? Accessed 12 May 2023: https://www.oxfordmartin.ox.ac.uk/downloads/academic/The_Future_of_Employment.pdf

Fried, Ina (2023). 1 Big Thing: How We All Became AI's Brain Donors. *Axios*, 24 April. Accessed 26 April 2023: https://www.axios.com/newsletters/axios-login-4fc52afb-3c90-4bea-ad37-35b90c77ed9f.html

Friedman, Milton (1970). A Friedman Doctrine—The Social Responsibility of Business Is to Increase Its Profits. *New York Times*, 13 September. Accessed 21 December 2022: https://www.nytimes.com/1970/09/13/archives/a-friedman-doctrine-the-social-responsibility-of-business-is-to.html

Gabor, Daniela (2021). The Wall Street Consensus. *Development and Change* 52: 429–459.

Gabor, Daniela (2022). The Wall Street Consensus at COP27. *Phenomenal World*, 19 November. Accessed 3 August 2023: https://www.phenomenalworld.org/analysis/the-wall-street-consensus-at-cop27

Gault, Matthew, and Jason Koebler (2021). Biden's Right to Repair Order Covers Electronics, Not Just Tractors. *Vice Motherboard*, 9 July. Accessed 12 July 2023: https://www.vice.com/en/article/y3d5yb/bidens-right-to-repair-executive-order-covers-electronics-not-just-tractors

Giblin, Rebecca, and Cory Doctorow (2022). *Chokepoint Capitalism: How Big Tech and Big Content Captured Creative Labor Markets and How We'll Win Them Back*. Boston: Beacon Press.

Gidley, Jennifer M. (2017). *The Future: A Very Short Introduction*. Oxford: Oxford University Press.

Gitelman, Lisa (ed.) (2013). *"Raw Data" Is an Oxymoron*. Cambridge, MA: MIT Press.

Gornall, Will, and Ilya A. Strebulaev (2020). Squaring Venture Capital Valuations with Reality. *Journal of Financial Economics* 135: 120–143.

Gotham, Kevin Fox (2009). Creating Liquidity Out of Spatial Fixity: The Secondary Circuit of Capital and the Subprime Mortgage Crisis. *International Journal of Urban and Regional Research* 33 (2): 355–371.

Graeber, David (2012). Of Flying Cars and the Declining Rate of Profit. *The Baffler*, March. Accessed 4 September 2023: https://thebaffler.com/salvos /of-flying-cars-and-the-declining-rate-of-profit

Graeber, David (2013). A Practical Utopian's Guide to the Coming Collapse. *The Baffler*, April. Accessed 7 September 2023: https://thebaffler.com /salvos/a-practical-utopians-guide-to-the-coming-collapse

Graeber, David, and David Wengrow (2022). *The Dawn of Everything: A New History of Humanity*. London: Penguin Press.

Graham, Mark, and Mohammad Amir Anwar (2019). The Global Gig Economy: Towards a Planetary Labour Market? *First Mind* 24 (4). https://doi.org/10.5210/fm.v24i4.9913

Gray, Mary L., and Siddharth Suri (2019). *Ghost Work: How to Stop Silicon Valley from Building a New Global Underclass*. Boston: Houghton Mifflin Harcourt.

Greene, Daniel (2022). Landlords of the Internet: Big Data and Big Real Estate. *Social Studies of Science* 52 (6): 904–927.

Greene, Daniel, and Daniel Joseph (2015). The Digital Spatial Fix. *TripleC* 13 (2): 223–247.

Gregory, Karen (2021). "My Life Is More Valuable Than This": Understanding Risk among On-Demand Food Couriers in Edinburgh. *Work, Employment and Society* 35 (2): 316–331.

Gregory, Karen, and Miguel Paredes Maldonado (2020). Delivering Edinburgh: Uncovering the Digital Geography of Platform Labour in the City. *Information, Communication & Society* 23 (8): 1187–1202.

Gregory, Karen, and Jathan Sadowski (2021). Biopolitical Platforms: The Perverse Virtues of Digital Labour. *Journal of Cultural Economy* 14 (6): 662–674.

Griffith, Erin, and Cade Metz (2023a). Anthropic, an A.I. Start-Up, Is Said to Be Close to Adding $300 Million. *New York Times*, 27 January. Accessed 9 May 2023: https://www.nytimes.com/2023/01/27/technology/anthropic -ai-funding.html

Griffith, Erin, and Cade Metz (2023b). "Let 1,000 Flowers Bloom": A.I. Funding Frenzy Escalates. *New York Times*, 14 March. Accessed 9 May 2023: https://www.nytimes.com/2023/03/14/technology/ai-funding-boom.html

Griffith, Erin, and Cade Metz (2023c). A New Area of A.I. Booms, Even amid the Tech Gloom. *New York Times*, 7 January. Accessed 19 February 2024: https://www.nytimes.com/2023/01/07/technology/generative-ai-chatgpt-investments.html

Haila, Anne (1988). Land as a Financial Asset: The Theory of Urban Rent as a Mirror of Economic Transformation. *Antipode* 20 (2): 79–101.

Han, Byung-Chul (2017). *Psychopolitics: Neoliberalism and New Technologies of Power*. Translated by Erik Butler. London: Verso.

Hara, Kotaro, Abigail Adams, Kristy Milland, Saiph Savage, Chris Callison-Burch, and Jeffrey P. Bigham (2018). A Data-Driven Analysis of Workers' Earnings on Amazon Mechanical Turk. *Proceedings of the 2018 CHI Conference on Human Factors in Computing Systems (CHI '18)*, Paper 449, pp. 1–14.

Haraway, Donna (1988). Situated Knowledges: The Science Question in Feminism and the Privilege of Partial Perspective. *Feminist Studies* 14 (3): 575–599.

Harris, Malcolm (2017). *Kids These Days: Human Capital and the Making of Millennials*. New York: Little, Brown.

Harris, Malcolm (2023). *Palo Alto: A History of California, Capitalism, and the World*. New York: Little, Brown.

Harvey, David (2006). *Limits to Capital*. London: Verso.

Harvey, David (2008). *A Brief History of Neoliberalism*. Oxford: Oxford University Press.

Harvey, David (2010). *The Enigma of Capital and the Crises of Capitalism*. London: Profile.

Harvey, David (2014). *Seventeen Contradictions and the End of Capitalism*. London: Profile Books.

Harvey, David (2017). *Marx, Capital and the Madness of Economic Reason*. London: Profile Books.

Hedgecoe, Adam (2010). Bioethics and the Reinforcement of Socio-Technical Expectations. *Social Studies of Science* 40 (2): 163–186.

Hicks, Mar (2018). *Programmed Inequality: How Britain Discarded Women Technologists and Lost Its Edge in Computing*. Cambridge, MA: MIT Press.

Hoffmann, Anna Lauren (2021). Terms of Inclusion: Data, Discourse, Violence. *New Media & Society* 23 (12): 3539–3556.

Hong, Sun-ha (2022). Predictions without Futures. *History and Theory* 61 (3): 371–390.

Hong, Sun-ha (2023). Prediction as Extraction of Discretion. *Big Data & Society* 10 (1): 1–11.

Hook, Leslie (2016). The Humans behind Mechanical Turk's Artificial Intelligence. *Financial Times*, 26 October. Accessed 16 May 2023: https://www.ft.com/content/17518034-6f77-11e6-9ac1-1055824ca907

Horan, Caley (2021). *Insurance Era: Risk, Governance, and the Privatization of Security in Postwar America*. Chicago: University of Chicago Press.

Houghton, Jeremy, and Shuwen Wong (2020). Case Study—AIA Vitality. *Shared Value Project*, August. Accessed 5 July 2023: https://sharedvalue.org.au/wp-content/uploads/2020/08/AIA-Vitality_Case-Study.pdf.

Houlder, Vanessa, and Nathalie Thomas (2023). Lex In Depth: How Investors Are Underpricing Climate Risks. *Financial Times*, 17 August. Accessed 18 August 2023: https://www.ft.com/content/899472a8-e5e2-4fde-bc91-7e548ba35294

Howard, Phoebe Wall (2018). Data Could Be What Ford Sells Next as It Looks for New Revenue. *Detroit Free Press*, 13 November. Accessed 19 February 2024: https://www.freep.com/story/money/cars/2018/11/13/ford-motor-credit-data-new-revenue/1967077002/

IBM (2014). A World Made with Data. Made with IBM. YouTube, 27 May. Accessed 12 April 2023: https://www.youtube.com/watch?v=QCgzrOUd_Dc

Intagliata, Christopher (2011). The Origin of the Word "Robot." *Science Friday*, 22 April. Accessed 16 May 2023: https://www.sciencefriday.com/segments/the-origin-of-the-word-robot/

Irani, Lilly (2015). The Cultural Work of Microwork. *New Media & Society* 17 (5): 720–739.

Isaac, Mike (2023). Reddit Wants to Get Paid for Helping to Teach Big A.I. Systems. *New York Times*, 18 April. Accessed 24 April 2023: https://www.nytimes.com/2023/04/18/technology/reddit-ai-openai-google.html

Ivanovs, Alex (2023). Zoom's Updated Terms of Service Permit Training AI on User Content without Opt-Out. *Stack Diary*, 7 August. Accessed 8 August 2023: https://stackdiary.com/zoom-terms-now-allow-training-ai-on-user-content-with-no-opt-out/

Jacobsen, Benjamin N. (2023). Machine Learning and the Politics of Synthetic Data. *Big Data & Society* 10 (1): 2.

Jason (2023). If You're in Crypto Pivot to AI. Twitter post, 9 June. Accessed 24 November 2023: https://twitter.com/Jason/status/1666874821077250048

Jeanningros, Hugo, and Liz McFall (2020). The Value of Sharing: Branding and Behaviour in a Life and Health Insurance Company. *Big Data & Society* 7 (2): 1–15.

Jouvenal, Justin (2016). The New Way Police Are Surveilling You: Calculating Your Threat "Score." *Washington Post*, 10 January. Accessed 8 August 2023: https://www.washingtonpost.com/local/public-safety/the-new-way-police-are-surveilling-you-calculating-your-threat-score/2016/01/10/e42bccac-8e15-11e5-baf4-bdf37355da0c_story.html.

Kak, Amba, and Sarah Myers West (2023). *AI Now 2023 Landscape: Confronting Tech Power*. New York: AI Now Institute.

Kalluri, Pratyusha Ria, William Agnew, Myra Cheng, Kentrell Owens, Luca Soldaini, and Abeba Birhane (2023). The Surveillance AI Pipeline. *arXiv*, 26 September. Accessed 27 November 2023: https://arxiv.org/abs/2309.15084

Kaminski, Margot E. (2023). Regulating the Risks of AI. *Boston University Law Review* 103: 1347–1411.

Karp, Alex (2023). Our Oppenheimer Moment: The Creation of A.I. Weapons. *New York Times*, 25 July. Accessed 3 August 2023: https://www.nytimes.com/2023/07/25/opinion/karp-palantir-artificial-intelligence.html

Kastrenakes, Jacob (2022). Bored Ape Yacht Club Creator Raises $450 Million to Build an NFT Metaverse. *The Verge*, 22 March. Accessed 6 April 2022: https://www.theverge.com/2022/3/22/22991272/yuga-labs-seed-funding-a16z-bored-ape-yacht-club-bayc-metaverse-other-side

Kaye, Kate (2022). Inside Eric Schmidt's Push to Profit from an AI Cold War with China. *Protocol*, 31 October. Accessed 1 May 2023: https://www.protocol.com/enterprise/eric-schmidt-ai-china

Keegan, Jon (2023). Forget Milk and Eggs: Supermarkets Are Having a Fire Sale on Data about You. *The Markup*, 16 February. Accessed 12 April 2023: https://themarkup.org/privacy/2023/02/16/forget-milk -and-eggs-supermarkets-are-having-a-fire-sale-on-data-about-you

Kelly, Kevin (2010). *What Technology Wants*. New York: Viking Press.

Keynes, John Maynard (1936). *The General Theory of Employment, Interest and Money*. New York: Harcourt, Brace.

Kirby, David (2010). The Future Is Now: Diegetic Prototypes and the Role of Popular Films in Generating Real-World Technological Development. *Social Studies of Science* 40 (1): 41–70.

Kissinger, Henry, Eric Schmidt, and Daniel Huttenlocher (2021). *The Age of AI: And Our Human Future*. New York: Little, Brown.

Kiviat, Barbara (2019). The Moral Limits of Predictive Practices: The Case of Credit-Based Insurance Scores. *American Sociological Review* 84 (6): 1134–1158.

Klein, Ezra (host) (2021). Ezra Klein Interviews Ted Chiang [transcript]. *New York Times*, 30 March. Accessed 14 March 2023: https://www.nytimes.com /2021/03/30/podcasts/ezra-klein-podcast-ted-chiang-transcript.html

Klingler-Vidra, Robyn (2014). Building a Venture Capital Market in Vietnam: Diffusion of a Neoliberal Market Strategy to a Socialist State. *Asian Studies Review* 38 (4): 582–600.

Klingler-Vidra, Robyn (2016). When Venture Capital Is Patient Capital: Seed Funding as a Source of Patient Capital for High-Growth Companies. *Socio-Economic Review* 14 (4): 691–708.

Klingler-Vidra, Robyn (2018). Building the Venture Capital State. *American Affairs* 2 (3): n.p.

Knight, Will (2023). OpenAI's CEO Says the Age of Giant AI Models Is Already Over. *Wired*, 17 April. Accessed 24 April 2023: https://www .wired.com/story/openai-ceo-sam-altman-the-age-of-giant-ai-models -is-already-over/

Koebler, Jason (2018). Tractor-Hacking Farmers Are Leading a Revolt against Big Tech's Repair Monopolies. *Vice Motherboard*, 15 February. Accessed 20 July 2023: https://www.vice.com/en/article/kzp7ny/tractor-hacking-right- to-repair

Koebler, Jason (2020). Why Repair Techs Are Hacking Ventilators with DIY Dongles from Poland. *Vice Motherboard*, 9 July. Accessed 25 July 2023:

https://www.vice.com/en/article/3azv9b/why-repair-techs-are-hacking
-ventilators-with-diy-dongles-from-poland

Koebler, Jason (2023). Biden Administration Changes Mind, Says Car
Companies Shouldn't Ignore Overwhelmingly Popular Car Repair Law
Anymore. *404 Media*, 22 August. Accessed 23 August 2023: https://
www.404media.co/biden-administration-changes-mind-says-car
-companies-shouldnt-ignore-overwhelmingly-popular-car-repair-law
-anymore/

Konczal, Mike, and Nell Abernathy (2015). *Defining Financialization*. New
York: Roosevelt Institute.

Krippner, Greta R. (2005). The Financialization of the American Economy.
Socio-Economic Review 3: 173–208.

Krippner, Greta R. (2023). Unmasked: A History of the Individualization of
Risk. *Sociological Theory* 41 (2): 83–104.

Krippner, Greta R., and Daniel Hirschman (2022). The Person of the
Category: The Pricing of Risk and the Politics of Classification in
Insurance and Credit. *Theory and Society* 51: 685–727.

Krugman, Paul (2023). How Bad Was the Silicon Valley Bank Bailout? *New
York Times*, 14 March. Accessed 15 March 2023: https://www.nytimes.com
/2023/03/14/opinion/silicon-valley-bank-bailout.html

Krzywdzinski, Martin (2021). Automation, Digitalization, and Changes in
Occupational Structures in the Automobile Industry in Germany, Japan,
and the United States: A Brief History from the Early 1990s until 2018.
Industrial and Corporate Change 30 (3): 499–535.

Langley, Paul (2021). Assets and Assetization in Financialized Capitalism.
Review of International Political Economy 28 (2): 382–393.

Langley, Paul, and Andrew Leyshon (2017). Platform Capitalism: The Intermediation and Capitalisation of Digital Economic Circulation. *Finance and
Society* 3 (1): 11–31.

Lazzarato, Maurizio (2009). Neoliberalism in Action: Inequality, Insecurity
and the Reconstitution of the Social. *Theory, Culture & Society* 26 (6):
109–133.

Lee, Peter (2018). Innovation and the Firm: A New Synthesis. *Stanford Law
Review* 70 (5): 1431–1501.

Lee, Peter (2022). Enhancing the Innovative Capacity of Venture Capital. *Yale
Journal of Law and Technology* 24: 611–705.

Lehoux, Pascale, Fiona A. Miller, Geneviève Daudelin, and David R. Urbach (2016). How Venture Capitalists Decide Which New Medical Technologies Come to Exist. *Science and Public Policy* 43 (3): 375–385.

Lerner, Josh, and Ramana Nanda (2020). Venture Capital's Role in Financing Innovation: What We Know and How Much We Still Need to Learn. *Journal of Economic Perspectives* 34 (3): 237–261.

Levine, Matt (2021). Startups Sometimes Stretch the Truth. *Bloomberg*, 27 February. Accessed 7 February 2023: https://www.bloomberg.com/opinion /articles/2021-0226/startups-sometimes-stretch-the-truth?sref=1kJVNqnU

Levine, Matt (2023). Startup Bank Had a Startup Bank Run. *Bloomberg*, 11 March. Accessed 14 March 2023: https://www.bloomberg.com/opinion /articles/2023-03-10/startup-bank-had-a-startup-bank-run

Levitz, Eric (2020). America Has Central Planners. We Just Call Them "Venture Capitalists." *New York Magazine*, 3 December. Accessed 10 March 2023: https://nymag.com/intelligencer/2020/12/wework-venture -capital-central-planning.html

Levy, Steven (2023). What OpenAI Really Wants. *Wired*, 5 September. Accessed 8 September 2023: https://www.wired.com/story/what-openai -really-wants/

Light, Jennifer S. (1999). When Computers Were Women. *Technology and Culture* 40 (3): 455–483.

Lipartito, Kenneth (1994). When Women Were Switches: Technology, Work, and Gender in the Telephone Industry, 1890–1920. *American Historical Review* 99 (4): 1075–1111.

Lipton, Eric, Daisuke Wakabayashi, and Ephrat Livni (2021). Big Hires, Big Money and a D.C. Blitz: A Bold Plan to Dominate Crypto. *New York Times*, 29 October. Accessed 6 April 2022: https://www.nytimes.com/2021 /10/29/us/politics/andreessen-horowitz-lobbying-cryptocurrency .html

Lipton, Zachary C., and Jacob Steinhardt (2019). Troubling Trends in Machine Learning Scholarship: Some ML papers Suffer from Flaws That Could Mislead the Public and Stymie Future Research. *ACM Queue* 17 (1): 45–77.

Littlejohns, Peter (2020). Aviva's Colm Holmes on Claims Inflation, Stupid Drivers and Commercial Insurance. *NS Insurance*, 7 February. Accessed

16 August 2023: https://www.nsinsurance.com/analysis/aviva-colm
-holmes-claims-inflation/

Lu, Yiwen (2023). Generative A.I. Can Add $4.4 Trillion in Value to Global
Economy, Study Says. *New York Times*, 14 June. Accessed 29 August 2023:
https://www.nytimes.com/2023/06/14/technology/generative-ai-global-
economy.html

Luckey, Palmer (2018). Disrupting Defense: How Tech Can, and Should,
Support National Security. Web Summit, 16 November. Accessed 21
August 2023: https://www.youtube.com/watch?v=0G4FR1pepu4

Luitse, Dieuwertje, and Wiebke Denkena (2021). The Great Transformer:
Examining the Role of Large Language Models in the Political Economy
of AI. *Big Data & Society* 8 (2): 1–14.

Lunden, Ingrid (2023). France's Mistral AI Blows in with a $113M Seed Round
at a $260M Valuation to Take On OpenAI. *TechCrunch*, 14 June. Accessed
15 June 2023: https://techcrunch.com/2023/06/13/frances-mistral-ai-blows
-in-with-a-113m-seed-round-at-a-260m-valuation-to-take-on-openai

Luxemburg, Rosa (1951). *The Accumulation of Capital*. New York: Monthly
Review Press.

Maalsen, Sophia, and Jathan Sadowski (2019). The Smart Home on FIRE:
Amplifying and Accelerating Domestic Discipline. *Surveillance & Society*
16 (1/2): 118–124.

MacMillan, Douglas (2018). Tech's "Dirty Secret": The App Developers
Sifting through Your Gmail. *Wall Street Journal*, 2 July. Accessed 16 May
2023: https://www.wsj.com/articles/techs-dirty-secret-the-app
-developers-sifting-through-your-gmail-1530544442

Malm, Andreas (2016). *Fossil Capital: The Rise of Steam Power and the Roots of
Global Warming*. London: Verso.

Manovel, Ian, and Leigh Donoghue (2019). *Injecting Intelligence into Health
Care*. Sydney: Accenture Consulting.

Marcus, Gary (2022). Deep Learning Is Hitting a Wall. *Nautilus*, 10 March.
Accessed 16 December 2022: https://nautil.us/deep-learning-is-hitting
-a-wall-238440/

Marx, Karl (1843). Letter from Marx to Arnold Ruge. Accessed 9 February
2023: https://www.marxists.org/archive/marx/works/1843/letters/43_
09-alt.htm

Marx, Karl (1990). *Capital, Volume I*. Translated by Ben Fowkes. New York: Penguin Classics.

Marx, Karl (1992). *Capital, Volume II*. Translated by David Fernbach. London: Penguin Classics.

Marx, Karl (1993a). *Capital, Volume III*. Translated by David Fernbach. London: Penguin Classics.

Marx, Karl (1993b). *Grundrisse: Foundations of the Critique of Political Economy*. Translated by Martin Nicolaus. Harmondsworth, UK: Penguin.

Marx, Leo (1964). *The Machine in the Garden: Technology and the Pastoral Ideal in America*. Oxford: Oxford University Press.

Marx, Leo (1987). Does Improved Technology Mean Progress? *Technology Review* 71 (January): 33–41.

Marx, Leo (2010). Technology: The Emergence of a Hazardous Concept. *Technology and Culture* 51: 561–577.

Mau, Søren (2023). *Mute Compulsion: A Marxist Theory of the Economic Power of Capital*. London: Verso Books.

Mazzucato, Mariana (2013). *The Entrepreneurial State: Debunking Public vs. Private Sector Myths*. New York: Anthem Press.

Mazzucato, Mariana (2018). *The Value of Everything: Making and Taking in the Global Economy*. London: Allen Lane.

McElroy, Erin, and Manon Vergerio (2022). Automating Gentrification: Landlord Technologies and Housing Justice Organizing in New York City Homes. *Environment and Planning D: Society and Space* 40 (4): 607–626.

McFall, Liz, Gert Meyers, and Ine Van Hoyweghen (2020). The Personalisation of Insurance: Data, Behaviour and Innovation. *Big Data & Society* 7 (2): 1–11.

McIlwain, Charlton D. (2020). *Black Software: The Internet and Racial Justice, from the AfroNet to Black Lives Matter*. Oxford: Oxford University Press.

McKinsey & Company (2022). Value Creation in the Metaverse. Accessed 29 August 2023: https://www.mckinsey.com/capabilities/growth-marketing-and-sales/our-insights/value-creation-in-the-metaverse

McQuillan, Dan (2018). Data Science as Machinic Neoplatonism. *Philosophy and Technology* 31: 253–272.

Medina, Eden (2014). *Cybernetic Revolutionaries: Technology and Politics in Allende's Chile*. Cambridge, MA: MIT Press.

Merchant, Brian (2023a). *Blood in the Machine: The Origins of the Rebellion against Big Tech*. New York: Little, Brown.

Merchant, Brian (2023b). These Apps and Websites Use Your Data to Train AI: You're Probably Using One Right Now. *Los Angeles Times*, 16 August. Accessed 17 August 2023: https://www.latimes.com/business/technology/story/2023-08-16/column-its-not-just-zoom-how-websites-and-apps-harvest-your-data-to-build-ai

Merchant, Brian (2023c). What Stephen King—and Nearly Everyone Else—Gets Wrong about AI and the Luddites. *Los Angeles Times*, 31 August. Accessed 11 September 2023: https://www.latimes.com/business/technology/story/2023-08-31/column-stephen-king-i-love-you-but-youre-wrong-about-the-luddites-and-technological-progress

Metcalfe, Philippa, and Lina Dencik (2019). The Politics of Big Borders: Data (In)Justice and the Governance of Refugees. *First Monday* 24 (4): n.p.

Metz, Cade (2023). Generative A.I. Start-Up Cohere Valued at about $2 Billion in Funding Round. *New York Times*, 2 May. Accessed 9 May 2023: https://www.nytimes.com/2023/05/02/technology/generative-ai-start-up-cohere-funding.html

Meyers, Gert, and Ine Van Hoyweghen (2018). Enacting Actuarial Fairness in Insurance: From Fair Discrimination to Behaviour-Based Fairness. *Science as Culture* 27 (4): 413–438.

Meyers, Gert, and Ine Van Hoyweghen (2020). "Happy Failures": Experimentation with Behaviour-Based Personalisation in Car Insurance. *Big Data & Society* 7 (1): 1–14.

Miéville, China (2022). *A Spectre, Haunting: On the Communist Manifesto.* Chicago: Haymarket Books.

Minty, Duncan (2021). Is Settlement Walking Now Part of UK Insurance? *Ethics and Insurance*, 18 March. Accessed 16 August 2023: https://www.ethicsandinsurance.info/settlement-walking/

Minty, Duncan (2022). Why the Clearview Ruling Matters to Insurers. *Ethics and Insurance*, 25 May. Accessed 8 August 2023: https://www.ethicsandinsurance.info/why-the-clearview-ruling-matters-to-insurers/

MIT Technology Review Custom and Oracle (2016). *The Rise of Data Capital.* Accessed 12 April 2023: http://files.technologyreview.com/whitepapers/MIT_Oracle+Report-The_Rise_of_Data_Capital.pdf

Morozov, Evgeny (2013). *To Save Everything, Click Here: The Folly of Technological Solutionism.* New York: PublicAffairs Books.

Morozov, Evgeny (2022). Critique of Techno-Feudal Reason. *New Left Review* 133/134 (1): 89–126.

Morozov, Evgeny (2023a). AI: The Key Battleground for Cold War 2.0? *Le Monde Diplomatique*, May. Accessed 1 May 2023: https://mondediplo.com /2023/05/02china

Morozov, Evgeny (2023b). The Lessons of Chile's Struggle against Big Tech. *New Statesman*, 9 September. Accessed 11 September 2023: https://www .newstatesman.com/the-weekend-essay/2023/09/salvador-allende-fight -big-tech

Morozov, Evgeny (2023c). The Santiago Boys. Accessed 11 September 2023: https://the-santiago-boys.com/

Mozur, Paul (2018). Inside China's Dystopian Dreams: A.I., Shame and Lots of Cameras. *New York Times*, 8 July. Accessed 16 May 2023: https://www .nytimes.com/2018/07/08/business/china-surveillance-technology.html

Mueller, Gavin (2021). *Breaking Things at Work: The Luddites Are Right about Why You Hate Your Job*. London: Verso.

Murgia, Madhumita (2023). Why Computer-Made Data Is Being Used to Train AI Models. *Financial Times*, 19 July. Accessed 21 July 2023: https:// www.ft.com/content/053ee253-820e-453a-a1d5-0f24985258de

Nakamura, Lisa (2014). Indigenous Circuits: Navajo Women and the Racialization of Early Electronic Manufacture. *American Quarterly* 66 (4): 919–941.

Neel, Phil A. (2022). The Knife at Your Throat. *Brooklyn Rail*, October. Accessed 16 December 2022: https://brooklynrail.org/2022/10/field-notes/The-Knife-At-Your-Throat

Neocosmos, Michael (1986). Marx's Third Class: Capitalist Landed Property and Capitalist Development. *Journal of Peasant Studies* 13 (3): 5–44.

Nethercote, Megan (2023). Platform Landlords: Renters, Personal Data and New Digital Footholds of Urban Control. *Digital Geography and Society* 5 (December): 100060.

Newman, Kathe (2009). Post-Industrial Widgets: Capital Flows and the Production of the Urban. *International Journal of Urban and Regional Research* 33 (2): 314–331.

Newton, Casey (2018). Facebook Is Shutting Down M, Its Personal Assistant Service That Combined Humans and AI. *The Verge*, January 8. Accessed 16

May 2023: https://www.theverge.com/2018/1/8/16856654/facebook-m-shutdown-bots-ai

Nicholas, Tom (2019). *VC: An American History*. Cambridge, MA: Harvard University Press.

Noble, David F. (1979). *America by Design: Science, Technology, and the Rise of Corporate Capitalism*. Oxford: Oxford University Press.

Noble, David F. (1984). *Forces of Production: A Social History of Industrial Automation*. New York: Knopf.

Noble, David F. (1995). *Progress without People: New Technology, Unemployment, and the Message of Resistance*. Toronto: Between the Lines.

Nye, David E. (1996). *American Technological Sublime*. Cambridge, MA: MIT Press.

O'Gieblyn, Meghan (2016). As a God Might Be: Three Visions of Technological Progress. *Boston Review*, 9 February. Accessed 10 January 2023: https://bostonreview.net/books-ideas/meghan-ogieblyn-god-might-be

Omarova, Saule T. (2019). New Tech v. New Deal: Fintech as a Systemic Phenomenon. *Yale Journal on Regulation* 36 (2): 735–793.

O'Neill, Cathy (2016). *Weapons of Math Destruction*. New York: Crown.

Ongweso, Edward, Jr. (2023). The Incredible Tantrum Venture Capitalists Threw over Silicon Valley Bank. *Slate*, 13 March. Accessed 14 March 2023: https://slate.com/technology/2023/03/silicon-valley-bank-rescue-venture-capital-calacanis-sacks-ackman-tantrum.html

OpenAI (2023). *GPT-4 Technical Report*. Accessed 24 April 2023: https://cdn.openai.com/papers/gpt-4.pdf

OpenAI Charter. Accessed 24 April 2023: https://openai.com/charter

Pasquale, Frank (2015). *The Black Box Society: The Secret Algorithms That Control Money and Information*. Cambridge, MA: Harvard University Press.

Patel, Nilay, and Chris Dixon (2022). Chris Dixon Thinks Web3 Is the Future of the Internet: Is It? *The Verge*, 12 April. Accessed 17 April 2023: https://www.theverge.com/23020727/decoder-chris-dixon-web3-cryptoa16z-vc-silicon-valley-investing-podcast-interview

Patel, Raj, and Jason W. Moore (2018). *A History of the World in Seven Cheap Things: A Guide to Capitalism, Nature, and the Future of the Planet*. Oakland: University of California Press.

Peck, Jamie, and Adam Tickell (2002). Neoliberalizing Space. *Antipode* 34 (3): 380–404.

Perrigo, Billy (2023). Exclusive: OpenAI Used Kenyan Workers on Less Than $2 per Hour to Make ChatGPT Less Toxic. *Time*, 18 January. Accessed 9 May 2023: https://time.com/6247678/openai-chatgpt-kenya-workers/

Perry, Tekla S. (2023). 10 Graphs That Sum Up the State of AI in 2023: The AI Index Tracks Breakthroughs, GPT Training Costs, Misuse, Funding, and More. *IEEE Spectrum*, 8 April. Accessed 13 April 2023: https://spectrum.ieee.org/state-of-ai-2023

Phan, Thao, Jake Goldenfein, Declan Kuch, and Monique Mann (eds.) (2022). *Economies of Virtue: The Circulation of "Ethics" in AI*. Amsterdam: Institute of Network Cultures.

Pitchbook and NVCA (2022). *Venture Monitor: Q4 2022*. Accessed 20 March 2023: https://files.pitchbook.com/website/files/pdf/Q4_2022_PitchBook-NVCA_Venture_Monitor.pdf

Plantin, Jean-Christopher, Carl Lagoze, Paul N. Edwards, and Christian Sandvig (2018). Infrastructure Studies Meet Platform Studies in the Age of Google and Facebook. *New Media and Society* 20 (1): 293–310.

Pollock, Neil, and Robin Williams (2010). The Business of Expectations: How Promissory Organizations Shape Technology and Innovation. *Social Studies of Science* 40 (4): 525–548.

Powers, Devon (2019). *On Trend: The Business of Forecasting the Future*. Champaign-Urbana: University of Illinois Press.

Preston, Laura (2023). Human_Fallback. *n+1 magazine*. Accessed 15 May 2023: https://www.nplusonemag.com/issue-44/essays/human_fallback/

Prince, Anya E. R., and Daniel Schwarcz (2020). Proxy Discrimination in the Age of Artificial Intelligence and Big Data. *Iowa Law Review* 105: 1257–1318.

Puschmann, Cornelius, and Jean Burgess (2014). Metaphors of Big Data. *International Journal of Communication* 8: 1609–1709.

Ram, Aliya (2019). Europe's AI Start-Ups Often Do Not Use AI, Study Finds. *Financial Times*, 5 March. Accessed 9 May 2023: https://www.ft.com/content/21b19010-3e9f-11e9-b896-fe36ec32aece

Randall, Adrian (1998). The "Lessons" of Luddism. *Endeavour* 22 (4): 152–155.

Ricardo, David (2004). *The Principles of Political Economy and Taxation*. New York: Dover.

Richardson, Michael, Jake Goldfein, and Thao Phan (2021). Privatising the Sky: Drone Delivery Promises Comfort and Speed, but at a Cost to

Workers and Communities. *The Conversation*, 4 October. Accessed 10 May 2021: https://theconversation.com/privatising-the-sky-drone-delivery-promises-comfort-and-speed-but-at-a-cost-to-workers-and-communities-166960

Rikap, Cecilia (2021). *Capitalism, Power and Innovation: Intellectual Monopoly Capitalism Uncovered*. London: Routledge.

Roberts, Sarah T. (2019). *Behind the Screen: Content Moderation in the Shadows of Social Media*. New Haven, CT: Yale University Press.

Rogers, Dallas (2016). Uploading Real Estate. In *Housing and Home Unbound: Intersections in Economics, Environment, and Politics in Australia*, edited by N. Cook, A. Davison, and L. Crabtree, pp. 23–38. Melbourne: Routledge.

Rogers, Dallas (2017). *The Geopolitics of Real Estate: Reconfiguring Property, Capital, and Rights*. London: Rowman & Littlefield.

Romain, Manon, Adrien Senecat, Soizic Pénicaud, Gabriel Geiger, and Justin-Casimir Braun (2023). How We Investigated France's Mass Profiling Machine. *Lighthouse Reports*, 4 December. Accessed 31 December 2023: https://www.lighthousereports.com/methodology/how-we-investigated-frances-mass-profiling-machine/

Röschmann, Angela Zeier, Matthias Erny, and Joël Wagner (2022). On the (Future) Role of On-Demand Insurance: Market Landscape, Business Model and Customer Perception. *The Geneva Papers on Risk and Insurance—Issues and Practice* 47: 603–642.

Rucker, Patrick, Maya Miller, and David Armstrong (2023). How Cigna Saves Millions by Having Its Doctors Reject Claims without Reading Them. *ProPublica*, 25 March. Accessed 16 August 2023: https://www.propublica.org/article/cigna-pxdx-medical-health-insurance-rejection-claims

Rumsfeld, Donald (2002). DoD News Briefing: Secretary Rumsfeld and Gen. Myers. US Department of Defense, 12 February. Accessed 7 August 2023: https://archive.md/20180320091111/http://archive.defense.gov/Transcripts/Transcript.aspx?TranscriptID=2636#selection-401.0-406.0

Sadowski, Jathan (2019). When Data Is Capital: Datafication, Accumulation, and Extraction. *Big Data & Society* 6 (1): 1–12.

Sadowski, Jathan (2020a). Cyberspace and Cityscapes: On the Emergence of Platform Urbanism. *Urban Geography* 41 (3): 448–452.

Sadowski, Jathan (2020b). The Internet of Landlords: Digital Platforms and New Mechanisms of Rentier Capitalism. *Antipode* 52 (2): 562–580.

Sadowski, Jathan (2020c). *Too Smart: How Digital Capitalism Is Extracting Data, Controlling Our Lives, and Taking Over the World*. Cambridge, MA: MIT Press.

Sadowski, Jathan (2021a). Future Schlock. *Real Life Magazine*, 25 January. Accessed 5 September 2023: https://reallifemag.com/future-schlock/

Sadowski, Jathan (2021b). Who Owns the Future City? Phases of Technological Urbanism and Shifts in Sovereignty. *Urban Studies* 58 (8): 1732–1744.

Sadowski, Jathan (2022a). FIRE Watchers: The Centrality of Surveillance (Studies) for Finance, Insurance, Real Estate. *Surveillance & Society* 20 (4): 450–454.

Sadowski, Jathan (2022b). Lords of the Platform: Rentier Capitalism and the Platform Economy. In *Platform Labour and Global Logistics: A Research Companion*, edited by Immanuel Ness. London: Routledge.

Sadowski, Jathan (2023). Total Life Insurance: Logics of Anticipatory Control and Actuarial Governance in Insurance Technology. *Social Studies of Science*. https://doi.org/10.1177/03063127231186437

Sadowski, Jathan, and Kaitlin Beegle (2023). Extractive and Expansive Networks of Web3. *Big Data & Society* 10 (1): 1–14.

Sadowski, Jathan, and Roy Bendor (2019). Selling Smartness: Corporate Narratives and the Smart City as a Sociotechnical Imaginary. *Science, Technology & Human Values* 44 (3): 540–563.

Sadowski, Jathan, and Anthony Levenda (2020). The Anti-Politics of Smart Energy Regimes. *Political Geography* 81 (August): 102202.

Sadowski, Jathan, Kelly Lewis, and Zofia Bednarz (2024). Risk, Value, Vitality: The Moral Economy of a Global Behavioral Insurance Platform. *Economy and Society*. https://doi.org/10.1080/03085147.2024.2328992

Sadowski, Jathan, and Evan Selinger (2014). Creating a Taxonomic Tool for Technocracy and Applying It to Silicon Valley. *Technology in Society* 38: 161–168.

Sadowski, Jathan, Yolande Strengers, and Jenny Kennedy (2024). More Work for Big Mother: Revaluing Care and Control in Smart Homes. *Environment and Planning A: Economy and Space* 56 (1): 330–345.

Sadowski, Jathan, Salomé Viljoen, and Meredith Whittaker (2021). Everyone Should Decide How Their Digital Data Are Used—Not Just Tech Companies. *Nature* 595: 169–171.

Sambasivan, Nithya, Shivani Kapania, Hannah Highfill, Diana Akrong, Praveen Paritosh, and Lora Aroyo (2021). "Everyone Wants to Do the Model Work,

Not the Data Work": Data Cascades in High-Stakes AI. *CHI '21: Proceedings of the 2021 CHI Conference on Human Factors in Computing Systems.* Article no. 39.

Satariano, Adam, and Matina Stevis-Gridneff (2020). Big Tech Turns Its Lobbyists Loose on Europe, Alarming Regulators. *New York Times*, 14 December. Accessed 12 January 2023: https://www.nytimes.com/2020/12/14/technology/big-tech-lobbying-europe.html

Scharff, Christina (2016). The Psychic Life of Neoliberalism: Mapping the Contours of Entrepreneurial Subjectivity. *Theory, Culture & Society* 33 (6): 107–122.

Schaul, Kevin, Szu Yu Chen, and Nitasha Tiku (2023). Inside the Secret List of Websites That Make AI Like ChatGPT Sound Smart. *Washington Post*, 19 April. Accessed 24 April 2023: https://www.washingtonpost.com/technology/interactive/2023/ai-chatbot-learning/

Sclove, Richard E. (1995). *Democracy and Technology.* New York: Guilford Press.

Selin, Cynthia (2007). Expectations and the Emergence of Nanotechnology. *Science, Technology & Human Values* 32 (2): 196–220.

Selin, Cynthia (2008). The Sociology of the Future: Tracing Stories of Technology and Time. *Sociology Compass* 2 (6): 1878–1895.

Shaw, Joe (2018). Platform Real Estate: Theory and Practice of New Urban Real Estate Markets. *Urban Geography* 41 (8): 1037–1064.

Siemens (2014). Siemens Smart Data. YouTube, 4 September. Accessed 12 April 2023: https://www.youtube.com/watch?v=ZxoO-DvHQRw

Simon, Jonathan (1988). The Ideological Effects of Actuarial Practices. *Law & Society Review* 22 (4): 771–800.

Slobodian, Quinn (2023). *Crack-Up Capitalism: Market Radicals and the Dream of a World without Democracy.* New York: Metropolitan Books.

Smith, Adam (1999). *The Wealth of Nations, Books I–III.* London: Penguin Classics.

Solon, Olivia (2018). The Rise of "Pseudo-AI": How Tech Firms Quietly Use Humans to Do Bots' Work. *Guardian*, 6 July. Accessed 16 May 2023: https://www.theguardian.com/technology/2018/jul/06/artificial-intelligence-ai-humans-bots-tech-companies

Solon, Olivia, and Sabrina Siddiqui (2017). Forget Wall Street—Silicon Valley Is the New Political Power in Washington. *Guardian*, 3 September. Accessed

12 January 2023: https://www.theguardian.com/technology/2017/sep/03/silicon-valley-politics-lobbying-washington

Somerville, Heather (2021). Silicon Valley's Deal Machine Is Cranking: "I've Never Seen It This Frenzied." *Wall Street Journal*, 21 April. Accessed 27 April 2021: https://www.wsj.com/articles/startups-crack-records-as-more-money-flows-to-silicon-valley-11619004801

Son, Heonju (2015). The History of Western Future Studies: An Exploration of the Intellectual Traditions and Three-Phase Periodization. *Futures* 66: 120–133.

Srnicek, Nick (2017). *Platform Capitalism*. Cambridge: Polity.

Stacey, Kiran (2022). Meet the "Crypto Caucus": The US Lawmakers Defending Digital Coins. *Financial Times*, 31 March. Accessed 6 April 2022: https://www.ft.com/content/29f32905-1933-458e-aa29-7f1685109ea1

Standage, Tom (2002). *The Turk: The Life and Times of the Famous Eighteenth-Century Chess-Playing Machine*. New York: Walker.

Standing, Guy (2016). *The Corruption of Capitalism: Why Rentiers Thrive and Work Does Not Pay*. London: Biteback.

Stanford Graduate School of Business (2017). Andrew Ng: Artificial Intelligence Is the New Electricity. YouTube, 2 February. Accessed 12 April 2023: https://www.youtube.com/watch?v=21EiKfQYZXc

Stark, Luke, and Anna Lauren Hoffmann (2019). Data Is the New What? Popular Metaphors and Professional Ethics in Emerging Data Culture. *Journal of Cultural Analytics* 4 (1): 1–22.

Steiger, Paul E. (2014). What a Difference 25 Years Makes. *CNBC*, 2 May. Accessed 10 July: https://www.cnbc.com/2014/04/29/what-a-difference-25-years-makes.html

Steinert, Martin, and Larry Leifer (2010). Scrutinizing Gartner's Hype Cycle Approach. *Proceedings of PICMET 2010 Technology Management for Global Economic Growth, Phuket, Thailand*, pp. 1–13. https://ieeexplore.ieee.org/document/5603442

Strengers, Yolande, Jathan Sadowski, Zhuying Li, Anna Shimshak, and Florian "Floyd" Mueller (2021). What Can HCI Learn from Sexual Consent? A Feminist Process of Embodied Consent for Interactions with Emerging Technologies. *CHI '21: Proceedings of the 2021 CHI Conference on Human Factors in Computing Systems*. Article no. 405, pp. 1–13.

Swedloff, Rick (2020). The New Regulatory Imperative for Insurance. *Boston College Law Review* 61 (6): 2031–2084.

Sweet, Ken, Christopher Rugaber, Chris Megerian, and Cathy Bussewitz (2023). US Government Moves to Stop Potential Banking Crisis. *AP News*, 13 March. Accessed 14 March 2023: https://apnews.com/article/silicon-valley-bank-bailout-yellen-deposits-failure-94f2185742981daf337c4691bbb9ec1e

Taffel, Sy (2023). Data and Oil: Metaphor, Materiality and Metabolic Rifts. *New Media & Society* 25 (5): 980–998.

Tankus, Nathan (2023). Every Complex Banking Issue All at Once: The Failure of Silicon Valley Bank in One Brief Summary and Five Quick Implications. *Crises Notes*, 14 March. Accessed 15 March 2023: https://www.crisesnotes .com/every-complex-banking-issue-all-at-once-the-failure-of-silicon -valley-bank-in-one-brief-summary-and-five-quick-implications/

Tanninen, Maiju, Turo-Kimmo Lehtonen, and Minna Ruckenstein (2021). Tracking Lives, Forging Markets. *Journal of Cultural Economy* 14 (4): 449–463.

Taylor, Astra (2018). The Automation Charade. *Logic*, 1 August. Accessed 19 February 2024: https://logicmag.io/failure/the-automation-charade/

Thatcher, Jim, David O'Sullivan, and Dillon Mahmoudi (2016). Data Colonialism through Accumulation by Dispossession: New Metaphors for Daily Data. *Environment and Planning D* 34 (6): 990–1006.

Thiel, Peter, and Blake Masters (2014). *Zero to One: Notes on Startups, or How to Build the Future.* New York: Crown Business.

Thompson, E. P. (1966). *The Making of the English Working Class.* New York: Vintage Books.

Throsby, Karen (2009). Revisiting "The Machinery of Dominance: Women, Men, and Technical Know-How." *Women's Studies Quarterly* 37 (1/2): 274–276.

TrueBridge Capital Partners (2022). State of VC 2021: Breaking Every Record. *Forbes*, 14 June. Accessed 15 March 2023: https://www.forbes.com/sites /truebridge/2022/06/14/state-of-vc-2021-breaking-every-record/?sh= 654b75ad5fbe

Tubaro, Paola, Antonio A. Casilli, and Marion Coville (2020). The Trainer, the Verifier, the Imitator: Three Ways in Which Human Platform Workers Support Artificial Intelligence. *Big Data & Society* 7 (1): 1–12.

Turner, Fred (2006). *From Counterculture to Cyberculture Stewart Brand, the Whole Earth Network, and the Rise of Digital Utopianism.* Chicago: University of Chicago Press.

Turow, Joseph (2017). *The Aisles Have Eyes: How Retailers Track Your Shopping, Strip Your Privacy, and Define Your Power.* New Haven, CT: Yale University Press.

United Nations Conference on Trade and Development (2019). *Digital Economy Report: Value Creation and Capture; Implications for Developing Countries.* Geneva: United Nations.

van Doorn, Niels (2017). Platform Labor: On the Gendered and Racialized Exploitation of Low-Income Service Work in the "On-Demand" Economy. *Information, Communication & Society* 20: 898–914.

van Doorn, Niels, and Adam Badger (2020). Platform Capitalism's Hidden Abode: Producing Data Assets in the Gig Economy. *Antipode* 52: 1475–1495.

van Lente, Harro (2012). Navigating Foresight in a Sea of Expectations: Lessons from the Sociology of Expectations. *Technology Analysis and Strategic Management* 24 (8): 769–782.

van Lente, Harro, Charlotte Spitters, and Alexander Peine (2013). Comparing Technological Hype Cycles: Towards a Theory. *Technological Forecasting & Social Change* 80 (8): 1615–1628.

Viljoen, Salomé (2021). A Relational Theory of Data Governance. *Yale Law Journal* 131 (2): 573–654.

Vinsel, Lee (2019). You're Doing It Wrong: Notes on Criticism and Technology Hype. *Medium*, 2 February. Accessed 8 February 2023: https://sts-news.medium.com/youre-doing-it-wrong-notes-on-criticism-and-technology-hype-18b08b4307e5

Vogell, Heather (2022). Rent Going Up? One Company's Algorithm Could Be Why. *ProPublica*, 15 October. Accessed 20 July 2023: https://www.propublica.org/article/yieldstar-rent-increase-realpage-rent

Wacjman, Judy (2004). *Technofeminism.* London: Polity Press.

Wahome, Michel, and Mark Graham (2020). Spatially Shaped Imaginaries of the Digital Economy. *Information, Communication & Society* 23 (8): 1123–1138.

Ward, Callum, and Manuel B. Aalbers (2016). "The Shitty Rent Business": What's the Point of Land Rent Theory? *Urban Studies* 53 (9): 1760–1783.

West, Sarah Myers (2019). Data Capitalism: Redefining the Logics of Surveillance and Privacy. *Business & Society* 58 (1): 20–41.

Whittaker, Meredith (2021). The Steep Cost of Capture. *ACM Interactions* 28 (6): 50–55.

Winner, Langdon (1978). *Autonomous Technology: Technics-Out-of-Control as a Theme in Political Thought.* Cambridge, MA: MIT Press.

Winner, Langdon (1980). Do Artifacts Have Politics? *Daedalus* 109 (1): 121–136.

Winner, Langdon (1986). *The Whale and the Reactor: A Search for Limits in an Age of High Technology.* Chicago: University of Chicago Press.

Wolfe, Tom (1987). *The Bonfire of the Vanities.* New York: Farrar, Straus and Giroux.

Wood, Gaby (2002). Living Dolls: A Magical History of the Quest for Mechanical Life by Gaby Wood. *Guardian*, February 16. Accessed 16 May 2023: https://www.theguardian.com/books/2002/feb/16/extract.gabywood

Wright, Erik Olin (2010). *Envisioning Real Utopias.* London: Verso Books.

Wright, Erik Olin (2013). Transforming Capitalism through Real Utopias. *American Sociological Review* 78: 1–25.

xkcd (2017). Machine Learning. 17 May. Accessed 7 August 2023: https://xkcd.com/1838/

Zakrzewski, Cat (2022). Tech Companies Spent Almost $70 Million Lobbying Washington in 2021 as Congress Sought to Rein in Their Power. *Washington Post*, 21 January. Accessed 12 January 2023: https://www.washingtonpost.com/technology/2022/01/21/tech-lobbying-in-washington/

Zamir, Eyal (2014). Contract Law and Theory: Three Views of the Cathedral. *University of Chicago Law Review* 81: 2077–2123.

Zest AI. (n.d.). AI-Driven Credit Underwriting Software. Accessed 8 August 2023: https://www.zest.ai/

Zuboff, Shoshana (2019). *The Age of Surveillance Capitalism: The Fight for a Human Future at the New Frontier of Power.* New York: PublicAffairs.

Index

labor: capitalist exploitation, 40; capitalists work with, 141; cheap, 118; controlling, 41; cost of, 96; dead, 125; dynamics of, 26; exploitation, 106, 108, 112, 116, 119, 121; forms of, 17; human, 107, 110, 111, 117, 122, 124; Luddism, 42–43; markets, 122–123, 134; money for, 10; networks of, 106; organizing, 16; outsourced, 111; poorly-paid, 98; power of, 122; and profit, 13; relationship to capital, 130, 133; relation to technology, 127; rights, 163; role for, 126; and value, 129

landlords: acting like, 136; automating of, 148–152; central position of, 26, 137; corporate, 151, 153; internet of, 143, 146, 149, 154; ownership claims, 141; parasites, 132; and platforms, 152; predatory, 143; rent extraction, 130; value extraction, 131

Lee, Peter, 59, 60

legal systems, 6–7

Levine, Matt, 29

Lightsey, Harry, 144–145

Lord Byron, 41

Luckey, Palmer, 94–95

Ludd, Ned, 41, 44

Luddites: becoming, 46–47; craftsworkers, 41; futures, 209, 210–211; and innovation, 40, 43; Luddism, 39–40, 45–46; materialist alternatives of, 26; materialist analysis, 34; materialist approach, 48; myths about, 42–44; role model, 25, 42; today's Luddite, 44–45

Marx, Karl, 2, 9–10, 14, 74, 79, 82–83, 101, 124–125, 131, 209, 210

Marx, Leo, 22–23, 37–38

materialist action, 42

materialist alternatives, 26

materialist analysis, 27, 33–34, 38–39, 152, 157, 187

materialist approach, 25, 48, 187

materialists, 188

Mau, Søren, 11, 31, 133

Mazzucato, Mariana, 141

McClintock, Emory, 176

McElroy, Erin, 150

McElroy, John, 21

McKinsey trend report, 50

McQuillan, Dan, 88

mechanic, 25–26, 34–39, 42, 46–48, 209–211

Mechanical Turk, 104, 105–106, 112, 114, 117–118, 136

Merchant, Brian, 210

Meyers West, Sarah, 92

military: contracts with, 7, 22; deployed by capitalists, 44; interests, 120; military-industrial regime, 94–95; planners, 190; spending, 55; strategy positions, 94

Moore, Gordon, 195–196

Moore, Jason, 95

Morozov, Evgeny, 94

Mueller, Gavin, 42

multiplicities, 5

Musk, Elon, 53, 202

Napoleon, 41

Neumann, Adam, 73

Ng, Andrew, 83

technology *(continued)*
of quality, 96; blaming people for
consequences, 53; corporate
control of, 144; creation of, 189;
definition, 2–3; development of, 16;
embracing, 40; fears and anxieties
about, 18; and finance, 135–136;
FIRE sector, 156–157; and future,
192–194, 200; granting power to,
37; and human labor, 111, 124, 127,
129; hype about, 68; hype cycle,
198; improved, 22–23; industry,
196; information, 19–22, 55, 56, 77;
jobs replaced by, 123; and
landlords, 143, 150; links to
capitalism, 24; and Luddites,
40–41, 43, 46; Luddites not
opposed to, 211; media coverage,
31; narratives of, 202; perpetual
value machine, 122; as power, 3–8,
19–20; pretending to be human,
128; private planning for, 54;
rejecting, 40; in rentierism, 154;
right to repair, 145; risk, 158,
165–166, 168, 175–176, 184, 194;
social struggle, 210; start-up, 71,
134; strength of, 86; systemic
problems, 91; technology sector
explosion, 133; use of, 13; using,
106; venture capitalists, 57, 65;
Zoom, 138
Thiel, Peter, 95, 208
Thompson, E. P., 40
Toffler, Alvin, 192

utopias, 26, 188–189, 200–209

van Lente, Harro, 196
Vaucanson, Jacques de, 105
venture capital (VC): ascension of,
61; digital platforms, 148;
financial activities of, 68–69;
funding, 61; hype cycle, 109;
industry, 58, 64; innovation, 55, 62,
63, 156; investment, 105, 118; mark
of, 56; operations of, 54; planning
technology, 25–26; sustaining
operations and growth, 57; women
and people of color are low
percentage, 73
Vergerio, Manon, 150
Viljoen, Salomé, 89
Vinsel, Lee, 32

wealth divide, 15
Web3: absurdity, 64; capital, 67;
collapse, 92; constructing, 66;
crypto assets, 75; futures, 65;
investment cycle, 64; movement,
70; trend, 57
WeWork, 73
Williams, Robin, 195
Winner, Langdon, 175
women, as computers, 39
Wright, Eric Olin, 203

Zoom, 138–140
Zuboff, Shoshana, 32
Zuckerberg, Mark, 53